Praise for *Spectacular Bid*

"Winning a Triple Crown is an automatic stamp of immortality—think Secretariat, Citation, and the others—but what about those horses that didn't quite make it? Where do they fit in the hierarchy of Thoroughbred racing's history? Peter Lee makes a strong argument that Spectacular Bid deserves a place among the sport's elite despite coming up short in his bid for the Triple Crown. A once-in-a-lifetime horse for his owners, for a veteran trainer best known for his success with 'claimers,' and for an inexperienced jockey beset with problems, Spectacular Bid was the best of his generation. He swept the Kentucky Derby and Preakness Stakes and almost certainly would have won the Triple Crown if not for a bizarre accident that likely cost him the Belmont Stakes. Was Spectacular Bid really the last superhorse of the twentieth century? It's difficult to say, but Lee's well-written and thoroughly researched book is excellent fodder for the argument."—Milton C. Toby, author of *Taking Shergar: Thoroughbred Racing's Most Famous Cold Case*

"When I started Peter Lee's book, I knew of Spectacular Bid: the safety pin, the world record, and the failed Triple Crown run were the oft-repeated narrative about this dynamite-gray champion. This book showed me that the story of the Bid was much more: a horse with an average pedigree and superior talent; a blue-collar trainer who proved he could compete with the sport's elite; owners that genuinely loved and enjoyed their remarkable horse; and a jockey whose burning passion for horses and the sport of horse racing could not outrun the demons of success. I highly recommend this book to any reader who loves horse racing and wants to learn the full story of this champion."—Jennifer S. Kelly, author of *Sir Barton and the Making of the Triple Crown*

Spectacular Bid

Spectacular Bid

The Last Superhorse of the Twentieth Century

PETER LEE

Published by The University Press of Kentucky

Scholarly publisher for the Commonwealth,
serving Bellarmine University, Berea College, Centre
College of Kentucky, Eastern Kentucky University,
The Filson Historical Society, Georgetown College,
Kentucky Historical Society, Kentucky State University,
Morehead State University, Murray State University,
Northern Kentucky University, Transylvania University,
University of Kentucky, University of Louisville,
and Western Kentucky University.
All rights reserved.

Editorial and Sales Offices: The University Press of Kentucky
663 South Limestone Street, Lexington, Kentucky 40508-4008
www.kentuckypress.com

Cataloging-in-Publication data available from the Library of Congress

ISBN 978-0-8131-7780-9 (hardcover : alk. paper)
ISBN 978-0-8131-7783-0 (epub)
ISBN 978-0-8131-7782-3 (pdf)

This book is printed on acid-free paper meeting
the requirements of the American National Standard
for Permanence in Paper for Printed Library Materials.

Manufactured in the United States of America.

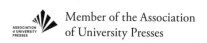

Member of the Association
of University Presses

*To my father, who instilled in me a love of writing,
and to my mother, my biggest fan.*

Contents

Introduction   1

1. Beginnings   4

2. Sold   13

3. Potential   30

4. The Field Shapes Up   50

5. Derby Fever   76

6. Home Again   95

7. One More for the Crown   109

8. Growing Pains   130

9. The Streak   156

Epilogue   187

Acknowledgments   207

Appendix A. Spectacular Bid's Pedigree   210

Appendix B. Spectacular Bid's Record   212

Glossary   214

Notes   217

Index   255

Introduction

WHEN SECRETARIAT CROSSED the finish line at Belmont Park, New York, on June 9, 1973, thirty-one lengths in front of Twice a Prince and faster than any horse had ever run a mile and a half, the crowd exploded in joy and pride—and relief.

Twenty-five years had passed since any three-year-old horse had done what Secretariat just did—win the Kentucky Derby, Preakness Stakes, and Belmont Stakes in a span of five weeks. The Triple Crown of Thoroughbred racing was reserved for an elite crop of horses: only eight horses had won it in fifty-four years. Many horse experts wondered if they would ever see another Triple Crown winner; some called it the Triple Crown jinx.

"If some 'big horse' doesn't win the triple [crown] soon, the racing crowd may forget what it's all about," wrote Steve Snider in 1963, when the drought was only at the fifteen-year mark. "For, since Citation last collared those three famous races for three-year-olds in 1948, the Triple Crown is something to talk about but not to witness." Former Calumet Farm trainer Jimmy Jones was even more cynical in 1966, before Kauai King made his unsuccessful bid for the Triple Crown in the Belmont Stakes. "We may never see another Triple Crown champion," he said.

Horse racing experts were at a loss to explain why no horse had won the Triple Crown. The main consensus was that Thoroughbred racing had become extremely competitive. In 1945, 5,819 foals had been registered with the Jockey Club. By 1970, that number had skyrocketed to 24,954. Others thought bad luck contributed to the dearth of winners; Tim Tam, Carry Back, Majestic Prince, and Cañonero II all had the Triple Crown within reach before suffering injuries before or during the Belmont.

1

The task that lies before these horses is daunting: Take a young, green three-year-old horse and make him race a mile and a quarter early in the spring (the Kentucky Derby). A short two weeks later, make him run in a slightly shorter race (the Preakness). Then, in three weeks, enter him in a mile-and-a-half marathon (the Belmont) that would take its toll on any horse, especially a three-year-old. Consider that in the Preakness and the Belmont, the horse will probably face fresh horses that did not run in the Derby, and it is difficult to string together three wins in a row.

But Secretariat ended the drought with three resounding victories in 1973, breaking track records in each race and a world record in the Belmont. Four years later, Seattle Slew, bought for $17,500 at an auction, defeated all competitors with relative ease to become the only undefeated Triple Crown winner.

The trend continued. Affirmed battled it out with his rival, Alydar, in all three races in 1978, thrilling crowds and winning the Derby by one and a half lengths, the Preakness by a neck, and the Belmont by a nose. For the first time ever, horse racing had two consecutive Triple Crown winners. Talk suddenly changed from a Triple Crown jinx to a Triple Crown glut. The question now turned on itself: why were there suddenly so many Triple Crown winners after a twenty-five-year drought?

Triple Crown winners seemed to come in bunches; there were three Triple Crown winners in the 1930s, four in the 1940s, and now three in the 1970s. No one knew exactly why, although some horse racing experts tried to rationalize the trend. First, horses were not experiencing the injuries that had befallen so many Triple Crown hopefuls in the past. Second, Bold Ruler, one of the great sires of all time, was making his presence known in his progeny; both Secretariat and Seattle Slew were descendants of the stallion. And finally, luck played a role. Just like drawing two straight flushes in poker, a freak occurrence could happen anytime—even three Triple Crowns in six years.

"To win the Triple Crown, a horse must first have outstanding ability," said Kent Hollingsworth, editor of *Blood-Horse*. "But he also must clearly dominate his division, and he must be lucky enough to stay sound and to find racing room when he needs it. I'm sure we're breeding better horses, just as we're getting better football players. Bronco Nagurski might have a tough time today making the all-pro backfield."

Fans did not care what the reason was. They flocked to racetracks;

attendance jumped 6 percent to 75 million in 1973 and reached 79.2 million in 1975. That year, the filly Ruffian took the horse racing nation by storm before sustaining a fatal injury in a match race with 1975 Kentucky Derby winner Foolish Pleasure. More than twice as many people were going to horse races as were going to baseball games.

But the sport was facing problems. In 1979, a federal grand jury indicted twenty-one people in connection with a multimillion-dollar scheme to fix horse races at several East Coast racetracks. More indictments were predicted for the following year. Other sports were rising in popularity. The National Football League expanded to include two more teams in 1976, and the National Basketball Association merged with the American Basketball Association to bring professional basketball to more cities. Even baseball was starting to gain fans again after the thrilling playoff and World Series games in 1975 and 1977.

Horse racing looked for a new hero to keep interest alive, much like Affirmed and Alydar had done in 1978. Fans waited to see what 1979 would bring, hoping for another superhorse to give the sport three Triple Crown winners in a row—and the hero it needed.

1

Beginnings

Good, big, strong colt. Shows quality.
> —Entry in 1976 foaling book, Buck Pond Farm

BUCK POND FARM lies about two miles off Highway 60 in Versailles (pronounced ver-SALES), Kentucky, just outside of Lexington. It consists of about 300 acres of rolling hills dotted with giant pin oak and maple trees—a tiny operation compared with Claiborne Farm's 3,000 acres. It is not as flashy as the fabled Calumet Farm, with its devil red–trimmed barns and white fences. Buck Pond Farm is simple and unassuming, its only impressive structure being the Georgian house at the end of the long drive. The hills that inundate the farm, though, are packed full of calcium and phosphorus, which leaches into the bluegrass that young horses love to eat. It gives them the nutrients they need to grow strong and healthy.

Originally a plantation called Buck Pond, it was founded in 1783 by Colonel Thomas Marshall, a hero at the Battle of Brandywine during the Revolutionary War. When a horde of British soldiers attacked his tiny regiment, Marshall kept his position and lost no ground until the regiment had nearly exhausted its supply of ammunition and more than half its officers and one-third of its soldiers had been killed or wounded. He was also with General George Washington during the harsh winter at Valley Forge and made the famous crossing of the Delaware River with him. When the war was over, Marshall was appointed surveyor general of the lands in Kentucky and established his office in Lexington in 1783. Two years later, he moved his family to Kentucky and built the main house at Buck Pond.

Major Thomas Clay McDowell, great-grandson of Kentucky states-
man Henry Clay, bought the estate from the Marshalls in 1925. Born
and raised in Kentucky, McDowell was a successful owner and trainer of
Thoroughbred horses. He trained Alan-a-Dale, the winner of the twenty-
eighth Kentucky Derby in 1902 and a son of Halma, who had won
the Derby in 1895 (the first father and son Derby winners).[1] Buck Pond
became a horse farm, and its massive fields were turned into pastureland.
Here, McDowell bred and raised his next crop of racehorses. Over the
next fifty years, the property changed owners a few times, finally settling
into the hands of George and Susan Proskauer, who, along with horse
expert Victor Heerman, bought the property in 1973.

On February 17, 1976, at about 8:25 a.m.—a relatively mild morning for the end of winter—a small, light gray, six-year-old mare felt the
pains of labor and could not make it back to the foaling barn at Buck
Pond Farm. The horses had been put out into the pasture to enjoy the
good weather while the farmhands prepared the foaling barn for several pending births. The workers were unaware of the mare's condition,
so she lay down where she was, at the bottom of a hill, and gave birth to
a colt. The foal, his legs still weak and wobbly, struggled to his feet and
immediately fell, ending up in a puddle. If a worker riding by on a trac-
tor had not noticed the foal stuck in the puddle, the horse might have
drowned, his matchstick legs not yet ready to bear his weight. Farmhands, surprised by the mare's quick delivery in the paddock, had to pull
the foal out.

The mare's name was Spectacular, and unlike many of the Thoroughbreds at Buck Pond Farm, she was not a Kentucky native. Spectacular was California bred and raised, owned by Madelyn Jason and
her mother, Grace Gilmore. The two women were heirs to a family fortune from the California steel, oil, and natural gas businesses. Grace's
late husband, William, had founded the Gilmore Steel Corporation in
1926, which developed into the largest independent steel company in
the West. He was also an accomplished equestrian and champion polo
player, and he operated a large Thoroughbred breeding ranch in Grass
Valley, California.

Wanting a place to race his horses, William Gilmore discovered
Golden Gate Fields in San Francisco, a new but struggling racetrack.
Heavy rains had made the clay surface so muddy and sticky that jockeys

refused to ride on it, and the track closed only six days after opening in 1941. Track assets were tied up in receivership, creditors squabbled with one another over payments, and the owners could do nothing to save the track. Gilmore got involved and became the major stockholder in Golden Gate Fields, and by 1957, it was admitted to the Thoroughbred Racing Association. He also helped bail out Tanforan Racetrack in San Bruno, California, becoming a major stockholder in that venture as well. Soon Gilmore was the largest breeder in California, and he worked hard to keep the sport clean. When he died in 1962, his daughter Madelyn stayed in the business and partnered with veterinarian William Linfoot.

One of their first purchases, Stop on Red, was a twin—a rarity in horse racing. Twins are not considered good horses and frequently have physical defects, such as a swayed back or a thin, ungainly appearance. "Once a mare has twins, you won't find anybody who wants to breed to her again," said Jock Jocoy, a Del Mar, California, veterinarian. "People get gun-shy, afraid she's going to have twins again." At that time, if owners discovered that a mare was carrying twins, one fetus was sometimes aborted to give the other the best chance for survival. Sometimes, both twins were destroyed. "Carrying two fetuses to term is very unusual," Jocoy said. "There's just not enough room in a mare's body for both twins to survive."

Walter Kelley, who trained horses at Max Gluck's Elmendorf Farm in Lexington, remembered when the twins were born. "They were so small. I told them to destroy them, or, if nothing else, give them away. Twins never make good racehorses." Gluck, however, insisted on keeping them and named them Stop on Red and Go on Green.

Both horses ended up racing—a rare feat. Stop on Red's first outing was on January 27, 1961, in the third race at Hialeah Park Race Track. She finished last. She finally broke her maiden in August of that year in Atlantic City, winning a six-furlong claiming race. She finished the year with one win, one second, and three thirds in twelve starts. Her career record was unimpressive: seven wins in fifty-one races. Go on Green's career was more successful; she finished in the money nineteen times in thirty-two starts. The twins did have four Kentucky Derby winners in their pedigree—Johnstown, Broker's Tip, Hindoo, and Ben Brush. On their sire's side they also had the great Colin—one of the only undefeated horses in modern racing.

William Linfoot's wife, Janet, was a veterinarian as well—one of the first female veterinarians in the United States. She had done extensive research on twins and believed that if breeding were possible, they could have valuable offspring. Her examination confirmed the ungainly appearance of Stop on Red, the twin her husband and Madelyn Jason had purchased: "[Stop on Red's] eyes drooped, her feet were turned out, and she had a very flat back. But she was an incubator. She was born to be a mother," Dr. Linfoot said.

Both Stop on Red and Go on Green were bred—breaking every rule horse professionals had about twins—and they both had foals, an even rarer occurrence. "I knew [Stop on Red] had to have a lot of stamina to have made it," owner Jason said. Linfoot and Jason bred Stop on Red to a stallion called Promised Land, an iron horse that had finished in the money forty-seven out of seventy-seven times in his career: winning twenty-one times, finishing second ten times, and placing third sixteen times. The offspring of Stop on Red and Promised Land turned out to be a beautiful gray horse born in 1970: Spectacular. Linfoot was not impressed with the filly and sold her at auction. Jason had a feeling about Spectacular, though, and she convinced Linfoot to buy her back; later, she and her mother bought out Linfoot's share of the horse for $10,250.

Spectacular's name did not describe her racing career. She never even raced as a two-year-old and ran mostly at fairgrounds, collecting four wins in ten starts. Her best races were a second-place finish in the My Fair Lady Stakes and a win in the City of Berkeley race at the Alameda County Fair in Pleasanton, California, where she broke a track record. One day earlier, her full brother, Go to Goal, had broken a track record on the same course. Her career earnings, though, amounted to only $16,633. "She broke that track record, but on other days she'd just kind of gallop along," Jason said. Friends and colleagues admired the filly's beauty—she was almost Arabian in appearance—and Jason thought that breeding her with the right stallion could yield a good horse.

When Madelyn Jason and Grace Gilmore decided they wanted to get out of the racing business, they sold some of their stock, including several Promised Land mares that could not run. But when it came to Spectacular, Jason had a feeling. "Spectacular showed me she had speed, so I kept her," she said. Before she bred Spectacular, Jason sought the counsel of Vic Heerman at Buck Pond Farm, who had served as a Gilm-

Spectacular, Spectacular Bid's dam. Note her long back. (Lyn Jason Cobb)

ore family adviser. Heerman saw a good match in a horse named Bold Bidder, a half brother to the immortal Secretariat. Their sire was Bold Ruler, the 1957 Preakness Stakes winner and the Three-Year-Old Champion Male and Horse of the Year. A leading sire in North America during the 1960s, Bold Ruler was inducted into the National Museum of Racing and Hall of Fame in 1973. Bold Bidder's dam, High Bid, was not a disappointing racehorse either, finishing in the money in twenty-one of thirty starts and earning $151,122.

Bold Bidder was larger than most of Bold Ruler's offspring. As a two-year-old, he had ankle problems that kept him from running. His ankles improved, though, and as a three-year-old, he won seven of seventeen races. A year later, he was the nation's leading older horse, winning five stakes races, including the 1966 Hawthorne Gold Cup Handicap, the Monmouth and Washington Park handicaps, and the 1966 Strub Stakes at Santa Anita Park, where he set a track record. That performance earned him Co-Champion Older Male Horse of the Year in 1966. In his thirty-three career starts, Bold Bidder finished in the money

Bold Bidder, Spectacular Bid's sire. (*Blood-Horse*)

twenty times, earning more than $478,000. He was retired to stud at Gainesway Farm in Lexington, Kentucky, where he was a success, siring the 1974 Kentucky Derby winner Cannonade.

"I wanted to breed [Spectacular] to somebody with desire, somebody who wanted to win, and that was Bold Bidder," Jason said. "She had good bone and a long back, so I was looking for a stallion that was short-coupled, and Bold Bidder was that, too."[2]

Californians bristled at the thought of sending a horse to Kentucky to be bred. They wondered why Jason did not breed Spectacular with a California-bred stallion. "When they heard we were going for Bold Bidder, [critics] asked, 'Don't you think you've overmatched your mare a bit?'" Jason said.

The breeding between the two horses cost Jason about $25,000, but it paid off, for Spectacular came into foal on the first try. Jason and Gilmore kept Spectacular in Kentucky throughout her pregnancy and stabled her at Buck Pond Farm. "Good, big, strong colt. Shows quality," wrote Vic Heerman in the foaling records for February 17, 1976, after the near disaster in the mud puddle where Spectacular gave birth. He recorded the time of birth as 8:45 a.m. The Proskauers were embarrassed to tell Jason and Gilmore that the foal had been born without the proper medical care, but Jason did not mind and thought it would make him even stronger.

Within hours of his birth, farmhands slipped a halter around the foal's head to get him used to having a human lead him around and to make him more manageable, trusting, and trainable. His diet early on consisted of mother's milk, hay, and grass; after two months, he started to eat horse feed, which contains the protein required for the horse to continue to grow.

The foal spent his first few days in the stall with Spectacular, then gradually ventured out into the paddock with her. Eventually, he spent his days in a pasture outside his stall, enjoying the fresh air and the pleasant Kentucky climate. He was shed raised, which means that although he was brought into a shed for feedings and examinations, he was free to roam the pasture regardless of whether it was raining, snowing, or sunny. Some horse experts believe this toughens the foal and allows it the freedom it desires at such a young age. Until Spectacular's foal was weaned, he stayed close to his mother, but he was able to explore his surroundings and frolic with the other foals. After he was weaned from Spectacular—a traumatic experience that took a few days to get used to—he stayed in a pasture with the other colts, which are more rambunctious than the fillies.

Ed Caswell, manager of Buck Pond Farm at the time, remembered him as "a nice-looking colt, intelligent acting. He didn't do anything wrong. He lived up in that paddock where he could go in that run-in shed if he wanted to." Heerman described him as a "smooth-moving colt. He was aggressive and nippy in the field but not a bully."

Jason eventually moved Spectacular and her foal to Wimbledon

Farm, just down the road from Buck Pond Farm. As the months progressed, Jason received invoices from Wimbledon Farm for the care of the foal. The first invoice was for a brown colt, the second invoice was for a bay colt, and the third was for a roan. She finally called the farm and asked whether the mare had had triplets. The colt's coat was changing as he got older, and over time, it developed into a deep battleship gray with darker and lighter spots—an unusual color for a Thoroughbred. According to Keeneland Racing and Sales, nearly 90 percent of the horses born each year are some variation of brown. The other 10 percent are distributed among bay, chestnut, dark bay or brown, and gray/roan. But despite the numbers, a gray horse has as much chance of winning as a brown or bay horse.

This fact was not always accepted by breeders and trainers, however. At one time, they believed that grays were slower and more susceptible to injury, their coats an indicator of premature aging. By 1815, only twenty-eight gray broodmares were recorded in England. Grays were so despised that near the turn of the twentieth century, the gray Thoroughbred line almost disappeared; they simply were not bred in the United States. In 1929, out of about 30,000 horses that raced during the season, only fifty-nine were gray. Grays seldom won because there were so few of them. "Gray horses may make good plow animals," wrote Gene Kessler of the *Lincoln Star*. "But they apparently don't go for speed." Bob Considine of the *Rockford Register-Republic* likened grays to "little more than yaks."

Most modern grays can be traced back to a horse named The Tetrarch, an Irish gray who went undefeated in seven starts in 1913. The Tetrarch's gray descendants included Mahmoud, the 1936 Epsom Derby winner; Determine, the 1954 Kentucky Derby winner; Determine's son Decidedly, the 1962 Kentucky Derby winner (up to then, the only two gray horses to win the Derby); and Spectacular, who had shown her bloodline only sporadically on the racetrack.[3]

When the colt became a yearling in 1977—all foals become one year old on January 1, regardless of when they were born the previous year—Jason and Gilmore put him up for sale; they were no longer in the racing business and wanted to focus on breeding. Staff at Wimbledon Farm readied the colt for sale by teaching him how to start and stop, how to react to a stranger's touch, and how to stand at attention. They also began the slow process of breaking the horse. First, grooms placed a saddle pad on the colt's back and cinched a band around his belly to mimic the feel of a saddle. An exercise rider then lay across the horse's back to introduce the sensation of weight. Slowly, the rider worked his way up to a seated position. At this point, they had done as much as they could with the horse; he was ready to be sold.

2

Sold

Here's your next champion.

—Harry Meyerhoff to Bud Delp after buying
Spectacular Bid for $37,000

YEARLING SALES AT Keeneland in Lexington are one of the premier Thoroughbred auctions in the country. While Keeneland is also host to some world-class races, thousands of racehorses are sold at its auctions, with winning bids ranging from $1,000 to $1 million. The first auction was held in 1938, and the first yearling sale was in 1943, when wartime restrictions on rail travel prevented Kentuckians from transporting their horses to the Saratoga sale in New York.

It is an event that attracts thousands of potential horse buyers, each one eager to find that special horse that will bring them fame and fortune. Owners bring their horses to the sale meticulously groomed, with braids in their manes and black polish on their hooves, as if they had been manicured. Each horse is assigned a hip number for listing in the catalog, which also indicates the horse's birth year, color, gender, and pedigree. Prospective buyers go from stall to stall, examining the horses' legs and looking for any weakness in the bone or any deformity. They check the bloodlines for evidence of success, seeing whether the yearling has what it takes to be fast and to be fast over a long distance. Some yearlings that cannot handle long distances might still be good candidates for sprints.

At the time, Keeneland held two yearling sales—the July Selected Yearling Sale and the September Yearling Sale.[1] Yearlings considered for the July sale were divided into three groups—A, B, and C—based on their conformation. As were almost always included in the summer sale, and Cs were usually thrown out of the auction. In 1977, Spectacular's colt was up for sale, and Madelyn Jason and Grace Gilmore were hoping to get at least $60,000 for him. However, he was graded a C—probably due to the twins on his dam's side—so they waited until the September sale. Eight Kentucky Derby winners had been sold at Keeneland, but only two—Dust Commander and Cañonero II—had been sold in September. Both won the Derby as long shots.

Jason and Gilmore waited as prospective buyers walked by the gray colt's stall, which was far away from the sales ring, where all the action took place. One buyer who seemed interested was Jim Hill, a veterinarian who had convinced Mickey Taylor to buy part of Seattle Slew, the 1977 Triple Crown winner, for the bargain price of $17,500. Hill looked at the colt three times, twice with Taylor, but he never made a bid. Vic Heerman remembered asking him why he did not bid on the colt, and Hill said, almost annoyed, "I just don't know. Maybe I went to the bathroom. Maybe somebody asked me out for a drink, and I forgot there was a horse I wanted to bid on." The colt did not seem to stick in people's memories for long.

One group of people that did remember him was the Meyerhoff family and their trainer, Grover G. "Bud" Delp. Fifty-year-old Harry Meyerhoff was part owner of several Thoroughbreds in Maryland. Along with his wife, Teresa, and his son, Tom, Meyerhoff ran Hawksworth Farm, a small stable that usually raced its horses at the nearby Pimlico and Laurel racetracks.

Harry was born in 1929 in Baltimore, Maryland, into a Jewish family. His father, Jacob Meyerhoff, was a real estate developer in partnership with his brother, Joseph. Harry graduated from Lehigh University with a degree in industrial engineering and was an all-American in lacrosse. He and his brother, Robert, went into the family business in 1950, and by 1959, they were running it. They took advantage of the housing boom in the late 1950s and early 1960s and graduated from low-income housing and apartment complexes to shopping centers, amassing a small fortune.

The business was stressful, though, and the two often went to the racetrack in the afternoons to relax. In 1961, they decided to see if their luck in real estate might extend to horse racing. "I was a racing fan for some time before I bought my first horse," Harry told the *Daily Racing*

Harry Meyerhoff, 1983.
(Keeneland Association
Library)

Form. "We had a young Dutch trainer, Reinier Vandernat, and Marlton Pike was our first horse, purchased privately from another stable.
We ran him twice, and he bowed a tendon. We didn't even know what
a bowed tendon was." The two brothers, who raced horses under the
name Bon Etage Stables, remained patient, and in the early 1970s, their
luck changed. They bought a filly by Bold Bidder named Bold Place for
$16,500, and after the horse had won several stakes, they sold her as a
broodmare for $250,000. Another horse of theirs, Ecole Etage, was the
early leader in the 1973 Preakness Stakes before Secretariat sped past the
entire field en route to a win. Ecole Etage finished a respectable fourth
and went on to earn $241,525 for the Meyerhoffs.

By 1973, Harry had had enough of the building business. He retired
as a millionaire and turned over the bulk of his real estate business to
his son, Tom. Harry and Robert also split their horse racing business in
1974; Robert preferred to buy mares and breed his own racehorses, while
Harry opted to purchase yearlings. In 1976, Harry bought a 320-acre
estate called Hawksworth. Built in 1810, the estate was on the Miles

River on the Eastern Shore of Chesapeake Bay and featured a guest-house, a 9-acre pond, tennis courts, and a pool. No horses were on the farm; instead, Harry raised corn and soybeans.

One day in 1973, Harry, who was married at the time, walked into O'Henry's, a Baltimore bar, and struck up a conversation with the young bartender serving him. Her name was Teresa Riberdy, and Harry was immediately smitten with her green eyes and dark blonde hair. The youngest of seven children, Teresa was born and raised in New York; her father was a dairy farmer. She got married and became pregnant during her senior year in high school. "You didn't stay in school if you were pregnant then," Teresa said. "I was lucky. They let me finish at home and get my diploma." About a year later, she had her second child and went to work while her husband went to school. In 1968, she moved to Baltimore, and by 1970, she had split up with her husband. All she had were her two sons, a high school diploma, and "an absolute certainty that there was more to life than she had seen, and an equally sure determination that she was going to see it before it was too late," wrote Judy Mann of the *Washington Post*.

In 1971, Teresa sent her children to live with their father's parents in Florida while she studied psychology at Antioch College. She supported herself by working as a secretary, switchboard operator, waitress, and bartender, including the job at O'Henry's. "[Harry] came in and that was it," she said. She was nineteen years younger than Harry, but the two bonded quickly. Teresa dropped out of college, and they started living together. They were married in February 1978, after Harry's divorce from his first wife became final. They moved into Hawksworth together, and Teresa's children came back to Maryland to live with them.

It was a Cinderella story, and Teresa appreciated her good fortune. She bristled at the notion that she had married for money. "I've worked before, and I can work again. Harry knows I didn't marry him for his money," she snapped when a reporter asked why she had married Meyerhoff. Yet she continued to feel that people were giving her looks and judging her choice in men. "There are subtle things," she said. "No one would ever say it to my face. It's intimations . . . 'Well, you came from a humble family and now you're wealthy.'" So she carried a laid-back style and often wore sweaters and jeans to the track to watch the horses work out, the only sign of her wealth being a large diamond ring on her finger.

Tom Meyerhoff was one of three children from Harry's first marriage. He was a sports fan and had been around horses his entire life. Harry used to tell his kids that if one of his horses won a race and the kids knew about it, he would give them $5. "I read the sports page every day. Cover to cover. I knew something about racing," said Tom, who got the lion's share of the rewards when Harry's horses won. A Boston University dropout, a stockbroker, and a racquetball and tennis player, Tom was considered one of the country's most eligible bachelors. He liked to wear expensive clothes and was a regular at many of the downtown Baltimore drinking establishments. "I've never been in jail, although I've been behind many bars," he joked.

When Tom was twenty-two, his father asked him and Teresa to become equal partners in his racing business. The three formed Hawksworth Farm, and Harry financed the stable. "We used to say, 'He is an equal partner, but he's a lot more equal than the two of us are,'" Tom said. Harry and Teresa were sometimes mistaken for father and daughter, and some thought she and Tom were husband and wife. This did not seem to bother Tom, who countered, "Dad and I argue about a lot of things, but the one thing we don't argue about is who sleeps with Teresa."

Harry, with his gray hair and long gray beard, looked like a trim Santa Claus, especially with his twinkling eyes and ever-smiling face. He preferred blue jeans and tennis shoes to a suit and tie, and he usually had a beer or vodka in his hand, no matter the time of day. Judy Mann of the *Washington Post* called Harry "the most laid-back millionaire to own a Thoroughbred . . . in years." Bill Tanton, sports editor of the *Baltimore Evening Sun,* agreed. "I used to see Harry in bars all the time, and I always thought he was just one of the guys. I knew he had money, but I never dreamt he was the type to own a classic racehorse."

Not that Harry lived like a miser. The Meyerhoffs spent much of their time either vacationing in Acapulco or cruising on their fifty-four-foot yawl, which they sailed to Bermuda on one occasion. They loved to throw parties and invited the upper crust of Baltimore society; in 1958, Harry threw a luau for 180 people that cost him $55 a plate—or about $175 in today's money. The family also enjoyed hunting and taking care of their Labrador retrievers.

Bud Delp. (*Blood-Horse*)

Accompanying the Meyerhoffs at Keeneland in 1977 was their trainer, Grover G. "Bud" Delp, who had been working with them for ten years. Bold, garrulous, and cocky, the forty-six-year-old Delp was a little pudgy and almost bald (his teenage sons called him "Baldy" behind his back). He sported tinted eyeglasses, expensive and sometimes loud casual suits, and patent leather shoes; he drove a Lincoln Town Car. Delp hyperbolized when he talked about his horses and boasted to excess. This did not make him popular among those in the horse racing establishment, who dressed in cowboy boots and understated their horses' abilities. To some members of the media, Delp gave short, sarcastic answers to questions he found pointless. He was from Maryland, not Kentucky, and found the New York racing establishment especially distasteful. "Racing up [in New York] doesn't impress me that much," he once said. He was like a runaway freight train and a loose cannon with journalists, who loved to get quotes from him, but he irritated horse racing's upper crust. Frank Phelps of the *Lexington Leader* wrote, "I doubt if the brash Delp ever will be any darling of the establishment."

Delp could brag because he was a big fish in a small pond. He dominated the Maryland circuit at the Pimlico, Laurel, and Bowie racetracks, which were considered second-tier facilities and inferior to tracks such as Belmont and Saratoga in New York. "They spent more money up there [in New York], and they had bigger purses," said King Leatherbury, one of Delp's rival trainers in Maryland. "And they drew better horses because of the better purses." However, Leatherbury's assistant, Nate Heyman, said Maryland trainers—and horses—could hold their own against New Yorkers and Kentuckians any time, any place, any day. They were born to race, he said, and Maryland trainers knew how to treat horses like individuals, not animals.

Delp made a name for himself in the claiming circuit, where all the horses running in a race are for sale. Delp would "steal" good horses out from under other trainers, getting them for low prices, and unload underperforming horses from his own stable for higher prices. To others in the business, he became known as "crazy ol' Bud," the trainer who did things a little differently. His stable was filled with both cheap and expensive claimers, mixed with middling horses that never amounted to much. But he did wonders with what little talent they possessed. "Most of [Bud Delp's] horses are claimers," wrote Bill Lyon of the *Boca Raton News*. "That's like being a used car dealer. Claiming horses, they say, is the ultimate act of putting your money where your mouth is, betting that you can do more with a horse than the man who used to own him could. This, obviously, requires the kind of self-confidence that borders on egomania. You need either a cat burglar's nerve or dictator's sense of inflated self-worth." Delp, it seemed, had a little bit of both.

He also had a temper and a way of belittling other horses to promote his own, which he fiercely defended. "In a way, the cockiness is a mask for the insecurity that still lurks in the recesses of his mind," wrote Billy Reed of the *Louisville Courier-Journal*. "Like a lot of self-made men, Delp can never quite forget where he came from, or how hard it was to get to the top. So sometimes he can't resist the urge to get even for the slights, real or imagined, that he has suffered in twenty years of scuffling.

Indeed, Delp seems to relish the idea that racing's bluebloods finally are forced to pay attention—and homage—to a guy who knows what it's like to be too broke to buy a hamburger."

He was tough on his crew and demanded perfection from them, and they often felt his wrath when things did not go according to his plans. But they were loyal to him and weathered his outbursts. "You gotta be careful," said Herman "Mo" Hall, Delp's main groom. "You can't miss nothing. I go along with him so there's no argument. A whole lot of times, he has gotten on to me, but I don't pay him no mind. If you say something, that's when you get in trouble."

Born in Creswell, Maryland, Delp was attracted to horses from an early age, playing hooky from school and going to the races. He would sneak into the racecourse by climbing over the fence and then bum $2 off people so he could make a bet. His father, Richard, was a dairy farmer; he died when Delp was three, drowning at a family reunion. Although Delp was too young to remember this tragedy, it left its mark. Delp's philosophy was to live life to the fullest, take chances, and not look back and regret things one should have done.

When Delp was nine, his mother married horse trainer Ray Archer. Delp worked with Archer, starting at the bottom by hot-walking horses for $35 a week. He was drafted into the US Army in 1952 and served as a postal carrier in Italy during the Korean War. In the army, he learned a valuable lesson: as a soldier, you did things the army way; there was no other way. He extended that point of view to his own life. "It was the Bud Delp way or the wrong way," said his younger son, Gerald, who helped him train horses. "And most of the time, he was right on."

After flunking out of the University of Maryland after just one semester, Bud began working for his stepfather again. In 1962, he parted ways with Archer and started his own training business with seven claimers at the Laurel, Maryland, racecourse. "I had no choice," said Delp, who by that time was married, had one baby and another on the way, and was making only $125 a week. One night in the fall of 1962, Delp left Delaware Park to go to Monmouth Park with six horses. He had barely enough gas in his car and just a little change to buy a meal. He told his stepfather that if he did not pay him more money, he would have to leave. Archer asked, "When are you leaving?" They parted ways soon after that.

When Delp left his stepfather, he got one of the two horses they owned: Our Rocky. Delp entered him in a claiming race, and the horse won; Delp collected $1,650—money he desperately needed. Our Rocky won five more times before he was finally claimed by another trainer. "I [eventually] carried sixty-five to seventy horses," Delp said. "I didn't have the clients to go to the sales, and I didn't have the big breeders to send me their well-bred horses. The only way I could survive was in the claiming business."

Delp continued to win on the small track. From 1963 to 1972, he was the leading trainer at Delaware Park in Wilmington. Over the next decade, a rivalry developed among Delp and three other trainers in Maryland—John Tammaro, Dick Dutrow, and King Leatherbury. Together, they were known as the "Big Four," and they claimed horses from one another "as if Thoroughbreds no longer were being bred," wrote Marty McGee of the *Daily Racing Form*. "As a result, rivalries boiled and tempers flared." Leatherbury recalled the time he put a fake bandage on a horse to make it look as if he had a bowed tendon—just so Dutrow would not claim him in a race. "[Bud Delp] was good, and he let people know he was good. People called him the 'King of Claimers,'" Gerald Delp said.

Dan Mearns of the *Thoroughbred Record* described Delp as carrying "a certain anger, a certain mistrust of others. . . . Delp is temperamental. He can be either gregarious or moody, charming or insulting, and even those closest to him must wonder how they stand at times." He was cocky, but he knew when he was right, and he would not hesitate to knock people down a few notches. Delp even described himself as "an ol' country boy from Maryland who has a big mouth that he likes to run whenever he has something to talk about."

On November 3, 1964, disaster struck. A stable hand at Laurel Park was smoking late at night, and his match started a fire in Barn 21—Delp's barn. As the man tried to stamp out the fire, he kicked over some flammable material, fueling the blaze. The fire swept through the wooden structure so fast that workers could not get the horses out of the stalls. Thirty of Delp's thirty-two horses died in the fire. Officials said they had never seen a fire go through a barn so quickly; nor had they seen a barn so completely gutted in such a short time. The champion horse Kelso was only five barns away in Barn 26 but was safe.

It was back to square one for Delp, who took it in stride. The next day, he started claiming new horses. He moved into Barn 32, which had been untouched by the fire, and track owner John Schapiro said he could remain there for as long as he wanted. Delp stayed there for the next forty years.

Steve Haskin of *Blood-Horse* wrote that the Big Four in Maryland were not known on a national scale like the trainers in New York, Kentucky, and California. "These were tough, resilient horsemen who braved the harsh winters at Bowie Race Course every year before moving on to Pimlico and Laurel. There wasn't a great deal of glory for these trainers. They trained mostly claimers and allowance horses and their livelihood depended on keeping these horses sound. Their goals were not the Kentucky Derby. . . . The big-time was having a horse in the Pimlico Special or the Black-Eyed Susan Stakes." It was as if there were two horse racing worlds, and trainers were not supposed to pass from one to the other. A trainer accepted his lot in life and worked hard in the world he was put in.

This did not mean that Delp did not dream. Like most trainers, he longed to find that special horse that came along once in a generation. "I've got a reputation as a trainer of claimers," he told the *Daily Racing Form* in 1967. "I think I could do just as well with a class horse, if I had one."

Delp continued to train horses, and eventually, quality horses found him. In 1968, he trained his first stakes winner, and two years later, he got his second. About that time, the Meyerhoff brothers knocked at Delp's door and asked him to train some of their horses. There was one problem: the Meyerhoffs had been working with another trainer at Laurel, an old-timer named Charlie White, and Delp turned them down, refusing to take horses away from White, who had once saved his career. "[White] was stabled right across from me at Laurel Park," Delp said. "The next day [after the fire in 1964], I claimed three horses. Charlie White opened his tack room to me and said, 'Anything I have here you're welcome to use. If you need room for your horses, you can have my empty stalls. You can use my equipment.' He helped me along in those days after the fire."

After some cajoling, the Meyerhoffs finally convinced a reluctant Delp to take them on as clients. They were interested in buying low at the fall yearling sales, where the horses were cheaper, and finding a dia-

From left: Bud Delp and Tom, Harry, and Teresa Meyerhoff at the 1979
Keeneland sale. (Keeneland Association Library)

mond in the rough that they could turn into a stakes winner. The Meyerhoff brothers had already made their fortune in the real estate business,
so Harry was more concerned with winning than with making money;
he needed Delp's expertise to find those hidden gems and develop them
into contenders. That partnership paid off. Delp recommended Ecole
Etage and Bold Place, and both horses performed well.

Woody Stephens, himself a Hall of Fame trainer at age sixty-five,
said, "There isn't a man alive who knows as much about horses as Bud
Delp." The Meyerhoffs realized this and stayed out of Delp's way. "We
all get along very well with Bud," Teresa Meyerhoff said. "We also know
we're not trainers—that's not our job."

When the Meyerhoffs and Delp arrived at the fall Keeneland sales in
1977, they went through their usual routine: Tom and Harry studied
each horse in the catalog and chose the ones they liked. "We basically

just looked at the sire's side, and we'd look at the dam's side, and then we'd approve the horse," Tom said. "The dam's side sort of told us how high we would have to go for any given sire." When the two saw the gray yearling with an unspectacular dam listed in the catalog, they were immediately interested. Delp noted in his catalog, "Looks like a runner." They liked Bold Bidder as a stallion; he had sired one of their big-money winners, Bold Place. They wanted the colt, and they were willing to pay as much as $60,000 for him—the amount Jason and Gilmore hoped to get for the horse. "We thought we might have to pay more than we did, but he had a twin in his dam's family, and Bold Bidder was not particularly popular as a sire," Harry Meyerhoff said. "[The colt] was a standout physically, a very well-conformed yearling who toed out a little in his right front [hoof]. That might have affected his price a little."

The colt was on the short list of horses that they all liked. "Bud was very quiet if he didn't like a horse. He knew it pretty quickly," Tom said. "We tried not to waste too much time on horses we didn't like, but the ones we did like, we might spend five minutes or more on them—just having them walk and looking at them from all angles and talking about them. We'd listen to what Bud was saying, and then after our notes were done, we'd go ahead and decide which ones we wanted to get, and what prices we were thinking."

Most horsemen thought the colt was not that beautiful; perhaps the bias against grays was still apparent among buyers. His dull gray coat spotted with brown created an unpleasant contrast to the other beautiful, shining brown and chestnut colts; one writer thought the horse looked like a tweed coat. He was somewhat small in stature, and his pedigree—especially the twins on his dam's side—was troublesome. His tail was somewhat scraggly. But the colt was muscular, and one trainer raved about the horse's "perfect ass." His rear end, where horses get their driving action, was well proportioned and promised power and speed.

Few people bid on the horse, and the auctioneer's gavel fell at $37,000—considerably less than what Jason and Gilmore wanted, and less than Meyerhoff was prepared to spend. Meyerhoff handed Delp the sales slip and, as he always did when he bought a horse, told the trainer, "Here's your next champion." Then they went back to the barn and had a drink.

Heerman was disappointed at the low price fetched by the Buck

Spectacular Bid as a yearling at Wimbledon Farm, 1977. (Keeneland Library Thoroughbred Times Collection)

Pond Farm colt. "I thought realistically that he would bring $60,000," he said. "But Mrs. Jason entered the colt in the sale to be sold, and we did not think about bidding him in. A number of interested people stopped by the barn to look at him. . . . Now those same people come to me and shake their heads and recall, 'He certainly was a nice-looking yearling.'"

Later, Keeneland defended its decision to place the colt in the fall sale, claiming that Bold Bidder was not a popular commodity. "Realistically, at the time, [Bold Bidder] was a borderline case. Since then Bold Bidders have sold very well. Like women's dresses, they're up and down," said William S. Evans, director of the sales. "The fact that [the colt] brought only $37,000 backed up the pedigree committee and justified its action [to reject the colt for the July sale]. Back then, we were averaging in the $80,000 area." That year at the fall sale, the average price of a yearling was $13,321, and the top price was $200,000. The top price for a Bold Bidder yearling was $82,000, and the lowest was $10,000. It seemed that the Meyerhoffs got a bargain with this Bold Bidder colt.

Now that they had the colt, the Meyerhoffs had to name it. At first, they went with a name using Bold Bidder's side of the family, offering Seven No Trump—a bold bid in the game of bridge. But the Jockey Club, which records and approves the names of all Thoroughbreds, rejected it.[2] Instead, the Meyerhoffs went for a mixture of both sides of the family—Spectacular and Bold Bidder. They submitted Spectacular Bid for consideration, and the Jockey Club accepted it.

The Meyerhoffs sent Spectacular Bid to the Middleburg Training Center in Virginia, where, under the tutelage of Barbara Graham, he learned how to be ridden. He was introduced to the bridle and the bit; he learned subtle hand signals conveyed by the jockey's use of the reins; he became familiar with the ever-important starting gate; and he learned the basics of training, such as breezing, or working at moderate speed. "At this stage, each individual progress[es] at its own rate," the center's website explains. "Both physical and mental soundness must be maintained in order to move to the next level. Horses must learn to pay attention to their own rider, despite lots of things going on around them, e.g., horses galloping by them, [and] other horses walking in the opposite direction."

"Barbara was quite impressed with him," Tom Meyerhoff said of Bid (his nickname). "She liked the yearling crop in general—we usually send our sale buys to her—but she said that Spectacular Bid was the best-looking yearling she had ever seen, and she's been a horsewoman for some time." Graham agreed. "He was a really nice colt," she told the *Daily Racing Form*. "With each new lesson, it seemed that he already knew what he was supposed to do."

About a year earlier, sixteen-year-old Ron Franklin had arrived at the same training center to learn how to be a jockey. Born in Baltimore in 1959 and raised in Dundalk, Maryland, he stood only five feet tall and weighed 106 pounds soaking wet. His mother, a nurse and one-time secretary to the mayor of Baltimore, remembered that he got into numerous fights at Patapsco High School over his size. "He couldn't stand people making fun of him or laughing at him," she said. At one point, she took her son to the doctor to see if he was maturing at the right pace, and the doctor said nothing was wrong.

"You had to take care of yourself," Ron Franklin said. "You know, there was always bullies. I was just a guy who didn't like people bully-ing." It was young Ronnie against the world, and the fights toughened him. He was known as a kid who would not take anything from any-body. He used baseball bats, bricks—anything he could lay his hands on—to defend himself, and it worked.

Franklin also hated the confines of school—or being confined in any building—and longed to be outside where he could fish, hunt crabs, or play sports. The ocean was one of his favorite places, its expansive waters seeming to go on forever, with nothing to block his view. He did not want to follow in his father's footsteps, working as a maintenance man at the American Can Company. "I didn't want to be behind no windows," he was fond of saying. His mother had only one wish: that her six children would at least graduate from high school, and maybe do more.

Franklin had no thoughts of that; from third grade on, he made it his goal to drop out of school. To pass the time, he played hooky, ran with gangs, drank, smoked cigarettes (and occasionally marijuana), and got into trouble for throwing mud balls and tossing dead fish into neigh-bors' swimming pools. During one stretch in seventh grade, he and his friends were absent from school for three weeks and two days straight, but school officials still promoted him. "I would say he's a gutsy little fellow. He had a lot of nerve," said John M. Benser, his English teacher. Benser remembered Franklin defying his teachers by marching around the desks when he got bored. "He'd say he was never afraid of anything."

Franklin tried out for the baseball team in tenth grade and was made the "designated walker." At four feet seven inches tall, he presented such a small strike zone when he went up to bat that pitchers usually walked him.

When he was sixteen, Franklin finally quit school, urged on by his teachers, who had had enough of him. He was the first in his family not to get a high school diploma (to his mother's chagrin). "He went to the eleventh grade, and he *hated* school so much, you know, that we just had a problem with him," his mother said. "He just didn't want to go, and he was skipping school, and the best thing for him to do was to quit."

He was a boy in search of a purpose—something that could hold his interest and keep him occupied. He joined the Boy Scouts because they spent a lot of time outdoors and went camping, but every time he returned from a camping trip, he quit. He asked his mother for a set of drums; she acquiesced, but he soon quit playing. Determined that he not spend his days lying around the house, Ron's mother told him to get a job. He first worked at a Roy Rogers Restaurant, cutting grass and painting picnic tables for $50 a week. But it was clear that he still had no direction and no skills—nothing he liked that could turn into a career.

One day, he was wrestling some kids in a yard that belonged to a neighbor, "Uncle" Hank Tiburzi. Impressed by Franklin's arm strength despite his size, Tiburzi asked the boy if he had ever thought about becoming a jockey. Franklin, who had never even been on a horse, said no, so Tiburzi invited him to Pimlico Race Course in Baltimore. From the moment he stepped through the Rogers Avenue gate at Pimlico, Franklin was hooked. He had found his calling.

He did not wait; that first day, as if he knew this would be his life's work, he began asking stable hands around the barn about employment. He failed to get a job, but he went back the next day and asked everyone he saw if they needed any help. After a few minutes, someone on the public-address system announced, "There's a young man at the stable gate looking for a hot walker's job." Franklin did not know what a hot walker did, but he waited for a response. Bud Delp heard the announcement and sent his nephew, Brian, to get the boy. Brian offered Franklin a job hot-walking horses for $75 a week. Franklin was honest with him. "Look, I've never been around horses, I don't know them, I don't know nothin'," he told Brian in his southern drawl, complete with double negatives and dropped g's. The younger Delp replied, "Don't worry, we'll teach you."

Franklin soon left his parents' house on Ormand Road and moved into the track's tack room, a cold and drafty place overrun with mice. Franklin spent his nights throwing darts at the animals; at four o'clock each morning, he got ready for work. Two weeks passed before Bud Delp even noticed him. But when he did, he thought Franklin was the perfect size for a jockey. Franklin agreed. "I really didn't dream about nothing until I came on the racetrack," he said. "I knew then I wanted to be a jockey. That was my dream. When I was sixteen, I knew right away. First time I can remember wanting to be somebody."

After Franklin had been hot-walking horses for about six weeks, Delp called him into his office. "You wanna ride, boy?" he asked.

"Well, that's what I'm trying to do," Franklin said.

And so, in November 1976, at the tender age of sixteen, Franklin went to the Middleburg Training Center, where he learned how to handle horses and get in shape. Riding looks easy—jockeys appear to just stick their feet in the stirrups, hold the reins, and hang on—but there is much more to the art of riding a horse. Jockeys must have the strength and stamina to control a thousand-pound animal for up to two and a half minutes. Simply maintaining a crouch on a horse for that amount of time requires so much leg strength that inexperienced riders cannot walk after dismounting. Medical testing has shown that jockeys rank in the top 10 percent of all athletes.

Jockeys must also possess great reflexes; they must be ready to move the horse at less than a second's notice if another horse moves into them or if they see an opening in a wall of horses. And they must have good judgment, knowing when to hold a horse back and when to make a move. If they move too soon, they could tire the horse out too quickly; if they move too late, it could result in a second- or third-place finish with a horse that is still fresh. Jockeys need to be fearless—timidity can get them blocked in or even tossed from a horse. They must be in control of the animal, recognize an opening when it exists, and not fear other horses and jockeys when squeezing through that opening.

Finally, jockeys need to learn the most difficult skill of all: "feel," or the indefinable communication between horse and rider that enables a jockey to coax the maximum performance from an animal. Horses ride well for some jockeys and refuse to perform for others. Delp saw that talent in Franklin. "Anyone can climb on a horse, but Ronnie can really communicate with a horse through his hands," he said. "Ronnie and horses. Horses run fast for him."

When Franklin returned from Middleburg, he galloped horses as part of their training regimen and soon became the barn's main rider. Delp took him into his home in Laurel, half an hour away from Dundalk, where he lived with his own boys, Doug and Gerald. The two formed a family bond that would last for years. In time, Delp would call Franklin his "third son."[3] This meant that he was subject to Delp's cutting tongue along with the hugs, the unrelenting demands along with the rewards.

3

Potential

The colt has all the necessary potential to be a Kentucky Derby winner, a Triple Crown winner.

—Andrew Beyer, *Washington Post*

IN JUNE 1978, while he was having dinner with Bud Delp, Ron Franklin, who had been riding Spectacular Bid as part of his regular schedule, said, "Boss, that's a helluva colt we got."

"How the hell would you know?" Delp asked in his grumpy but amiable way.

Franklin knew. Earlier in the day, the apprentice jockey had ridden Bid half a mile in a blazing forty-six seconds flat. A good time for an adult racehorse to run four furlongs during a workout is forty-eight seconds. And Bid was a baby, a two-year-old that was just learning to race and whose bones and muscles had not yet matured.

When he got off the horse, Franklin said, "This horse is great! He feels like two horses under you. When you pull him up, he wants to go again." Delp answered Franklin as a master would respond to an overeager apprentice: "What the hell are you talking about? What do you know about horses?" Delp himself did not want to admit it, but he was getting excited about this colt. Was this the horse he had been waiting for? Was this the horse that would lift him out of the claiming business? *Could he have a champion?*

Bid had returned from Middleburg Training Center in March 1978, along with the rest of Hawksworth Farm's crop, and Delp's assistant, Charlie Bettis, had been working with Bid for a few weeks. "Bud came over to see him," Bettis said. "He came away impressed, and said, 'He needs to be with me [at Pimlico].'" Delp had taken three of the Meyerhoffs' most promising colts from the Keeneland sale to Middleburg; when he saw Bid run against the other two colts, Seethreepeo and I Know Why,[1] he said, "I could see that Bid was best." Delp had to stop running Bid with the other two horses for fear that he would dishearten them with his speed. Franklin had to keep Bid under tight control to keep the other two horses on pace with the colt.

The more Bid trained, the stronger he got and the more he wanted to train. He was like an Olympic athlete, taking all he could from his trainer and wanting more. "The more I did with him, the more he thrived," Delp said. "He was telling me something about him, every day. But I had to be careful; you can overdo it, right from the get-go." Bid's racing style was unorthodox—he held his head unusually high, and his gait was so quick, so smooth and effortless, that it looked as if he were out for a short gallop—but it worked. His feet seemed to skim the ground as his "perfect ass"—as one trainer put it—transmitted a powerful snapping power to the hind legs, propelling him to a higher gear. Harry Meyerhoff used to joke that in every picture of Spectacular Bid, the horse's feet were off the ground. Delp likened his legs to tree stumps.

Pimlico general manager Chick Lang remembered Delp taking him into Bid's stall and saying, "Put your hand on him. Slap him." When he did, it was like hitting a piece of steel. "He's one big muscle. And when I felt his knees and ankles, it's like having a tray of ice in your hand. There isn't a bit of heat anywhere (the sign of an injury)." Delp told Lang he wanted to bring Bid along slowly after the 1978 winter break—just walking him around the paddock at first. "He said the horse was actually mad, raised hell all the way to his stall because he thought he was going to run and didn't," Lang recalled.

Bid's first test would be at Pimlico on June 30, 1978—the third race of the day at five and a half furlongs.[2] Word had not spread about Bid's potential yet, so odds were set at 6 to 1—not a long shot, but not a favorite either. He was the crowd's fourth choice in the race. Franklin recalled that Delp had hidden Bid from the people clocking the horses, exercising him in the early morning when it was still dark and the track was deserted. "He would've been 1 to 5 if they had seen him," Franklin said.

Delp had been using Franklin to exercise Bid occasionally, and the trainer wanted to see how the two meshed during a race, so he told

Bud Delp instructing young Ron Franklin. (Jim McCue)

Franklin that he would be riding Bid in the horse's first race. Franklin would benefit from the "bug rule," which allowed apprentice jockeys—or "bugs," as they are called—to carry five to ten pounds less than the other jockeys as an equalizer to their inexperience.

Franklin had ridden in his first race as an apprentice on February 4, 1978, at Bowie Race Course in Maryland on a horse called Pioneer Patty. Before a crowd of thousands cheering their hometown boy, Franklin brought her home, winning the seven-furlong race by three lengths. "A winning debut does not necessarily signal the beginning of a successful riding career, but Franklin might be an exception," wrote Dale Austin of the *Baltimore Sun*. Franklin, who worked the filly every day, had been confident enough to bet $50 on her, and he took home more than

$600 on the wager. Wedged inside Franklin's helmet was a nickel he had found outside Pioneer Patty's stall earlier in the day, and it turned out to be his good-luck charm.

The next day, he won his second race on board a three-year-old maiden named Deficit. Veterans around the racetrack speculated that Franklin might have been the first jockey to win his first two races. He soon got noticed around Bowie and was recognized as an exceptional apprentice jockey, leading to more mounts, even though Delp held his contract. "He is further along than any rider I've ever brought around," Delp said. "He's ready and has more confidence in himself than anybody I've ever known." Franklin was known around the track as a shy, quiet, polite boy who worked hard and did anything Delp asked of him. When Bowie's season was over, he moved to Pimlico and took the lead among jockeys there, with 34 wins in 142 mounts, a 24 percent winning record.

The day of Bid's first race was hot and humid; the temperature would reach ninety degrees that day. Bid was fed his regular breakfast, but not the usual amount. A few hours later, he went for his morning workout, but the rider limited him to a jog and would not let him run. At lunchtime, Bid received nothing. He grew annoyed and paced in his stall. Finally, his groom, Herman "Mo" Hall, came by to brush him, taking extra care, and then walked him to a paddock where other horses were waiting.

Hall had been with Delp for about nine years and had been caring for Bid ever since the colt came under the trainer's tutelage. Hall and Bid were close; the groom spent all his time washing the colt, bandaging his legs, preparing his food, mucking the stall, and applying first aid to any cuts he might have gotten from racing. Delp sometimes called Bid "Mo's Baby."

Hall and Delp put Bid's saddle on him, just as they would do for a workout. But they never spent so much time and care saddling him for a workout. Something different was happening that day. It was race day. Since the race was at nearby Pimlico, the Meyerhoffs were present to see their newest acquisition in his first race. "Bud usually says, 'If you want to come, come,'" Teresa Meyerhoff said. "But with Bid, he said, 'I think you should be there because I think he is going to run very well.'" They were treated to a show. Bid was light on his feet and pranced around in the post parade as if he were eager to get the race started. Franklin was wearing black and blue, the colors of Hawksworth Farm; Meyerhoff had chosen those colors because "that's how owners get treated in this game—they get beat on until they're black and blue."

The assistant starters loaded each horse into the starting gate, and Bid went in just as he had been taught at Middleburg. The bell signaled the start, the doors to the gate opened, and the track loomed ahead. Bid lumbered out of the starting gate and settled into fifth place behind the rest of the field. He took a while to get his long, clumsy legs into a rhythm, but they soon settled into a pattern, and he took off. He passed his competitors with ease as his effortless stride took hold of the track. Bid quickly claimed the lead and never looked back. Franklin hand-rode him the entire way and never had to use his whip, as the two-year-old romped to a three-and-a-quarter-length win over a fast-closing Strike Your Colors. His time was 1:04³/₅, two-fifths of a second away from the track record. It was his first race, and he was only two years old.

Upstairs in the press box, William Phillips of the *Daily Racing Form* turned to Pimlico general manager Chick Lang and said, "We've got ourselves a good one. We've got a Kentucky Derby horse!"

Lang replied, "He did look great, didn't he?"

The next day, Phillips wrote about Spectacular Bid in his column— a rare mention of a two-year-old's first race in the nation's premier horse racing periodical:

> Grover G. (Bud) Delp turned loose one of the promising two-year-olds from his barn in the third race here Friday. His name is Spectacular Bid and you'll probably be hearing more about him.
>
> He is a Kentucky-bred colt with a solid family background. A bay colt by Bold Bidder–Spectacular, by Promised Land, he is owned by the Hawksworth Farm of Harry Meyerhoff, his wife Teresa and son Tom.
>
> Spectacular Bid handled himself like a seasoned veteran in his first start. Three rivals outbroke him for the lead, but he moved between them to be in front by a half-length after the first furlong, and drew away under intermittent punishment from apprentice Ron Franklin to score by three-and-a-quarter lengths.

At a casual glance it might look like just another two-year-old maiden race, but the running time and the rivals he beat suggest it was much more. Carrying 115 pounds, his five-and-a-half-furlong time of 1:04⅗ over the fast track was just two ticks slower than Lucky Penny's track record. Because of the many other prospects in the race he paid $14.60.

Afterward, when Bid was in his stall enjoying a victory dinner that included a doughnut, Delp had a drink with the Meyerhoffs and confided in them: "You know, I really feel this is a special kind of horse." Never had Delp expressed such high praise for such a young horse. In the past, the Meyerhoffs had heard their trainer say, "We've got a good horse here," but he had always been referring to older horses. Never had he called a horse "special," and never had they heard such confidence after only one race. The three Meyerhoffs agreed with Delp. This horse might be the one they had been waiting for—a champion and maybe even a Kentucky Derby contender.

Delp lined up a second matchup for Spectacular Bid—another five-and-a-half-furlong race at Pimlico three weeks later, on July 22. This time, the crowd had heard of his previous performance and sent him off as a 3 to 10 favorite, which meant that bettors would win just 60 cents on a $2 bet.[3] Bid started slowly again, running third in the early going, but Franklin bided his time and waited until the far turn to make his move. Once he did, Bid took command, steadily drew away, and won by eight lengths over Silent Native. The time of 1:04⅕ was a track record.

The competition was too easy for this colt. Delp knew he should enter Bid in a stakes race—the top echelon of racing. Only the best horses got to compete in stakes races, and even fewer won them. So Delp entered Bid in the August 2 Tyro Stakes at Monmouth Park in Oceanport, New Jersey. So many horses were entered that the race had to be run in two heats. Although the distance was the same as Bid's first two races—five and a half furlongs—the competition in the Tyro would be better than the horses he had faced in his first two races.

As luck would have it, the rains came long and hard on race day. The track was a complete mess, full of standing water and mud. It would be hard for the horses to gain traction, and any horses in the back of the pack would have mud thrown up on their chests and in their faces—

something many horses do not tolerate well. Jockeys racing in the slop sometimes wear three or four pairs of goggles, slinging each one off when it gets too muddy.

Concerned about Bid slipping in the mud and injuring himself, Delp considered scratching him from the race but decided against it. Instead, he opted to give the colt some experience, while taking precautions to keep him safe. Knowing that he had an inexperienced jockey on a valuable horse, he instructed Franklin to "protect the horse, no matter what happened, just hold him together and make sure he [doesn't] get hurt. . . . I went to the jocks' room three times that afternoon and I said to Ronnie, I said, 'Now Ronnie, you leave that gate, get a hold of him, get him in the middle of the track and sit there—don't move on him the whole race.'"

It was the first time Spectacular Bid had raced in the slop; he was not used to the mud splashing him in the face and on the stomach. Racing in the second division of the stakes, Bid buck-jumped and leaped over mud puddles, doing everything but run; it was almost comical. He broke out of the gate last and was still twelve lengths behind halfway through the race. Franklin followed Delp's instructions and just sat on him, keeping Bid out of trouble and making sure he did not slip in the mud. The colt loafed to the finish line seven lengths behind the winner, Groton High. But despite his slow foray through the slop, his natural speed still enabled him to capture fourth place out of eight horses. It was disappointing, but considering the conditions, Bid's behavior, and Franklin's cautious ride, it was a respectable finish. Later, Delp would regret entering the horse in the race, but it was a learning experience for the colt.

In the first division of the race, a chestnut colt named Coastal, the son of 1969 Kentucky Derby winner Majestic Prince, scored a mild upset. Coastal (the second choice in betting) went to the front and then dropped to second as the favorite, Admiral Buck, took over. Coastal regained the lead one-sixteenth of a mile from the finish and won by six lengths—an impressive performance by the young colt.

Other juvenile horses were also making names for themselves. One of the most impressive two-year-olds was General Assembly, a son of Secretariat and the spitting image of his father, right down to the white stockings on his feet and the white blaze on his face. His dam was Exclusive Dancer, the offspring of Hall of Fame inductee and 1954 Horse of the Year Native Dancer. General Assembly was undefeated in three races, having won the Saratoga Special Stakes and the Hopeful Stakes, and he looked like he might carry on his sire's and grandsire's legacies.

Another highly regarded colt was Tim the Tiger, a son of the champion Nashua and a product of Calumet Farm. Calumet had been the premier name in racing from the 1940s through the 1960s and had produced eight Kentucky Derby winners and two Triple Crown winners. But aside from Alydar, the hard-luck runner-up to Affirmed in 1978's Triple Crown races, the farm had fallen on hard times. Tim the Tiger was not impressive to look at—he was big and ungainly—but he could run. Trainer John Veitch let him race, and Tim surprised everyone by winning his first four races.

On September 27 the two hopefuls met in the Cowdin Stakes, and Tim the Tiger handed General Assembly his first defeat, catching him in the last fifty yards and extending his record to five wins in five races. The margin of victory was just a neck, and people were discussing a rematch in the Champagne Stakes on October 7 and anticipating an Affirmed-Alydar–type rivalry between the two. The Eclipse Award for Champion Two-Year-Old Male could be settled in that race.

There was one more outstanding two-year-old colt: Flying Paster, a California-bred colt that had won five races in a row on the West Coast. (His owner and breeder was B. J. Ridder of the Knight Ridder newspaper chain, and the horse was named after a device that replaces rolls of newsprint without stopping the presses.) Ridden by veteran jockey Don Pierce, "The Paster" possessed a huge homestretch kick that overwhelmed his rivals. He could come from out of nowhere during the far turn and take the race with ease.

Delp wanted revenge for Bid's humiliating loss in the Tyro Stakes, and Hawksworth Farm put up $5,000 to enter Spectacular Bid as a supplementary addition to the Sapling Stakes at Monmouth Park on August 12, where Groton High was set to run. However, the day before the race, Bid's veterinarian informed Delp that the horse had a touch of colic, so the trainer announced that Bid would not be running in the race.

Instead, Bid raced in the Dover Stakes at nearby Delaware Park on August 20. This time, Bid, the bettors' favorite, got out of the gate in second position, then settled back and let a few horses pass him. Ron Franklin's inexperience showed as he allowed Bid to get caught behind two horses on the rail. Franklin had a split second to move to the outside and go around the horses, but he hesitated, and Strike Your Colors, who had finished second to Bid in his maiden win, pulled up beside him. He was boxed in. He could not go left because he was beside the rail; he could not go right because there was a horse beside him. There were two horses in front of him as well. Locked into fourth place, Franklin again failed to take advantage of an opening between horses at the half-mile pole while Bid strained at the reins, eager to take off. Strike Your Colors made his move on the outside and took the lead heading into the stretch, but Franklin did not follow him until it was too late. He took Bid around the row of horses at the five-sixteenths pole,[4] flew by them, and was aiming his sights on Strike Your Colors, but he did not have enough track. Bid finished second by two and a half lengths.

It was the second defeat in a row for Bid. His record in four starts was two wins, one second, and one fourth—respectable, but not outstanding. Delp was furious with the young jockey for getting Bid trapped on the rail. "No way the horse should have got beat," Delp said. "If Ronnie hadn't had him in trouble, he'd [have] won by ten."

Delp realized that if he had a special horse on his hands, he would need a special jockey. The Meyerhoffs' first choice was eighteen-year-old Steve Cauthen, the whiz kid behind Affirmed's Triple Crown run the year before. He was the same age as Franklin, but his experience made him look like a thirty-year-old. He was the first jockey to win $6 million in one season and was the nation's most winning jockey in 1977. In 1978 he was named *Sports Illustrated* Sportsman of the Year.

Delp called Cauthen's agent, Lenny Goodman, and asked about the jockey's availability. He told Goodman he had a special horse, one that could win the Triple Crown, and owners with deep pockets. He wanted Cauthen to ride Spectacular Bid in all his races, starting with the World's Playground Stakes in Atlantic City, New Jersey, on September 23. Goodman was coy, telling Delp he would think about it and get back to him. Delp did not like to be played with, so he went with Franklin again for the World's Playground. The seven-furlong race would feature some of the more talented two-year-olds, including Strike Your Colors and Groton High, the two horses that had defeated Bid in his last two races. That would not be the case this time.

Franklin took Spectacular Bid to the lead after the pacesetter, Honest Moment, posted a blistering quarter mile in twenty-two seconds. Bid was ahead by two lengths after a half mile and six lengths after six furlongs. "After that it looked like bowling pins falling over," Delp said. "One horse after another coming at him and falling back." Bid kept going and did not let up; he finished the final furlong in eleven and four-fifths seconds, crossed the finish line fifteen lengths ahead of Crest of the Wave, and set a new track record in the process—an astounding 1:20⁴/₅. His margin of victory is still a record. Usually, by the end of a race, the split times are much slower because the horses are tiring, but Bid's final furlong was almost as fast as his first. Coastal, the horse that had won the other division of the Tyro Stakes in the slop, was a badly beaten fifth, seventeen lengths behind Bid.

"We knew Spectacular Bid was a serious talent going in, but what he did at Atlantic City, winning by fifteen lengths in 1:20 and change, well . . . two-year-olds just don't do that," said Brian Zipse, senior writer with *Horse Racing Nation*. Bid had made his statement. And the horse racing community turned its collective head toward Atlantic City and raised its eyebrow at this horse owned, trained, and ridden by a group of Marylanders.

Lenny Goodman called Delp the next day, and the trainer's son Doug took a message: "Lenny . . . Cauthen . . . Idiot . . . Please call." When Goodman finally talked to Delp, he reiterated his earlier message—he had been an idiot—and asked if the offer for Cauthen to ride Bid was still available. Delp replied that he would take a rain check and hung up.

With Bid's win at the World's Playground, the competition for the Eclipse Award championship became more complicated. The winner might be determined in the Champagne Stakes, which was held at Belmont Park in Elmont, New York—a track where Delp had entered only fifteen horses in his career and had won just twice. General Assembly would be there, as would Tim the Tiger. Horse racing experts had expected these two to battle it out for Champion Two-Year-Old Male, but Bid's showing in the World's Playground brought a new dimension to the race.

Determined to have Bid win the Champagne Stakes, Delp told Franklin that he was being replaced by veteran jockey Jorge Velasquez. "Ronnie's only ridden for about seven months," Delp explained to the press, "and he's not familiar with this big track. I picked out Jorge because he's an old pro. I want no mistakes. Ronnie understands. He wants the best for the horse." Franklin's poor performance in the Dover Stakes was still in the back of his mind.

Spectacular Bid was bettors' third choice behind General Assembly and Tim the Tiger. He started the race from the inside number-one post—never a good position for a horse because of the possibility of getting boxed in along the rail by the other horses, a situation Bid had encountered in the Dover Stakes. Bid left the post in his usual plodding manner, while the quick-moving Breezing On went straight to the front to set the first-quarter pace in a moderate twenty-three and one-fifth seconds.

Three furlongs into the race, Velasquez recognized the slower pace and chirped into Bid's ear. Instead of moving on his own, as he usually did, the gray colt responded like lightning. With his light, seemingly effortless gait, he quickly put real estate behind him, passing several horses and moving into second place. He then pulled up alongside Breezing On and eyed the front-running colt. Breezing On tried to do the same, but he could not look Bid in the eye. Discouraged and intimidated, Breezing On dropped back immediately while Bid surged to the front, traveling along the rail. At the half-mile pole, he held a one-length lead over General Assembly, with Breezing On third and Tim the Tiger fourth. General Assembly tried to challenge him, but Bid kicked it into a higher gear on the homestretch, with some urging by Velasquez. Tim the Tiger was inexplicably fading, and fading fast.

Bid stretched his lead to four lengths before Velasquez tightened the reins, trying with all his might to slow him down. Bid was ahead by two and three-quarters lengths when he hit the finish line. The time for the mile-long race was a fast 1:34⁴/₅, only two-fifths of a second slower than the stakes record set by the great Seattle Slew in 1976. If Velasquez had let him race through the finish line, Bid could have beaten that record. General Assembly finished second, and Crest of the Wave was third. Tim the Tiger was a well-beaten fourth, nine lengths back.

What made the difference in this race was the discovery of a new, higher gear—something Bid would continue to use throughout his career. According to writer William Nack, "He had two or three different gears. Bid could move in a race, and then be steadied and then move again. He was one of those horses." Just when he seemed to be out of it, or when he seemed to tire, or when he faced a challenger, he would find that faster pace and accelerate ahead of any competition.

Russ Harris of the *Thoroughbred Record* did not put much stock in comparing records from different years, which involved different surface conditions, different equipment, and different competition. Instead, he looked at the other mile-long event on the program that day, which took place under the same conditions and on the same track. In that race, a four-year-old mare won in 1:38^{1}/5. Bid's time was more than three seconds faster than that of a horse *two years older* than he was.

"He's a nice horse," Velasquez said. "He didn't break too sharp, but he still made it by what, three lengths? We got to the eighth pole, and nobody was coming. I'm keeping my fingers crossed and hope he gets [to the Triple Crown races]."

When asked whether he was disappointed about losing the mount on Bid, Franklin said he took things as they came and was not upset about it. "I haven't been riding for very long," he admitted. "I guess my time will come later when I can ride up here. Maybe next year."

Meanwhile, things were not looking good for Coastal, the horse that had won the first division of the muddy Tyro Stakes but then finished fifth to Bid in the World's Playground Stakes. Running in the Marlboro Nursery Stakes at Bowie on October 14, 1978, Coastal finished fifth again, seven lengths behind winner Clever Trick. During the race, a clod of dirt flew up in his face, injuring his right eye; an abscess developed, and veterinarians had to operate, leaving him partially blind in that eye. His owner and trainer did not know whether Coastal would ever race again.

Delp's confidence in Spectacular Bid was growing, and he crowed about him. "If they want the [Two-Year-Old Male Horse of the Year] crown they will have to come to Laurel," he told the New York media after the Champagne Stakes. He was referring to the upcoming Laurel Futurity on October 28 at Laurel Park, Maryland. "I wouldn't have been here if I didn't expect to win. I told Velasquez not to let him loaf— I wanted to show who's the champ from the quarter pole home." The New York racing establishment seethed at the idea of a Maryland trainer winning such an important New York race and then gloating about it. When asked whether horse trainers would ever forgive Delp's remarks, one of his friends replied, "Never. They'll tolerate him, as long as he has the horse, but they'll never forgive him."

After the race, Harry Meyerhoff insured Bid for $5 million.

Velasquez was up on Spectacular Bid again for the colt's first race around two turns, the Young America Stakes at the Meadowlands in East Rutherford, New Jersey, on the evening of October 19. Bid was the bettor's favorite at 3 to 10 odds, but he almost blew it. Or, rather, Velasquez almost did.

At the start, the Canadian gelding Port Ebony swerved toward the outside and ran into several horses, including Bid. The collision caused Bid to veer off course, slow down, and fall back to seventh place, boxed in behind a wall of horses coming around the first turn. He regained his form, moving between horses in the first turn until he reached third place. Down the backstretch, he continued to make a strong move, challenging the leader, Make a Mess. But Velasquez held Bid back, allowing Make a Mess to hang around and battle for the lead. Again, Bid fought against the reins, wanting the lead for himself.

For three-quarters of a mile, the two ran as one, with Bid coming at Make a Mess multiple times until the latter tired. Then, with one furlong left, Strike Your Colors, the horse that had beaten Bid in the Tyro, inched ahead. Another horse named Instrument Landing also surged toward the leaders, and in the final 500 feet, it was a three-horse race. The crowd of 18,219 leaped to their feet as the three horses raced neck and neck. Velasquez threw everything into his mount—using the whip liberally— as Bid tried to inch ahead in the final yards. Digging his hooves into the dirt, reaching as far as he could with each stride, and breathing heavily, he could not find that extra gear and pull away. Perhaps the battle with Make a Mess had tired him. Maybe Strike Your Colors and Instrument Landing were too fresh. It was a photo finish. The crowd waited for the stewards to examine the photo and post the winner. The horses walked around the oval, cooling down and blowing hard after such a heated battle, as the jockeys continually checked the scoreboard.

Velasquez's urging had worked: the finish-line photo showed Spectacular Bid winning by a neck over Strike Your Colors, who edged out Instrument Landing by a head for second. For all his troubles—being boxed in, having to go around several horses, slowing down, and going after Make a Mess numerous times—he finished the mile-and-one-sixteenth race in 1:43^1/$_5$, just one second off the track record.

Delp was not happy with Velasquez's performance. "Going up the backside, the colt wanted the lead real bad," said an irritated Delp, who had wanted another runaway win in front of the New York crowd. "Velasquez reached down and took a hold on him. So the colt relaxed and stayed with the horse alongside him. That made it a hard race." If it sounded like Delp was criticizing Velasquez instead of Bid, he was. "It was a bad ride in the sense that he didn't follow instructions," Delp said of the jockey. "He didn't know Bid was a great horse." According to Delp, Velasquez had also suggested modifications in Bid's equipment before the race, including changes to his bit and use of a full blinker on the right side. Then there was the jockey's wife. After both of Velasquez's victories aboard Bid, his wife had beaten Teresa Meyerhoff to the winner's circle and beamed as the photographers took her picture. "That didn't sit well with the Meyerhoffs," Delp said.

And with that, Ron Franklin was back on Bid. However, Delp hinted that the move might be temporary. He admitted that his and the Meyerhoffs' first preference was the legendary Bill Shoemaker, winner of more than 7,000 races, but Shoemaker was not available. "He's the best there is, and we want the very best for this colt," Delp said. "But I'm not knocking Ronnie. He handled the colt well enough, but when you can get a Shoemaker, you just do." However, even when Shoemaker became free, neither the Meyerhoffs nor Delp called him.

Delp was still unhappy when he returned home to Maryland for the fifty-sixth Laurel Futurity on October 28. The track conditions at Laurel leading up to the race were "cuppy," which meant that the racing surface was dry and loose, tending to break away under a horse's hooves. This kind of surface can make a horse slip, risking injury, or it can cause him to tire as he fights through the sandy surface to gain traction. Delp and LeRoy Jolley, General Assembly's trainer, threatened to pull their horses from the race unless track officials did something about the conditions. "This isn't a racetrack," Delp said. "I don't know what it is, but it ain't no racetrack. And if they don't do something about it, we're not running. It's as simple as that."

John Veitch scoffed at Delp's threat and accused him of having

"Eclipsitis" (the great undefeated British horse Eclipse had scared away the competition in many of his races), implying that Delp did not want Bid to face Tim the Tiger. Delp, never afraid to engage in a war of words, said, "If Alydar (who was trained by Veitch) had switched trainers with Affirmed last year, Alydar would have been the Triple Crown winner. I'm sure Veitch's daddy (Sylvester, a Hall of Fame trainer) is the greatest, and John has great horses. But having great horses doesn't make a great trainer. Veitch and his crowd just don't like an outsider to step on their territory."

Track officials sided with Delp. Days before the race, Laurel staffers scraped and firmed the track until he and Jolley were satisfied. As evidence of the improvement, Bid ran a half mile in forty-seven and one-fifth seconds. The other change was to the finish line. Track officials erected a second finish line to account for the race's extra sixteenth of a mile over the mile oval. Delp had Franklin ride several mounts that day to get accustomed to the second wire. He did not want inexperience to ruin this race, no matter what he thought of Franklin's ability.

In addition to Spectacular Bid, Tim the Tiger, and General Assembly, there would be a new challenger at Laurel. Clever Trick had won his last three outings, all stakes races, and was getting some notice from turf writers. It was rare for a Kentucky horse to come to Maryland for a race—people regarded Maryland racetracks as a notch below those in Kentucky and New York. But, determined not to let the "Maryland invaders" take away the Two-Year-Old Male Horse of the Year honor, the Kentucky and New York establishment had come to Maryland to face Bid, who was running in his second race in nine days. Had he had enough time to recuperate from the tough race at the Meadowlands?

People also questioned Delp's decision to put the young Franklin back on Bid. Before the race, Delp advised him, "I'm not going to tell you how to ride this horse because nobody ever knows what's going to happen in a race. You know the horse and I don't want you tied down by orders. But if you find yourself in a position settling into the stretch run, ride him out. Keep him driving because he loves to run, and I want these people to see how much horse he really is."

Franklin responded with a superb ride, keeping Bid at the front of a slow pace and leaving him with enough stamina to finish strong. Bid held a half-length lead over Clever Trick after the first quarter mile and widened that lead to two lengths after a half mile. When General Assembly made his move on the far turn, coming to within a head of Bid, Franklin waited; then, when it seemed as if General Assembly was going to catch Bid, he loosened Bid's reins and used the whip, hitting him ten times. Bid had never been hit like that before, and he took off like a bullet, his powerful strides lengthening. The other horses seemed to stand in place. Bid turned the race into a rout, crossing the finish line eight and a half lengths ahead of General Assembly and twenty and a half lengths in front of third-place Clever Trick. He broke the track record, set by a four-year-old in 1972, by nearly a full second. He had run his final quarter of a mile in twenty-four and one-fifth seconds and the last sixteenth of a mile in six and one-fifth seconds—an astounding time for the end of a race, when the horses' legs are rubbery and they are breathing heavily. Instead, Bid came back to the barn dancing and playing, as if he had just gone out for a morning breeze. Tim the Tiger finished in last place, twenty-four lengths behind Bid.

"I got within a head at the top of the lane," said Steve Cauthen, General Assembly's jockey. "I thought I had him because I felt like I had a lot of horse left. But [Bid] just took off. Man, [Franklin's] horse was running." Again, Bid's extra gear, coupled with Franklin's vigorous use of the whip, put him in front by a significant margin. Franklin became the only apprentice rider ever to win the Laurel Futurity.

A joyous Bud Delp kissed Franklin on the cheek when the jockey got off the horse. Harry Meyerhoff reserved some hotel rooms in Louisville for the first weekend in May. A confident Delp confessed that he had made his reservations after Spectacular Bid won the World's Playground.

Franklin defended his liberal use of the whip. "I just wanted to keep busy on my mount so he'd keep his mind on business. He's the easiest kind of animal to ride, but you have to keep after him, or he'll start relaxing on you, like a lot of them are prone to do." Still, some questioned hitting a quality horse that often when he already had control of a race. But Delp had no problems with Franklin's ride. "It was very cool. I mean cool. Letting General Assembly get that close to him without making a move. I don't know that I could have been that cool."

Andrew Beyer of the *Washington Post* saw something special when he looked at horses' times for the Laurel Futurity in previous years and track conditions on race day in 1978. Had the last seven Laurel Futurities been run on the same track Bid had raced on, he would have had the fourth fastest time, just behind Secretariat and two-fifths of a second off the best time set by Affirmed and Alydar just the year before. A similar analysis of the Champagne Stakes using the same methodology showed that Bid was faster than both Seattle Slew and Affirmed. "The colt has all the necessary potential to be a Kentucky Derby winner, a Triple Crown winner," Beyer concluded. Someone finally agreed with Delp about the horse's potential.

The next day, Delp went back to the claiming game, claiming a horse for the Meyerhoffs for $8,000. Fame had not relieved him of his other responsibilities, and he continued to participate in the game at which he had made a name for himself. He was Bud Delp, the Claiming King of Maryland.

Delp wanted Bid to run in one more race—the Heritage Stakes on November 11—which, if he won, would help Franklin become Apprentice Jockey of the Year. Some questioned why Bid needed to run in the Heritage, since he had all but wrapped up Two-Year-Old Male Horse of the Year honors. It was only two weeks after the Laurel Futurity, and they thought the horse deserved a rest after a grueling two-year-old campaign in which he had won six of eight races. But Delp was used to criticism. That might not be the way they did things in Kentucky, but it was the Bud Delp way.

On November 7 the Meyerhoffs got a curious telegram from a person named Bob James, who said he represented "a very prominent industrialist, sportsman, and breeder in the United States and Europe" who was interested in buying Spectacular Bid for between $8 million and $9 million. The Meyerhoffs politely declined.

At Keystone Racetrack in Philadelphia on November 11, Bid ended an outstanding two-year-old season with a dominating six-length victory in the Heritage Stakes. This time, he came from behind; Delp wanted to see whether the colt could stalk the leaders from just off the pace and then make his move around the final turn, when the leaders tired. Sure enough, he was seven lengths off the lead through the first turn and into the backstretch before he got tired of watching the horses in front of him. After half a mile, he made his move; heading into the final turn, he passed three other horses with ease and was suddenly astride Terrific Son, who had just taken the lead from a tiring Breezing On. Once again, Bid looked Terrific Son in the eye, and the other colt acquiesced. Bid bounded to a one-length lead at the three-eighths pole, putting daylight between himself and Sun Watcher, the second-place finisher. Terrific Son finished third.

Delp and Harry Meyerhoff admitted that this race had been only a learning lesson for Bid. Delp had entered Bid in the Heritage only because he knew he would win, but the trainer acknowledged that the horse needed a break. "If there had been anybody in there hard, we might have left him at the stall in Maryland," he said.

Spectacular Bid was showing some maturity. He had shown that he could take the lead or come back from last place; he could lurk behind the leaders and still win. What would it take to beat him, besides running on a sloppy track or trying to box him in? Yet he had shown that as long as he could find an opening, he could pass the other horses on the outside and still win, despite the longer trip around the track.

Delp's confidence in his colt was growing, and he let the press know it. "I think only an act of God will stop Spectacular Bid from winning the Triple Crown next year," he told reporters. That was a rare statement to make about a two-year-old colt, and the Kentucky establishment scoffed at his boasting. Going out on a limb and predicting a colt's place in horse racing history so early in the horse's career was risky. Many horses have had promising two-year-old campaigns, only to falter as three-year-olds. In 1968, for instance, Top Knight was named Two-Year-Old Male Horse of the Year after victories in the Champagne, Hopeful, and Futurity stakes. He finished fifth in the Kentucky Derby, and his final record was eleven wins in forty-six races. Protagonist received the 1973 award after winning four of seven races, including the Cowdin, Champagne, and Laurel Futurity. But he lost his first two races as a three-year-old, finishing last in the Gotham Stakes, and he did not race in the Kentucky Derby. His final record: four wins in ten starts.

So far, though, Bid showed nothing but promise. He had won his last five races, all major stakes, on five different tracks. In fact, his nine starts had been on eight different tracks. "Not too many two-year-olds do that," wrote Bob Maisel of the *Baltimore Sun*. "He definitely does not have to carry his racetrack around with him. Put him out there in good condition, and he does his job."

On the morning of November 18, disaster almost struck young Ron Franklin. He was exercising a horse named Fortent along the rail at Laurel Park. Traditionally, when exercising, slower horses gallop closer to the outside fence, and faster horses run near the rail. Exercise rider Mike Smith, riding a mare named Spring Switches, was moving slowly along the rail and refused to make room for Franklin and Fortent, causing them to collide with the rail. Delp blew his top and warned Smith that he would be looking for him after he finished exercising the mare. Smith dismounted and dared Delp, "Come up to the stable gate and say that." Delp chased Smith to the security booth, where he slapped the surprised rider several times on the helmet and accused him of endangering the lives of Franklin and the horse. Smith was not hurt—Delp said the slap probably hurt his hand more than it did the exercise rider—but the stewards at Laurel Park handed down a twenty-day suspension for the attack. Since most racetracks honored suspensions in other states, it meant that Delp was barred from Gulfstream Park near Miami, Florida, where Bid would be spending the winter while training for his three-year-old season.

Delp did not deny hitting the exercise boy. "I was wrong in hitting the boy, for damn sure. But he could have caused Ronnie to get hurt. He hit the fence as it was, and he could have been severely hurt. If Ronnie was in the hospital now with a broken vertebra, this would all be secondary." The suspension would not end until January 19, 1979, leaving Delp little time to train Bid for his first race as a three-year-old, which was scheduled to be the Hutcheson Stakes on February 7.

Delp shipped Bid to Gulfstream anyway, along with twenty-three other horses from other stables, for his first winter in Florida. He left the bulk of his horses with his brother, Richard. If all went according to plan, Delp would not come back to Maryland until after Bid had won all the Florida prep races, the Blue Grass Stakes in Lexington, and the Kentucky Derby in Louisville. Bid had finished the season with seven wins and one second in nine starts and had earned $384,484. "Spectacular Bid has it all: Personality, poise, attitude and eats and rests like a champion," wrote Dave Feldman of the *Chicago Sun-Times*. "He never stopped eating his hay as I watched him at close range for more than an hour. All great horses are great doers. They eat everything in sight. They tell me Spectacular Bid eats thirteen quarts of oats a day." Feldman quoted Bid's exercise rider, Robert Smith, who echoed Delp's prediction: "If he doesn't meet up with an injury he'll win the Triple Crown with ease."

On December 11 Tom Meyerhoff received another telegram from Bob James, the representative for the mysterious person interested in buying Spectacular Bid. James reiterated his client's credentials and then upped the offer to $13 million. "This offer would more than likely be a world record for any individual purchase for a two-year-old colt, let alone any Thoroughbred for that matter," the telegram read. James said the buyer would retain Delp as trainer. Again, the Meyerhoffs declined to entertain the offer.

On December 13 the Eclipse Awards were announced, honoring the champions of the sport for the previous year. Affirmed won Horse of the Year for his Triple Crown run, Spectacular Bid won Champion Two-Year-Old Male, and Ron Franklin won Best Apprentice Jockey, having won 262 races and $1.75 million in purses. He had just turned nineteen years old and had been racing for less than a year.

Meanwhile, Flying Paster was flying out west. On December 30 he won his sixth straight race, the California Breeders' Championship Stakes at Santa Anita Park. Lying back in the pack, the Paster flew past the field on the far turn and drew away, winning by nine lengths and tying the stakes record. His times in all his races were impressive; he was becoming known as the West's best hope for a Derby contender. The victory at Santa Anita was his seventh in ten starts. Some horse racing experts had been pushing for Flying Paster to be named Two-Year-Old Male Horse of the Year. An equine civil war was brewing—East versus West.

4

The Field Shapes Up

He's a Rolls Royce, and I'm his regular rider.

—Ron Franklin

IN JANUARY 1979 the Jockey Club staged its annual Experimental Handicap, a hypothetical race in which the club assigned weights to horses based on their past performance. Handicappers would put extra weight on good horses and less weight on inferior horses, the belief being that the extra weight would slow down the good horses and make the race more competitive. The higher the weight, the better the handicappers considered the horse. This was a good barometer of which horses the Jockey Club felt were the ones to watch in 1979. In the last seven years, five colts that had led their class as two-year-olds and had been assigned the top weight in the Experimental Handicap had won the Kentucky Derby.

That year, the club assigned weights to 333 Thoroughbreds that had raced as two-year-olds—183 colts and geldings and 150 fillies. The top five were Spectacular Bid at 126 pounds, Flying Paster at 123 pounds, General Assembly at 122 pounds, and Strike Your Colors and Tim the Tiger at 121 pounds each. If the Eclipse Award had not proved it, the Experimental Handicap confirmed it: Spectacular Bid was the horse to beat in the 1979 Kentucky Derby.

While Delp was serving his suspension at a rented home near Gulfstream Park, his assistant Charlie Bettis and Delp's two sons, Doug and Gerald, carried out his instructions for training Spectacular Bid. Once the suspension was lifted, Delp saw Bid work six furlongs at 1:12—a perfect time, twelve seconds for each furlong. A week later, he breezed the same distance in 1:13.

On January 30 Delp gave Bid a workout at Gulfstream to prepare for the Hutcheson Stakes. Horse experts all over the park witnessed the colt cover six and a half furlongs in a sensational 1:15²/5, just two-fifths off the track record *for a race*. He galloped out seven furlongs in 1:21⁴/5, just one second away from another track record. Word about the unbelievable workout spread. Some trainers liked to give a horse a blowout before a race to tighten him up, but this was different. A workout this fast and this long just days before a race was unheard of.

Horatio Luro, trainer of the champion Thoroughbred Northern Dancer, was known for saying, "Never squeeze the last drop out of a lemon when you're preparing for the big ones." But Delp loved the workout. "Yes, the track was mighty fast this morning, and this, of course, contributed to the speed of the move," he said. "But more important was the fact that the colt handled his assignment like breaking sticks. He was moving along with an easy, flowing stride and actually had something left. I am really pleased."

Trainer Joe Petrucione agreed. "That's the most impressive work I've ever seen in my life," he said. "He answered all the questions this morning—at least all the questions I had. I know the track is very fast, but the way he did it just knocked your eye out." Some jumped on the bandwagon and compared Bid to Seattle Slew and Affirmed. Delp, however, knew that racing luck had something to do with it. "What could happen is an act of God, but every realistic precaution is being taken to ensure his safety and well-being," he said.

Members of the old guard of horse racing questioned Delp's training techniques and said he did not know how to handle a champion horse. To them, he was just a small-time trainer who was treating Bid as if he were one of his claimers. No good trainer would work a horse that fast one week before a race; it would be like running two races in one week, and it was bound to take its toll on the horse—especially one that had raced so frequently as a two-year-old. Some muttered about Delp's overconfidence in Spectacular Bid. "He talks as if he takes a Kentucky Derby for granted," a reporter overheard someone say.

The establishment could not believe that this crew of Marylanders was taking the racing scene by storm. In their opinion, Bid had the wrong owners, the wrong trainer, and the wrong jockey. The Meyerhoffs were upstarts who had gotten lucky with a colt they had bought for a song. Most members of the racing establishment, several of whom had breeding shares in Secretariat, were pulling for General Assembly.

At the Hutcheson Stakes, Bid would be facing a whole new slate of contenders, including Northern Prospect, who had won three starts in a row; Lot o' Gold, who had won the Kentucky Jockey Club Stakes the previous fall and had never finished out of the money; and the two-year-old Canadian champion Medaille d'Or.

Also making his three-year-old debut, three hours after the start of Bid's race on the other side of the country, was Flying Paster, who would be running in the San Vicente Stakes at Santa Anita. The Paster was staying in his home state of California for the winter and would not be contesting Bid. Fans might have to wait until the Kentucky Derby to see the two race each other—if they both made it.

Although twenty-four horses were nominated for the Hutcheson, only Northern Prospect, Lot o' Gold, and Medaille d'Or were brave enough to face Bid. The rest of the possible contenders dropped out, intimidated by Bid's meteoric workout. Some surmised that Delp had let Bid loose in that workout to scare off the competition: the fewer horses in the race, the less chance of Bid getting boxed in. And, as it turned out, Bid drew the number-one post—the perfect slot to get boxed in if a large field were on the course.

February 7 was gray and rainy—not a good omen for Bid. The track was wet, but that did not stop 17,374 people from attending—the largest crowd in the history of the twenty-five-year-old race. Going off as the 1 to 20 favorite, Bid started quickly but soon settled in behind the leader, Northern Prospect, and let him take a one-and-a-half-length lead. Then Lot o' Gold made his move and passed Bid as well, to the shock of the fans at Gulfstream Park. Was this a replay of the Tyro? Did Bid hate the mud that much? It was time to see. Franklin tapped Bid on the shoulder with his whip, and away he went, his shod hooves struggling to gain traction in the slop. He passed Lot o' Gold, moved to the inside of Northern Prospect, and easily pulled ahead going into the homestretch. At the wire, he had extended his lead over Lot o' Gold to three and three-quarters lengths. Had Franklin not eased him up at the end, the margin would have been even greater. Northern Prospect was finished, seven and a half lengths back. On a wet track, his first since the disastrous Tyro Stakes, Bid had covered the seven furlongs in 1:21²/5, only three-fifths of a second slower than the track record. It was his sixth win in a row.

Not only was Bid getting better and faster; he also proved that an off track would not hurt his chances. He had gotten over his disappointing romp in the mud at the Tyro Stakes and had run a perfect race. "A little rain wouldn't have bothered me," Delp said. "But when it started coming down hard I went back to the barn and got another vodka. Whenever he leaves his stall I'm apprehensive. But he came back without a nick on him and looks beautiful. . . . He'll go back to the barn now thinking that mud is terrific."

Franklin admitted that Bid lost his footing on the turn. "I took a little hold of him. Then I tapped him on the shoulder, and he took off again. I hit him twice, but I never rode him hard. It was one of the easiest races he's ever had." Delp had some criticism for Franklin, though. The jockey had eased up on Bid in the stretch, and the trainer warned him, "Don't ever do that again. You're teaching the colt bad habits that will be hard to break. I want you to go past the finish line driving."

After the race, Delp and the Meyerhoffs held an impromptu party at the barn, drinking Heinekens while Mo Hall tended to Bid's hooves. On the way back from the race, a photographer had gotten too close to Bid, and the horse had kicked the photographer's camera, causing a small cut on the colt's right rear ankle.

"I should have slugged that photographer," Delp said.

"No, I should have," his son Gerald said. "You can't afford another twenty days."

In the San Vicente Stakes, Flying Paster dominated the field of seven, winning by six lengths. Carrying a top weight of 124 pounds, he went the same distance as Bid but finished one-fifth of a second faster.

Once Delp knew that Spectacular Bid had come out of the race sound and uninjured, he boarded a plane for San Francisco, where he accepted the Eclipse Award for Champion Two-Year-Old Colt of 1978. Meanwhile, Tom Meyerhoff visited Churchill Downs, the site of the Kentucky Derby, to check the location of the owners' boxes and map out the best

route to the winner's circle. His horse was no Top Knight or Protagonist. If anything, Spectacular Bid had gotten even better over the winter.
Recognizing this, Harry Meyerhoff upped Bid's insurance to $10 mil-
lion, which was believed to be the largest policy ever issued on an animal. Premiums would be upward of $500,000 a year. "In my opinion,
the new policy covers half of Spectacular Bid's value," Harry said. "He's
worth twenty million dollars . . . and he might be worth more than that
after he wins the Triple Crown."

Harry also had to deny rumors that Bid was for sale. He rejected
reports that Bid had been sold to English sportsman Robert Sangster for
$16 million. "Neither Mr. Sangster, nor his agents, have approached me
with regard to this colt," Meyerhoff said. "Spectacular Bid is not for sale."

Reporters, handicappers, and other horse experts were gushing over
Bid's performance and talent. "It's almost unreal," said Gulfstream Park's
Joe Tannenbaum. "Almost unreal that Thoroughbred racing, in just a
few seasons, has produced such Triple Crown champions as Secretariat,
Seattle Slew, and Affirmed. And now we've got the best horse of the century." Horse racing expert Luther Evans agreed. "The workouts he turns
in are phenomenal, even though it's common knowledge that he hasn't
been pushed," he said. "They work him just fast enough to scare off some
challengers." Even Andrew Beyer of the *Washington Post,* who was usually conservative in his praise of horses, could not hold back. "He is, I
believe, the genuine article. I say this as a habitual knocker of the pre-
Derby favorite, as a skeptic of Affirmed and a hater of Seattle Slew in the
past two seasons. But Spectacular Bid is running faster at this stage of
his career than any Thoroughbred of my lifetime. Including Secretariat."

Next up for Bid was the Fountain of Youth Stakes at Gulfstream
Park on February 19. Once again, Delp had scared away most of his com-
petition; Spectacular Bid would be joined by four other horses, including
Lot o' Gold; Bishop's Choice, who had recently won the Tropical Park
Derby; and Rivalero, another Calumet Farm prospect.

W. A. "Smiley" Adams, Lot o' Gold's trainer and a longtime Ken-
tuckian, was angered by Delp's overconfidence and by his horse's defeat
in the Hutcheson. Adams predicted that Lot o' Gold would beat Bid in
the Fountain of Youth. "Next time we'll beat him. Put that in the paper.
My colt ran a real good race [in the Hutcheson]. The winner ran a helluva

race. He's a good one, for sure, but I say he can be beat." Smiley Adams was wrong.

The onslaught continued. Sent off at 1 to 10 odds, Bid broke slowly, and Franklin stayed back slightly as Bishop's Choice and Rivalero went to the lead. Finding himself boxed in, he swung Bid wide and took over second, a length behind Rivalero. Then Bid found his higher gear and made his move; by the middle of the backstretch, he had opened a one-and-a-half-length lead over Rivalero. Bishop's Choice tried to mount a rally, but Franklin hit Bid several times between the three-sixteenths pole and the one-eighth pole, and Bid responded, pulling away by two, three, four lengths. The response was incredible, efficient, effortless. And the margin kept getting wider. Bishop's Choice gave up second to Lot o' Gold, who finished eight and a half lengths behind Bid.

"He was just galloping down the backstretch," Franklin said. "As soon as he got clear, I knew it was over." It was an impressive win for Bid; he missed the stakes record by only one-fifth of a second. "He's a Rolls Royce, and I'm his regular rider," Franklin exclaimed. Except for the traffic problems early in the race, it seemed that all Franklin had to do with this colt was strap on his seatbelt and enjoy the ride. "He was push-button to race," Franklin later said of Bid. "Sometimes, I felt like he was taking *me* for a ride."

It was Bid's seventh straight victory—the same streak as Flying Paster. The odds were so stacked in Bid's favor that Gulfstream Park had a minus pool on its hands—that is, it had to pay out more money to the winners who bet on Bid than it took in that day.

The Meyerhoffs almost missed the race. Flying in from their rented vacation home in Acapulco, Mexico, they arrived in Miami three hours late. They sped to the racetrack in a cab, arriving just thirty minutes before the race. They were lucky to witness one of Bid's most impressive victories yet.

According to Delp, Bid had not been challenged in the Fountain of Youth Stakes and had not maxed out a good performance yet. "In fact, it put something into him. He's going to be even better for the Florida Derby." The Florida Derby would be a race to remember, but not the way Delp hoped it would be.

❧

The racing establishment was not so sure about Ron Franklin. The formula had worked with Steve Cauthen—put a young jockey on a super-horse, and sometimes things just clicked. Delp thought the same was true of Franklin and believed the jockey had a special bond with Bid. "The horse just seems to run for Ronnie," Delp was known to say. Franklin, however, had just finished his tenure as an apprentice jockey and did not yet have a full season of regular jockeying under his belt. Only three years earlier, he had never even ridden a horse. Critics cautioned that his inexperience might catch up with him.

Before the Florida Derby, Franklin bought a $265 saddle for Bid—a gift for himself and his horse. He hoped the saddle would bring them good luck. But bad luck stalked him throughout the race in the form of a pair of jockeys: Angel Cordero Jr. and Bid's former jockey, Jorge Velasquez.

Angel Cordero was known as a tough jockey and a fierce competitor. He was born in Santurce, Puerto Rico, the son of a jockey and trainer. He first sat on a horse at five months old and was riding a pony by himself at age three. When he became eighteen, his mother reluctantly let him pursue a career as a jockey, even though she was afraid for his safety. He began his career at El Comandante Race Track in Puerto Rico and headed to the United States in 1962. He went straight for the big time—New York—and failed miserably. He returned home to Puerto Rico beaten, but three years later he was back in New York, determined not to fail this time. To survive, he conditioned himself. He rode with abandon, becoming known for his aggressive tactics, which often led to inquiries and suspensions. Word spread among jockeys: you didn't get in Cordero's way when he thought he had a chance to win.

In 1970 Cordero bumped jockey Bob Woodhouse's mount so many times that Woodhouse slashed Cordero across the back with his whip, resulting in a ten-day suspension for Woodhouse. In 1973 Cordero was suspended for ten days for careless riding at Hialeah Park. The next year, weeks after winning his first Kentucky Derby on Cannonade, Cordero was suspended for seven days for bumping another horse, forcing him to miss the Belmont Stakes. Six months later, he was cited again for careless riding at Aqueduct Racetrack. In March 1975 he was out for seven days after hitting another horse with his whip. Although the stewards called it inadvertent, they also called it careless.

Perhaps most serious, though, were allegations of race fixing. In 1975 a trainer testified under oath that Cordero was part of a group of jockeys who fixed races and cashed in winning tickets amounting to $250,000 a day. Cordero denied the charges, saying, "Look at my record. I made over $200,000 each of the last three years. I'm the second leading money winner for the last four years. My heart is clean." The day before the hearing, Cordero's mounts had been disqualified twice for rough riding, but nothing came of the inquiry; the New York State Racing and Wagering Board called the trainer's allegations "irresponsible."

In 1978 accusations of race fixing surfaced again. This time, *Sports Illustrated* reported that "master fixer" Tony Ciulla claimed he had paid Cordero, among several other popular jockeys, to fix hundreds of races. According to the magazine, Ciulla paid Cordero as much as $6,000 to control a race. Cordero demanded a retraction from *Sports Illustrated,* which stood by its story.

That same year, Cordero was riding Shake Shake Shake in the Travers Stakes against the two greats Affirmed and Alydar. Cordero let Shake Shake Shake drift to the outside, allowing his good friend Jorge Velasquez to sneak Alydar in on the rail. Affirmed later bumped Alydar on the rail, causing Alydar to check sharply and leading to Affirmed's disqualification.

Cordero never apologized for his rough riding and insisted he wasn't the bad boy the press made him out to be. "Sometimes I do things and say things that I don't mean," he said. "But I'm not a troublemaker. People have the wrong impression and many of them will always have that impression. I don't know if I can change that but I'm gonna try. I'm not a bad person, really."

The *New York Times* labeled him "The Jockey Fans Love to Hate." "Cordero believes in taking every edge that the stewards allow—squeezing through tight holes, intimidating while not impeding his opponents—and a few that they do not," the *Times* wrote. The article referenced hundreds of suspensions and fines. Cordero was flamboyant, cocky, daring, and sneaky—a lesson Franklin was about to learn.

March 3 started like any other day. Bid was in an ill mood and feeling rambunctious. As they put Franklin's new saddle on him, he snorted and grunted. Mo Hall looked frightened. "This horse is a killer," he said. "He's always like this before a race. He wants to run now."

Spectacular Bid was the 1 to 20 favorite against a field that included some familiar rivals: Lot o' Gold, who had finished second to Bid in their last two races, along with Medaille d'Or, Musical Phantasy, Sir Ivor Again, and Brach's Dancer. Even before the race started, trainers had been trying to think of a new way to beat Bid. "To beat him, you've got to lay close, breathe on him," said Smiley Adams. "A little bad breath might bother Spectacular Bid. In the Florida Derby, I'm going to be breathing on him. If he beats me, I'm going to make him run." To this Delp replied, "Spectacular Bid will just love that. We'll just go and go. Instead of getting beaten by eight and a half lengths, as he was in the Fountain of Youth, Lot o' Gold will get beat by thirteen lengths."

Franklin was helped onto Bid's back, and as the post parade began, Bid was hopping and prancing along, shaking his head in impatience. But once the horses were settled into their post positions and the gates opened for the Florida Derby, Bid was in trouble. The colt banged hard against the left side of the gate—so hard that Franklin almost fell off the horse. Although he managed to stay on Bid and settle him down, the bump prevented Bid from getting a quick start. He had to settle for fifth place in the seven-horse field as the horses entered the first turn.

Franklin first tried to go outside, as usual, but Medaille d'Or was in the way, and Bid almost ran into him. Had he done so and impeded the other horse's progress, Bid would have been disqualified. So Franklin waited. After a while, Cordero, aboard Sir Ivor Again and running in front of Bid, drifted to the outside, leaving a hole for Franklin to go through on the inside. It was a trap.

Franklin hesitated at first, then decided to go through. As soon as he went for the hole, Cordero moved back inside, blocking his way. Franklin had to check Bid drastically to avoid a collision, slowing him down even more and causing him to almost clip the heels of Medaille d'Or, who was right behind him—a second near miss. Fourteen lengths behind and desperate to get back in the race, Franklin swung the colt outside. Bid passed Sir Ivor Again and made a furious run down the backstretch to catch the three pacesetters, making up eight lengths in a short distance. Franklin tried to go through an inside hole again, but when he was halfway through the opening, Velasquez, riding Fantasy 'n

Reality, drifted over toward the rail. Franklin panicked and, fearing that Bid would get pinned against the rail, put the brakes on the colt a second time. This time, he went around the three horses, and they were four horses wide on the final turn. Spectacular Bid, after three near accidents and a long trip around the far turn, including several changes in speed, was fighting for the lead.

Franklin hit Spectacular Bid hard several times, and the colt stepped on the gas once more, passing the three leaders in less than 100 yards and pulling away by four and a half lengths. It was an amazing performance by a horse that won despite his jockey. Once again, Bid proved that he could make several moves during a race, coming back time after time before prevailing in his final move.

Delp was furious. He ran over to the winner's circle and yelled at Franklin in front of hundreds of spectators. "You idiot!" he screamed. "You could have got the horse killed!" An embarrassed Franklin dismounted, acting like a son who had wrecked his father's prized automobile; he hung his head in shame as tears welled in his eyes. Groom Mo Hall turned and looked the other way, wishing he were somewhere else. Franklin's mother, Marian, and one of his sisters were on hand to watch the race and witnessed everything, as did about 50 reporters and some 30,000 fans. Delp turned around, noticed some photographers close to Bid, and shouted, "Get away from my horse. He'll kick you right into next year. . . . I hope he does."

He was not finished with Franklin. "You were pulling up in that first turn when all you had to do was go by him," he boomed at Franklin. "Why didn't you go by that S.O.B.? And what are you doing, going on the inside back there? You go *outside* with this S.O.B." Later, Delp still had not calmed down. "The smartest thing about Ronnie Franklin is that he knows how dumb he is," he told a reporter. "When you're running against horses like Flying Paster and General Assembly, you can't afford to make mistakes like this. I've been watching races for a long, long time and Ronnie really screwed it up."

That night, Delp stayed up late waiting for Franklin to come home. He finally fell asleep, and when he awoke at about four in the morning, Franklin was not in his bed. Delp found him curled up in Gerald's room, seeking comfort from one of his best friends. Delp covered him with a blanket and let him sleep where he lay.

Criticism of the jockey's performance came from the media. Andrew Beyer of the *Washington Post* called the ride "inept" and "dreadful" and said Franklin showed "bad judgment" and "panic." Billy Reed of the *Louisville Courier-Journal* wrote, "Only nineteen, with little more than a year's riding experience, Franklin had just been taught a lesson about what a cut-throat game racing can be at the highest level. That he won the race was almost entirely a tribute to Spectacular Bid's ability."

Some newspapers took a shot at Delp. "There is absolutely no excuse for such an incident in Thoroughbred racing or, for that matter, anywhere else," read an editorial in a local Maryland paper. "The thought of a horse trainer publicly threatening to kick a jockey is disgusting. . . . We shudder at the thought of what future temper tantrums will do to the image of racing and, while we're at it, the image of Maryland."

After the race, Franklin told reporters that the other jockeys had teamed up on him, and he could do nothing about it. When asked why they would do that, he said, "They want my horse. . . . They were yelling all over the place. 'Go to the inside, go to the outside.' They ain't got no class at all." Nearby, Cordero and Velasquez, who were friends, were yelling to each other in Spanish. Franklin muttered, "Listen at them. You can't even understand what they're saying—Spics!"

When asked about Franklin's accusations, Velasquez did not deny them. "When you're riding the best horse in the race, everybody's against you. Everybody's taking their best shot, so you have to do your best." When asked if he would like to ride Bid again, he answered, "Sure, everybody would like to ride the best horse in the country."

By the next day, Delp had calmed down somewhat and even defended Franklin. "He's a whipped puppy. I was too hard on him. He felt bad. In his mind all night last night, he thinks he's never going to ride this horse again. And he may never. It's the owners' decision to make. But I love him." Delp also reiterated the long-held belief that Latino riders stuck up for one another. "[Cordero and Velasquez] are buddies and they work together. I don't like either one of them. I think they're low class, [and if] they want to continue to intimidate him, then the proper authorities will have to watch it and see what happens," he said.

One jockey agreed with Delp but said that was the name of the game. "Of course they're going to try to intimidate Franklin. He's on the big horse. Wait until he gets into the Kentucky Derby and he'll find out what intimidation is." The *Thoroughbred Record,* however, noted that Bid's long trip around the track was almost as long as the Derby's distance, and he had displayed three stages of speed during the race.

Marian Franklin, Ron's mother, said it was difficult to watch her son be verbally abused in front of everyone. She and her oldest daughter had driven twenty hours to see Franklin race in the Florida Derby. "When we went back to the jock's room afterwards, Ron didn't say anything," Marian said. "He's the type of boy that keeps everything bottled up inside. I don't think he wanted to see me hurt."

Delp was not joking when he expressed doubts about Franklin riding Spectacular Bid again. He announced that he and the Meyerhoffs would discuss Franklin's future as Bid's regular jockey. Delp even had a short list of other jockeys to call on, including Bill Shoemaker, Sandy Hawley, Darrel McHargue, and Jacinto Vasquez. He told Franklin, "You're in select company. If you get submarined off the horse by one of them, you'll be submarined by a champion."

Jack Mann with the *Washington Star* placed odds on who Bid's next jockey would be. According to Mann, the odds-on favorite was Jacinto Vasquez at 9 to 5; Bill Shoemaker, 4 to 1; Darrel McHargue, 12 to 1; and Franklin as the long shot at 20 to 1. The Meyerhoffs were supposed to announce their decision on Friday, March 9, but they delayed it until Monday, whipping the media into a frenzy as they waited for the announcement.

When the day came, it was like Oscar night. Delp, surrounded by television cameras and reporters, stepped up to a podium set up outside Barn 5 at Gulfstream Park, opened a white envelope, and, with tears in his eyes, read a statement from the Meyerhoffs: "The primary thought has always been what is in the horse's best interest. The horse always runs very well for Ronnie Franklin. They have an affinity for each other. Ronnie is a good jockey on his way to being a great jockey. We, therefore, have decided to ride Ronnie Franklin in all of Spectacular Bid's races."

Delp did not reveal what his own recommendation had been, but he described himself as "happy as a lark" for Franklin. According to Delp, Franklin was "overwhelmingly happy" and cried. The jockey had taken a vacation to get away from all the stress, but he would be back in time for the Flamingo Stakes on March 24. "Ronnie never makes the same mistake twice. He's a smart kid and a dedicated one. He listens good."

Delp then added, "After watching the race again on ABC-TV Saturday, really, if he couldn't get him beat then, I don't see how he could ever get him beat." When asked whether he feared criticism for remaining with Franklin, Delp replied, "I don't give a damn."

The criticism came from everywhere. Andrew Beyer wrote that Franklin's ride had been "the most egregious stakes ride of modern times. Delp remains almost alone in [his] assessment of Franklin. . . . If Franklin was undistinguished in run-of-the-mill competition, he showed in the Florida Derby that he is completely out of his element in the upper echelons of racing." Billy Reed of the *Courier-Journal* wrote, "The kid has little experience in a game where experience means virtually everything."

Later, Delp admitted that if it had been his choice, he would have taken Franklin off the mount. But emotionally, he wanted the young jockey to keep the ride, so he left the decision to the Meyerhoffs. The family thought long and hard and watched tapes of Franklin's races versus Velasquez's two races on Bid. They noticed that Bid ran more smoothly under Franklin, and there seemed to be a connection between rider and horse. As Delp said, Bid just seemed to run for Franklin. Hence the decision to stay with the boy.

Delp admitted that his anger at Franklin's actions during the race had been due to his fear that something might happen to the horse. Teresa Meyerhoff agreed, saying Delp's primary concern was for the horse. "He lives and breathes for that horse, he has the horse's welfare topmost in his mind at all times. He loves that horse and, would, I think, sacrifice himself for the sake of that horse."

Delp had also been unhappy with the surface at Gulfstream that day. He said it was "like a beach" and refused to let Bid work out, since a sandy track can lead to strained muscles. "This is a risky game," he said. "I've seen everything happen to a horse and I want to eliminate any hazards with this horse. If something happens to him, let it happen when he's on the racetrack, heading for that bull's-eye, and not because of some stupid act that could have been prevented."

He responded to criticism from members of the Kentucky racing establishment, who said Delp did not know how to handle a horse of Spectacular Bid's caliber. Many accused Delp of treating Bid like one of his claimers in training, forcing the colt to go as fast as possible during workouts. "As far as I'm concerned, he can take a helluva lot more than I'm giving him," Delp said. "If anything, he's undertrained. Definitely. And look what he's done. So how good is he?"

Members of the media continued to question his decision to put such a young, inexperienced jockey on such a promising colt as Spectacular Bid. Delp ignored them—or, rather, he answered them in his own style. "Ronnie's my man. Fits Bid like a glove," he said. "Yeah, Ronnie looked bad in Maryland part of last year. But we won a lot of races. People were poking fun and we were laughing all the way to the bank. Now Ronnie looks good and rides better. He doesn't rattle. The only thing that bothers me at all is that all the furor might get to him at the Derby. I'm going to hide him out. If he rattles, he'll be the first to know he has to come off Bid. I'm not looking for that to happen. I've never seen Ronnie show the first sign of nervousness."

"Here's how I see it," he told another reporter. "He'll win everything in Florida . . . which will mean the shortest Derby field in history. Then we come home to Baltimore for the Preakness. Nobody will want to try us here. Then we go to the Belmont, where there will be a few who doubt, foolishly, that he can go a mile and a half. Let's face it. I've got a straight flush. And it's just not often that somebody else gets a higher one."

But reporters thought Delp had gone too far when he was asked what he thought of Secretariat, Seattle Slew, and Affirmed. "I'd rephrase the question," he said. "It ought to be: How do they compare with Spectacular Bid? He's done everything he's been asked to do so far, and I think he's the best horse who's ever looked through a bridle." Really? Was Spectacular Bid better than Man o' War, Citation, and Secretariat? The horse had yet to win even one Triple Crown race, and Delp was calling him the greatest ever. Was the trainer jinxing Bid? "Hell no, the horse can't hear," he said. "The horse doesn't believe in crossing fingers or making lucky wishes. You just point the son of a gun and go with him. He will run you to death. . . . He's going to make me famous and rich. And accepted in all the turf clubs in the world." Even a maverick like Delp cared about being accepted by the higher echelons of racing, if only to rub it in the faces of the establishment.

Flying Paster and Spectacular Bid had both won seven races in a row, but in the San Felipe Handicap on March 17, Pole Position broke the Paster's streak. The colt, bred by Grace Knoop (sister of Madelyn Jason, the breeder of Spectacular Bid), beat Switch Partners by a head. The Paster, who carried the top weight in the race at 127 pounds and gave up 8 pounds to the winner, finished third by a nose. Switch Partners carried only 114 pounds.

Jockey Don Pierce was puzzled by the Paster's performance and said the colt had never run that way before. "He didn't seem to be trying. If he'd half-tried, he could have won even with the weight." He thought the horse's two speedy workouts before the race might have tired him somewhat.

Another colt—Golden Act—made some noise by winning the Louisiana Derby by one and three-quarters lengths. It was the eleventh time in eleven starts that the colt had finished in the money. Golden Act's jockey expected him to run in the Derby, but another jockey, Eddie Delahoussaye, said Golden Act was not ready for Spectacular Bid. "Golden Act is a good horse, but he'll have to run to beat Spectacular Bid," he said. "I ran against him, and I know."

"The most important thing in racing is luck," Tom Meyerhoff was known to say. So far, Bid had been lucky, but he narrowly escaped some bad luck on March 23 during his final workout for the Flamingo Stakes. As Robert Smith, Bid's exercise rider, took him around the oval, Bid got scared by another horse that got too close and he jumped, almost throwing Smith. Delp was watching and ran out onto the track, shouting obscenities. No punches were thrown, but his temper went through the roof. "I know that jerk," he said. "He does it all the time. He wants his picture in the paper. Who does he work for? If I had him here now I'd knock his teeth out."

It reminded Delp that anything could go wrong with a horse. The Meyerhoffs had upped the insurance policy on Bid to $14 million, paying an annual premium of $700,000. "The worrisome time for me is not in the afternoon or at night," Delp said, "but in the morning at the racetrack, with a bunch of idiots around him. I'm talking about people who want to have their picture taken and who want to get close to the horse. . . . This horse would never get hurt in his stall. He's smart; I never worry about him in there. . . . I know what happens to some horses. It's some stupid, ignorant thing that ends a horse like this."

The Friday before the Flamingo Stakes was the Flamingo Ball, a formal event held under a tent on the grounds of Hialeah Park. It was a cancer benefit that included games and an auction of stud services of the top Florida stallions. It was *the* place to be seen in Miami, and the Meyerhoffs, owners of the odds-on favorite in the next day's race, were not invited. "I am a little curious why," Teresa Meyerhoff wondered. No explanation was given. "We're not looking to crash into the inner circle—if there is one," she said. "There are some great people in racing—and some not so great." It was another reminder that team Bid was not part of the establishment—a social slap in the face. Harry laughed it off. "Somebody made a mistake," he said, trying to rationalize the snub. "No big deal. We had a nice dinner with friends in Palm Beach." But the Meyerhoffs faced rejection everywhere, especially in New York. According to Meyerhoff, a reporter kept digging into his family tree to prove that he was not "establishment." "I'm not sure I know what establishment is," Meyerhoff said, grinning.

"Oh, you know, the Phippses, the Whitneys," the reporter replied. "You weren't invited to the Flamingo Ball, were you?"

Meyerhoff laughed it off, but the reporter continued, mentioning that an upper-crust magazine had noted that it was too bad the Meyerhoffs' bloodlines were not as good as Spectacular Bid's. "Oh," Meyerhoff said, "I didn't know the horse's were that good."

Perhaps the reporter was referring to Meyerhoff's Jewish heritage. Anti-Semitism was not new to horse racing. Although racing financier August Belmont was Jewish and was admired by many, others were not so lucky. Hirsch Jacobs, the first Jewish trainer to be inducted into the National Museum of Racing and Hall of Fame, faced anti-Semitism along the way. He had been refused membership in the exclusive Jockey Club. In fact, Jews were barred from the Jockey Club until 1951. Several people close to Harry Meyerhoff suggested that his heritage had something to do with the continual snubbing his family experienced from the racing elite.

Others, however, embraced the Marylanders' laid-back attitude toward horse racing. "What a welcome breather they are from the stuffy, snout-in-the-air, horse-owning aristocrats who often prance around the Triple Crown tracks, picking and choosing the persons to whom they will speak," wrote Betty Cuniberti of the *Washington Star*. Teresa Meyerhoff agreed with the assessment. "We were comfortable with the everyday people at the track because that's who we were basically. I mean, yes, Harry had money, but he was never a snob, and we just considered ourselves regular people." The Meyerhoffs enjoyed having their horse in the spotlight; they enjoyed getting dressed to the nines for the races and all the trips to the winner's circle. But they longed to be back home at Hawksworth Farm. "It is very strange getting into the public eye. It's tough getting used to it," Teresa said.

Delp also had his backers—the everyday workers who groomed, fed, and exercised the horses. He had always been one of the little guys, until Spectacular Bid came along. "His expertise has allowed Delp to love the good life for some time, but his name and face have never been familiar to the general public," wrote Randy Schultz of the *Palm Beach Post*. "They soon should be." Delp agreed. "I'm a working trainer who's been here for a lot of years and I thought I'd get a top horse one of these days. I didn't think it would be one like this one, though."

As luck would have it, when post positions were drawn for the Flamingo Stakes, Franklin's and Velasquez's mounts were side by side: Bid in the eighth post, and Velasquez's horse, Strike the Main, in the seventh. Franklin issued a stern warning to Velasquez before the race: "I'll knock him over if he comes near me. I know how powerful my horse is. He won't come near me if he knows what's good for him." Velasquez stayed above the fray, saying only, "I'll ride my own race and try to win." But when pressed about Franklin's ability as a jockey, he could not resist. "I'm friendly with anybody, and if he (Franklin) was a friend, he'd tell you that I was the only one who came up to him before [the Florida Derby] and wished him luck. If he gets beat with that horse, he's got to be the worst rider in the world." Andrew Beyer predicted a rout, while taking a backhanded slap at Franklin: "Spectacular Bid holds such a margin of superiority over his seven rivals in the Flamingo Stakes Saturday that even jockey Ron Franklin should not be able to find a way to get him beaten."

The morning of the Flamingo was hot and humid, with a little rain in the forecast. Franklin was nervous. This was his first ride since the disastrous Florida Derby. Fans shouted, "Don't choke, kid," and "Can you manage to sit on him, Ronnie?" Even Delp admitted after the race, "All I was worried about was what would happen if Ronnie fell off coming out of the starting gate. What would I have done then?" Secretly, though, Delp was confident. He half-jokingly invited the Meyerhoffs over to his house near Gulfstream Park to hang out by the pool and watch the race on television.

Bid must have felt Franklin's nervousness; in the walking ring before the race, the colt was feisty and high-spirited. He had never liked crowds, but he was particularly unruly on this day. "I was afraid he was going to kick somebody. . . . He could've gotten hurt if he kicked a camera, but somebody could've gotten killed if he had kicked them," Delp said. "When he kicks, he kicks. He has a helluva punch. It's worse than Muhammad Ali's."

Six other horses dared to challenge Spectacular Bid this time, and some trainers admitted they were running for the $29,800 check for second place. Bid broke out of the gate loafing, passed the clubhouse turn four wide, and was running third after a quarter of a mile. On the backstretch, Franklin chirped into the big horse's ear, "Let's go, Big Daddy." As if he understood the words, the colt accelerated, flew past Gallant Serenade without urging, and overtook Native Sir, inching his way to a half-length lead at the half-mile mark. Exploding into second gear, he stretched the lead to eight lengths after three-quarters of a mile. Jockey Jerry Bailey, aboard Need More Time, said that Franklin "never even moved . . . [Bid] just opened up four or five lengths. Effortless."

In the homestretch, Franklin hit Bid six times, and the colt responded; the final margin was twelve lengths, as the rest of the pack gamely followed Bid in the cuppy sand of Hialeah Park. The time for the one-and-one-eighth-mile race was an unremarkable 1:48²/₅—at least unremarkable by the lofty standards Bid had established. It was two seconds off the stakes record set by Honest Pleasure in 1976. But Delp was unconcerned about the time. Bid became only the twelfth horse to win both the Florida Derby and the Flamingo Stakes since the Florida Derby began in 1952.

Franklin had managed a perfect ride. In the winner's circle, Delp slapped hands with his "third son," then clasped them in his own and said, "I've always had faith in you"—quite a reversal of opinion, considering his reaction after the Florida Derby. It was Bid's ninth straight win, and in those races, he had defeated his rivals by sixty-one and a half lengths—nearly seven lengths per win.

The one question about Franklin's ride was his liberal use of the whip—six times was considered excessive for a twelve-length win. Once again, Franklin attributed it to Bid's tendency to slow down in the absence of a challenger. "I went to the whip because he got to loafing a little bit," he said. "He was in front of the other horses a long way, and I wanted him to keep his mind on business." His explanation was in line with Delp's admonition not to coast under the wire but to keep him driving all the way through the finish line.

The critics, however, were not so kind. Andrew Beyer wondered whether the colt's training regimen—and Franklin's use of the whip— was starting to "squeeze the lemon" out of Spectacular Bid, as Horatio Luro would have put it. "If he had been facing any decent opposition, Spectacular Bid's margin of victory would have been perilously narrow," Beyer wrote. "Could Spectacular Bid possibly have peaked so early in the season? The answer is emphatically yes."

Beyer called Franklin's ride "typical": "This was the action of a jockey with no self-confidence. Having been the target of so much criticism, Franklin rode as if he could not afford to take any chances—even with a ten-length lead." Franklin was racing worse than ever, he claimed. "He has been running his mounts into walls of horses and losing control of his horses in the stretch. If he were steering cars instead of Thoroughbreds, his license would be revoked for reckless driving instead of the mere five-day suspension he is serving right now for one such bad trip." (The suspension began on the Monday after the Flamingo Stakes.)

Frank "Pancho" Martin, who had trained Sham, Secretariat's main competitor during his Triple Crown races, was impressed with Bid, acknowledging that he was a better horse than Secretariat at this point in his career. "This horse, he's a tough horse," he said. "He loves to run. He can win the Triple Crown very easy. He's a super horse."

In the stands at the Flamingo was Seth Hancock, president of Claiborne Farm. He had put together a deal to put Secretariat out to stud, and this young three-year-old was piquing his interest.

Out west, Flying Paster had returned to form, taking the prestigious Santa Anita Derby by six and a half lengths. Starting from the outside post, he was five horses wide at the first turn and was fifth in the backstretch before making his move on the far turn. By the time he hit the homestretch, he was in first place and lengthening his lead. Veteran jockey Don Pierce only had to tap him on the shoulder a few times to get the response he needed. "I'll tell you, he beat some real runners today," Pierce said. "I'm really excited about the Kentucky Derby, and until Spectacular Bid shows he can beat us, I'm confident about my colt's chances." The two colts seemed to be equals on the track, and Flying Paster's trainer Gordon Campbell agreed with Pierce.

The rivalry was on. Other East-West battles had become classics: Swaps versus Nashua in 1955 and Majestic Prince versus Arts and Letters in 1969. Leon Rasmussen of the *Thoroughbred Record* mentioned the quality of the horses Flying Paster was beating. "It is just a feeling that the horses Flying Paster has been beating in the West are pounds better than those Spectacular Bid has been beating in Florida." Delp had to stir the pot, saying of Flying Paster, "He'll have to be as good as Secretariat or [the Kentucky Derby] won't even be a race. Every horse that has run against [Spectacular Bid] and tried him has never been the same. When they look this colt in the eye, they get demoralized." "We'll wait and see about that," quipped B. J. Ridder, Paster's owner. Taking a shot at Delp's Maryland background, he added, "As far as I'm concerned, [Delp] hasn't trained anything but claimers. Most trainers keep their mouths shut. He's made some ridiculous statements." Delp didn't mind. "If nothing happens to [Bid], he'll probably never lose another race."

Meanwhile, Golden Act continued his winning ways in the Arkansas Derby. Far behind for most of the race, he put in a final kick in the homestretch to run down Smarten and win by a neck. Despite spotting his rivals three to eleven pounds, he finished in the money for the twelfth straight time.

General Assembly was making a comeback. After several losses to Bid in 1978, he won the Gotham Stakes at Aqueduct Racetrack by three lengths over Belle's Gold. The colt, fifth after the first half mile, moved up to second with five-sixteenths of a mile to go. He then surged in front at the top of the stretch and remained in the lead for the rest of the race. Screen King, trained by Luis Barrera (brother of Affirmed's trainer Laz Barrera), was the even-money favorite but finished third.

Bid needed one good tune-up before the Derby, and Delp planned to enter him in the Blue Grass Stakes at Keeneland on April 26, where he had been sold a year and a half earlier. Once again, Smiley Adams was entering Lot o' Gold, and he was trying to out-Delp Bud Delp in the overconfidence wars. "His horse had better be in good shape. If he's not he's sure as hell going to get beat," Adams said. "He won't want to make no mistakes. I know my horse is in good shape." Adams again sneered at Delp's claiming career. "You can't take it away. [Bid]'s a nice horse," he said. "But [Delp] let that go to his damn head. I guess this is the best horse he's ever had and he's won them races around Maryland, few little stakes here and there, and got one horse and just thinks there's no hereafter."

Even the Kentucky establishment took a few shots at Bid, even though he had been born in Kentucky. Trainers said he looked like he should gallop with a cane; he had something wrong with his gait, they said, with his toe facing outward and his neck held high. Delp came back with a ferocity aimed not at the trainers but at Brownell Combs, president of Spendthrift Farm. He called a press conference and alleged that Combs was planning to syndicate Bid for future breeding rights before the Kentucky Derby and that after the syndication, the Meyerhoffs would replace Delp with another trainer before the Preakness Stakes. "I know Combs is a big, big man down here, and I also know that he'd like to shut me up," Delp said. "Racing is a cut-throat game all the way down the line. Every trainer living will cut your throat if he gets a chance." Delp denied that the Meyerhoffs were considering either syndication or replacing him, and Harry concurred.

Combs vehemently denied Delp's accusations. "There's no substance to his allegations," he said. "We have made no offer to syndicate the horse and the owners have solicited none. Apparently, another breeder is trying to plant false rumors to thwart any future offer we might make." He admitted he was interested in syndicating Bid but said he would not make any offer until the Triple Crown races were over. The allegation further divided Delp and several members of the establishment who found his statements intolerable and inexcusable, without foundation or explanation. But that was Bud Delp.

Spectacular Bid's fame was growing. More than 10,000 people came out to Keeneland on a Tuesday to watch the colt *practice*. He breezed seven furlongs in a blazing 1:22³/5 between the second and third races, then galloped out a mile in 1:35²/5. Joe Hirsch of the *Daily Racing Form* called it "one of the fastest and most impressive moves by a classic candidate at Keeneland in many years." The crowd applauded as Bid worked around the track, and the colt appeared to love the attention, kicking his heels a few times. "He needed it badly," Delp said afterward. "This probably is the most serious workout of this colt's career. This is the work which sets him up for the Kentucky Derby."

Blue Grass Day came on April 26 with overcast skies that threatened rain at Keeneland Race Course. The Meyerhoffs, sensing some animosity from the hardboots, declined an invitation to lunch at the track with the board of directors of the Keeneland Association, preferring to stay at the Hyatt Regency and arrive at the track later. Spectators began to fill the seats at around 11:00 a.m.

Once again, Bid's workouts had scared away most of the other horses. At one time, trainers of twenty-eight horses had considered running them in the Blue Grass. By post time, that number had dwindled to four: Bid; Lot o' Gold, a horse he had defeated three times already; Bishop's Choice, another colt he had beaten; and Pianist.

The horses walked through the post parade and into the starting gate, and when the bell clanged and the gates opened, all four leaped out together. The pack went four wide around the clubhouse turn, with Bid, starting in the number-four position, on the outside. Although Frank-

Spectacular Bid winning the Blue Grass Stakes by such a large margin that the rest of the field is not in the photo. (Keeneland-Pille)

lin urged Bid on from the start, he did not respond. Once they reached the backstretch, Bid was last. Pianist held the lead, and Lot o' Gold made a move on the inside to challenge. Finally, Bid decided it was time to run and made a move for the leaders on the outside. For a moment, Lot o' Gold held the lead by a neck. Then Franklin whipped Bid twice, and that was all the gray colt needed. Routinely, almost effortlessly, he responded, passing Lot o' Gold and increasing his lead to two lengths. Seeing as no one was challenging him, he loafed out of the far turn and into the homestretch—causing Franklin to hit him with the whip a few times. The final margin of victory was seven lengths. The time of 1:50 for the one-and-one-eighth-mile race was two seconds slower than Bid's time in the Flamingo Stakes. He took thirteen and four-fifths seconds to cover the last furlong, whereas a good training time for a furlong is twelve seconds. Spectators wondered, "What's wrong with Spectacular Bid?"

Franklin claimed that Bid needed another horse to challenge him to do his best. "He moved on his own down the backstretch to make the lead, just playing around and not leveling. I just hope Flying Paster is enough horse to pressure Spectacular Bid because I'd like to see what he can do. If he's pressured enough in the Derby I think he can break the track record."

"Who the hell were we supposed to impress?" Delp asked when questioned about the slow time. "All we had to beat was Lot o' Gold, and we beat him all the time." He spoke glowingly of Spectacular Bid: "He's

The Meyerhoffs, groom Herman "Mo" Hall, and jockey Ron Franklin on Bid after the Blue Grass Stakes. (Keeneland-Pille)

getting smart. After he took the lead at the five-eighths pole, he realized he didn't have to exert himself, and he was just playing with them the rest of the way." Bid had not responded to Franklin at first because he knew it was not time to go yet. It was Bid's race, and he had decided when to take the lead.

Still, the list of doubters was growing. Leading the pack once again was Andrew Beyer, who wrote, "At the very least, the slow time of Spectacular Bid's race has injected a great element of uncertainty into what appeared to be an open-and-shut Kentucky Derby." Another doubter was Smiley Adams. Spectacular Bid had now beaten his horse, Lot o' Gold, four times—badly in most cases. "Spectacular Bid is a nice horse," Adams said, "but he's no damned super horse. If he's a super horse, he's gotta run a mile and an eighth better than [one minute] fifty." When asked who was better, Flying Paster or Spectacular Bid, Lot o' Gold's jockey Darrel McHargue said, "I don't think there's more than two or three lengths difference between either horse."

The Associated Press published a story about Delp's training regimen, claiming that Bid was working twice as hard as most other horses preparing for the Derby. "Most horses gallop about a mile a day, but Spectacular Bid goes two miles, and he goes fast. The regimen established by [Delp] has drawn criticism from some who have watched the horse train, but Delp says the tall roan colt thrives on it."

There was even a rumor that Bid was injured and had been visited by a veterinarian. According to the *Daily Racing Form,* Bid's veterinarian, Dr. Alex Harthill,[1] had been called to examine a horse at Hialeah Park. While he was there, he visited Delp, an old friend whose services the trainer had used occasionally, and the two talked for about half an hour. Within minutes, the rumor mill was grinding. A reporter got a call from someone saying, "Spectacular Bid has bowed [a tendon]. He is out of the Derby." According to another rumor, the horse had a virus that would keep him from going to Churchill Downs. Reporters tried to contact Delp but could not reach him. By this time, panic had set in.

"Of course there's nothing wrong," Delp said when he was finally reached. He had left the phone off the hook for a few hours to keep the reporters frothing at the mouth. "Matter of fact, if things were any better I'd have reason to be alarmed. Spectacular Bid is just fine . . . great. He's never been better. As you see, I worked him Friday morning after all of those ridiculous reports."

The Paster kept up the chase in California. Despite stumbling at the start of the Hollywood Derby, he won by an astounding ten lengths, putting up a better time than Affirmed had the year before and bettering Bid's Blue Grass time by about three seconds. He was in third place after a half mile, eased into second by the three-quarter pole, and took the lead rounding the far turn. "It was definitely the best race in his career," said jockey Don Pierce. "He did it so easy that I didn't even have to put the stick to him." Darrel McHargue, who rode the runner-up Switch Partners, said the Paster would represent the West Coast well at the Derby. "He's going to be about the only opposition really for Spectacular Bid. . . . Flying Paster beat everyone on the West Coast about the same way that Spectacular Bid beat everybody on the East."

Barry Irwin of the *Thoroughbred Record* was sold on the pride of the West. He was ready to put the Paster in the same class as Sham and

Majestic Prince, two other colts that wintered in California. And after his latest blowout victories, Irwin believed that Flying Paster "must be considered the equal, at the very least, of Affirmed," another horse whose prep races had been run in California. Trainer Gordon Campbell said the Paster was an intelligent horse with exceptional skills. "He has the ability to run just about anywhere you want. He has speed to use when you need it—early, late, whenever. He's just a good all-around colt . . . the best I've ever had."

The Derby picture got fuzzier, however, when General Assembly faltered again. Racing in the Wood Memorial, he was upset by Instrument Landing, who won by a nose over a fast-closing Screen King. General Assembly had trouble fighting traffic in the field of ten, and although he closed the margin in the homestretch, he finished a disappointing fifth. Instrument Landing had finished a close third to Spectacular Bid in the Young America Stakes; Flying Paster had beaten him by sixteen lengths in the Santa Anita Derby.

All the criticism was starting to wear on Delp. Shortly before the Blue Grass Stakes, he lashed out at the "Kentucky hardboots," who, he said, were "not rooting for us." The Kentucky racing establishment saw him as an outsider, "an irreverent popoff, a claiming-horse trainer from Maryland who happened to get lucky and stumble into a great horse." "The hardboots ain't gonna help Bud Delp," he said to a crowd of reporters who were asking him about Ron Franklin—insinuating that Kentucky owners and trainers were refusing to put Franklin on their horses. "That's why I got these horses of mine here. I got to keep this jock fit. I'm gonna send three horses to Churchill Downs with another trainer. I'm going to run each one of them over there twice next week so Ronnie will know where that finish line is. I'm not asking any of these hardboots to use him. I never asked 'em for anything in my life, and I'm not going to now."

Franklin generally spent his time alone in the jockeys' room; he did not have many friends. He attributed this to his shyness, his recent arrival on the racing scene, and other jockeys' jealousy of him riding Spectacular Bid. Jockeys talked about him, and trainers did not let him ride their horses. All he had was Delp—and Bid.

5

Derby Fever

I am sure of one thing: Spectacular Bid is by nature the best
horse in the Derby field. He may be one of the best Thoroughbreds of all time.

—Andrew Beyer, *Washington Post*

THE KENTUCKY DERBY is the most prestigious horse race in the
United States. Open only to three-year-old colts, geldings, and fillies, it
was the brainchild of Colonel Meriwether Lewis Clark Jr., grandson of
William Clark of the famed Lewis and Clark expedition. On a trip to
England in 1872, Clark attended the Epsom Derby at Epsom Downs
and decided that America needed its own version of the race—something
that would capture the hearts of racing fans across the country. Returning home to Kentucky, Clark organized the Louisville Jockey Club to
raise money to build a racetrack for the city. He leased eighty acres of
land from his uncles, John and Henry Churchill. The track would soon
become known as Churchill Downs.

On May 17, 1875, about 10,000 people turned out to see Aristides
pull an upset in the inaugural Kentucky Derby. Hall of Fame trainer
Ansel Williamson had entered Aristides in the race to act as a "rabbit,"
a fast pacesetter that would tire the other horses and allow his prized
horse, Chesapeake, to come from off the pace and win in the homestretch. Aristides, however, built up such an early lead that no one challenged him. When jockey Oliver Lewis looked up into the stands at
owner H. P. McGrath, to see what he was supposed to do, McGrath
just waved him on. Aristides won by two lengths; Chesapeake finished
eighth.

Although the first race proved to be a success, the track itself ran into financial difficulties. Track officials built the famous twin spires in 1895, the same year Halma won the Derby, but the race continued to limp along. They tried shortening the race from one and a half miles to its current one and a quarter miles in 1896, hoping to persuade more conservative owners to race their young three-year-olds early in the spring, but it did not help; in both 1892 and 1905, only three horses ran in the race. Clark, who had lost a fortune in the 1893 stock market collapse, committed suicide in 1899, just twelve days before the twenty-fifth running of the Derby.

But help was on the way. Colonel Matt Winn of Louisville, a big Derby fan, put together a syndicate of executives to buy Churchill Downs in 1902. Under Winn, Churchill Downs prospered. Pari-mutuel machines were brought to the track, and bookmakers were outlawed. Soon, with the addition of a larger purse, the Kentucky Derby became the preeminent stakes race for three-year-old Thoroughbreds in North America.

The race has become larger than life in its 140-plus years of existence. Each year, more than 100,000 fans come to witness "the most exciting two minutes in sports," and millions more watch it on television. Those horses that win have their names etched in history: Exterminator, Sir Barton, Gallant Fox, Omaha, War Admiral, Whirlaway, Count Fleet, Assault, Citation, Swaps, Northern Dancer, Secretariat, Seattle Slew, Affirmed, Alysheba, Sunday Silence, American Pharoah, and Justify.

On April 30, 1979, the *New York Times* featured a Kentucky Derby preview on its sports page. Titled "East vs. West: Spectacular Bid Meets Flying Paster at Last," it featured two photographs of Flying Paster and Spectacular Bid in profile, facing each other nose to nose, along with their vital statistics—birthplace, sire, dam, color, and owner. It was like a prizefight's tale of the tape. "Even Bud Delp agrees that the East-West confrontation in next Saturday's 105th running of the Kentucky Derby could be a war," the *Times* commented.

The comparison showed an even matchup: The two colts' birthdays were only a week apart. Each horse had had fourteen career starts; Bid had won twelve times compared to the Paster's ten, but the Paster had never finished out of the money. Bid had won ten races in a row—the longest winning streak going into the Derby since Morvich won eleven in 1922. The two horses' earnings were just $12,000 apart, with Bid taking more than $729,000 so far. The Paster's time for one and one-eighth miles was faster by almost a second, but California tracks were known to be faster than the sandier eastern tracks.

When the *New York Times* polled the last five trainers who had won the Derby, three gave the edge to Flying Paster, one favored Bid, and the other called it a toss-up. Lucien Laurin, the trainer of Riva Ridge and Secretariat (the 1972 and 1973 Derby winners), chose Flying Paster. "Flying Paster is getting better and better. He was very impressive in the Hollywood Derby. . . . Broke a stakes record and won in hand,[1] just galloping. . . . Now he is getting three weeks to freshen up. He should be dynamite."

LeRoy Jolley, trainer of General Assembly and 1975 Derby winner Foolish Pleasure, gave a slight edge to Flying Paster. He noted that the competition in California was tougher than it was in Florida, so the Paster had defeated better horses in his prep races. "Look at Instrument Landing. He only won about $2,000 in three California races. Then he came back to New York and won the Wood Memorial," Jolley said.

Laz Barrera, trainer of 1978 winner Affirmed, agreed with Laurin and Jolley. He thought the competition in California was tougher and that Pierce's experience would prove vital in such an important race. "He's not just more experienced than Franklin, he's more experienced than almost any jockey you can name. He knows what kind of horse he's got, so he keeps him out of trouble. He stays to the outside. When it comes to a stakes race, Pierce is hard to beat."

Woody Stephens, trainer of 1974 Derby winner Cannonade, predicted a win for Spectacular Bid. "He's a very tough individual. He's strong, he's sound, and he's got [a] good disposition. If you've got the best horse, you'll win your share."

Only Billy Turner, trainer of 1977 Derby winner Seattle Slew, threw up his hands at any comparison. "I honestly can't separate Spectacular Bid and Flying Paster. I can't give an edge to either one. They're dead-even, in my opinion."

Almost all the trainers agreed that it was a strong Derby field, and one of the other horses such as General Assembly, Golden Act, or Screen King could make a splash or even pull an upset. However, they believed that if all went according to form, it would be a two-horse race, and fans might see a thrilling finish in each of the Triple Crown races, similar to the battle between Affirmed and Alydar in 1978.

What troubled experts the most were Bid's slow times in both the Flamingo and Blue Grass Stakes. Andrew Beyer was the most puzzled, wondering if Bid had peaked too soon. As an example, he pointed to Honest Pleasure, who had been a superhorse at age two but, after lackluster wins in the 1976 Florida Derby and Blue Grass Stakes, had finished second to Bold Forbes in the Kentucky Derby. However, Secretariat had finished second in the Wood Memorial, his warm-up to the Kentucky Derby, and Affirmed's races leading up to the Derby had not been remarkable either.

Delp dismissed the Blue Grass time. "Off form? There's no way possible. He's perfect. The day after the Blue Grass I couldn't hold him on the ground. He's ready to run the race of his life Saturday."

Spectacular Bid arrived at Churchill Downs on Saturday, April 28—one week before the Derby—and moved into Barn 41. Flying Paster had arrived two days earlier, needing time to become acclimated to his new surroundings after the long trip from California.

The Monday before the Derby, Flying Paster went through his final workout. According to Don Pierce, the horse nodded as he cooled down—a sign of lameness. Pierce brought this to the attention of trainer Gordon Campbell, but according to the jockey, Campbell just turned his head. The pressure was too great to even consider scratching the Paster so soon. "[Owner B. J. Ridder] forced [Gordon Campbell] to run the horse anyway, and he shouldn't have run," Pierce later claimed. However, none of the stable hands or assistants at the track mentioned any lameness. If there was an injury, the Paster's handlers were keeping it quiet.

As soon as Bid got to Churchill Downs, Bud Delp, always ready with a quip and a quote, put on a show for reporters. It was his first time at Churchill Downs since 1967, when he had watched from the stands as the great Damascus finished third to Proud Clarion. When Delp was asked if he had caught the Paster's final Derby training run on Monday, he answered, "Naw, I had to go to the bathroom." Although he believed it would be a two-horse race, Delp was not taking the Paster too seriously. In a rare moment of good sportsmanship, Delp said of Bid's rival, "He may be as good as Secretariat. I'm looking forward to the race just like everyone else. If he beats me fair and square, I'll congratulate Mr. Ridder and I'll congratulate Gordon Campbell (Flying Paster's trainer)—maybe not ten seconds after the race, but five or ten minutes later. That's the way I am."

As always, Bid was Delp's priority. He said, "You can prepare a horse for a claiming race, and if something happens and you miss it, you can come back in eight days. But if something happens this week, I'm going to miss the Derby. That's the pressure. If he comes around this corner and kicks the side of the barn or walks out and feels good and jumps up and comes down on a pebble and bruises a foot, that's the end of the ballgame. That's where the pressure is."

Delp told one reporter, "I never dreamed about it or anything, but I always did wonder what set these horses apart. That's been the most interesting part of the whole experience for me. Everything about him— his eyes, his legs—it all works for that one common purpose. He wastes no motion, and he uses every fraction of his talent every second."

Gordon Campbell was the antithesis of Delp—a quiet, modest, unassuming man who rarely provided a colorful quote. The only time he got offended during the buildup to the Derby was when someone asked if California horses were on par with eastern horses. (Only three California-bred colts had won the Derby, the last being Decidedly in 1962.) "We get the impression people hardly think we exist back there," Campbell said. "Racing is exceptionally good back there. But it's the same as Eclipse Award balloting. All your votes are back here and we have no chance. The same thing applies to right now. All the publicity applies to Spectacular Bid, so naturally he's going to be the favorite. That's all people think about." When reporters pressed him for other quotes— any ammunition they could use against Delp, Campbell instead talked about golf and gardening, complaining that the gophers and birds kept eating his plants.

Meanwhile, where was Ron Franklin? He was sneaking from one barn to the next to escape reporters, who would inevitably ask him whether he belonged on such a great horse as Spectacular Bid. "In the 105-year history of the Kentucky Derby, there never before has been a jockey whose every action has been so studied, analyzed, and disseminated for public debate," wrote Randy Harvey of the *Chicago Sun-Times*. Reporters discussed Franklin's short history with horses, his errors in the

Florida Derby, and whether he should be riding Spectacular Bid in the Derby. Billy Reed continued Harvey's hyperbole. "This is the biggest gamble in Kentucky Derby history," he wrote. Joe Hirsch of the *Daily Racing Form* added, "This is like putting in an untested rookie to pitch the seventh game of the World Series."

Franklin acknowledged the pressure, even though Delp told reporters that nothing got to the young jockey. "He grew up in the streets; he knows how to take care of himself," he said. Franklin knew that if he made a mistake and lost the Derby, he would never hear the end of it from the media, trainers, and backstretchers.

As Delp had promised back in February, he rented a house about half an hour away from Churchill Downs, isolated and in the woods. It belonged to a cousin of Dr. Alex Harthill. Delp was determined to keep the press away from Franklin as much as possible and give them access only on his terms.

On Tuesday, Bid worked five-eighths of a mile in 1:00²/₅, galloping out three-quarters in 1:15¹/₅. Delp called the workout "perfecto." He announced that Bid would gallop for two miles on Wednesday and Thursday and then work an easy three-eighths of a mile on Friday. A reporter asked Delp if Bid liked the Churchill Downs track. "My horse is ready to go a mile and a quarter in a plowed field," he said. Then he quickly added, "but I'm not comparing the Churchill Downs track to a plowed field."

Delp continued to play it up for the media, asking television reporter Howard Cosell if he had an extra toupee he could borrow. He recited a poem he had made up on the way over to the track: "If Bid wins by two, that'll do; if he wins by five, we'll jive; if he wins by nine, that'll be fine." It was Muhammad Ali at his worst. One reporter, interviewing Delp for the first time, leaned over to a colleague and asked, "Is he always like this?"

Another reporter asked, "What if Spectacular Bid loses? What about all the boasting you've done? How will you react?" Without batting an eye, Delp said, "I will probably look in a mirror and say, 'Delp, you're a dumb S.O.B.'"

On Tuesday evening the Meyerhoffs attended the Derby Trainers' Dinner at the Executive West Hotel. Delp, claiming he was mentally and physically exhausted, excused himself from the festivities. This may have been true. Clive Gammon of *Sports Illustrated* had noted an "impulsiveness" in Delp, a "seeming lack of control under stress" since Bid had come into the spotlight last year. One horseman had said of Delp, "He'll be a basket case before he gets to the Derby." But there may have been other reasons as well. The trainer was fed up with the Kentucky establishment. Franklin was having trouble getting other mounts at Churchill Downs—just as Delp had predicted.

Delp's absence from the dinner meant that the Meyerhoffs had to answer all the questions asked by a panel of reporters. The first question to Harry Meyerhoff was why he was staying with Ron Franklin. Why stick with him when the Meyerhoffs could have any jockey in the world? Having answered this question countless times before, Harry had his talking points together. "We're sticking with him because we think he's the best jockey for the horse," he said. "I think he already has proved that. I think he's the best jockey for the horse. What else can I say?"

The next day, General Assembly turned heads as he blazed five furlongs in fifty-seven and two-fifths seconds. It was the fastest workout on the week of the race since the great Forego[2] recorded a fifty-seven-second run in 1973 (the year Secretariat won the Derby). Trainer LeRoy Jolley was pleased with the results. "General Assembly seems to run best after he works best, somewhat like Foolish Pleasure (Jolley's 1975 Derby winner)."

On Thursday, officials drew the post positions. There would be a field of ten for the Derby—small compared to today's typical field of twenty. Spectacular Bid drew the number-three post; Flying Paster, number nine; General Assembly, number six; Screen King, number five; and Golden Act, number one. Some surmised that even at number three, Bid might have trouble getting out of traffic, encountering the same situation he had faced in the Florida Derby. Delp disagreed. "He can start from number eight or eighty-eight," he said. "You've got better than a quarter mile to run from the starting gate to the first turn. If a horse can't get in position in more than a quarter mile, he don't belong in the race."

Tim the Tiger was not in the field, having chipped a hind ankle in January. That had put him out of the running at the start of his three-year-old campaign. He was another example of a promising two-year-old whose future as a three-year-old did not materialize—this time through bad luck.

One surprise entry—at the last minute—was a horse called Great Redeemer. Although he was entered about twenty minutes after the deadline on Thursday, officials had decided to accept entries until the draw for post positions. Great Redeemer had not won in six career starts, and he had lost those races by a combined eighty-four and a half lengths. He had been crushed in the Derby Trial on Tuesday as a 91 to 1 shot, finishing third out of five horses, eleven and a half lengths behind the winner.

Great Redeemer's owner, Dr. James Allison Mohamed, was a radiologist and a self-described breeding expert. He had been running ads in the *Daily Racing Form* and *Thoroughbred Record* promoting his book on breeding theories. He had predicted that Spectacular Bid would not win any Triple Crown race, "nor will General Assembly or Flying Paster." His favorites were Pianist, Roman Coffee, and Unconscious Lad—none of which were even entered in the Derby. "Spectacular Bid can't go over a mile," he said, ignoring the fact that Bid's last three victories had been more than a mile.

Mohamed had bought the horse for $2,100 at auction. Great Redeemer's sire, Holy Land, had fallen in the 1970 Derby, unseating his jockey, and ran the rest of the race riderless. Great Redeemer's trainer was so upset that Mohamed had entered the horse in the Derby that he quit, so Mohamed had to activate his own trainer's license and train the horse himself. "I don't think he has a chance," Mohamed said, "but I have a conviction and I have to follow it." When told of the late entry of Great Redeemer, Delp said of Mohamed, "He must be some kind of nut. It's his money, though."

Odds came out on Friday, and Bid was the 3 to 5 favorite. Flying Paster was listed at 5 to 2; the double entry of General Assembly and Sir Ivor Again (both trained by Jolley), 7 to 1; Screen King, 7 to 1; Golden Act, 16 to 1; Lot o' Gold, 35 to 1; King Celebrity, 50 to 1; and Shamgo, 102 to 1. Great Redeemer was listed at 30 to 1 because the oddsmaker had no idea what odds to put on him, and fans bet on him out of curiosity instead of pedigree and previous performance.

When sportswriters announced their Derby predictions, fifteen out of thirty chose Spectacular Bid, nine chose Flying Paster, three chose

Screen King, and three chose General Assembly. Andrew Beyer was perhaps most effusive in his praise of Spectacular Bid. "I am sure of one thing: Spectacular Bid is by nature the best horse in the Derby field. He may be one of the best Thoroughbreds of all time. Just as the time of the Blue Grass stirred doubts about his current condition, the time of his previous victories proved his brilliance."

On Friday, the eve of the race, the Meyerhoffs held a birthday party for Tom, who was turning twenty-six. Partygoers presented Tom with a cake, and after he had blown out the candles, they smashed the cake in his face. Tom only laughed. Nothing could diminish his enthusiasm for the Derby.

Also on Friday, something happened to make Bud Delp unhappy: it rained. It rained all day, and water poured out of the gutters of Barn 41. The racing surface became as sloppy as the day Bid had taken a mud bath in the Tyro Stakes. This put another knot in Delp's gut, and he prayed that Saturday's forecast of clearing skies would come to fruition.

Teresa Meyerhoff had invited family and friends to watch the Derby with her. She seemed confident and nonchalant, telling one friend, "I'm not really worried about it. I think we'll win." However, she tossed and turned on the night before the race. Harry had trouble sleeping as well. The two admitted that since the success of Spectacular Bid, they had not slept well. "He's everything right now," Teresa said. "He's an obsession. We wake up in the night thinking of him."

The skies cleared at Churchill Downs on the morning of the Derby, and a light wind helped dry out the track. Officials labeled it fast, but it had dried so quickly that it became cuppy. Trainers likened it to running on sand dunes. It was also cold—thirty-nine degrees in the morning, and it never got above the mid-sixties the whole day, making it the coldest Derby in twenty-two years. The gates to the infield opened at eight o'clock in the morning, and thousands of people streamed in equipped with blankets, tents, chairs—and lots of alcohol. One person even had whiskey in an intravenous bag. As it grew warmer, the crowd played volleyball and threw Frisbees, drinking and wagering throughout the day and occasionally running over to the chain-link fence separating the crowd from the track to watch the next race on the schedule.

For the owners and trainers, it was a waiting game. Penny Chenery, owner of Secretariat, once said, "I tell you, waiting for the Derby to start is the longest day of your life. . . . It's just a unique time of thrill and tension and worry." Delp experienced the same feeling, arriving at the track at 5:45 a.m., as usual, to see how his horse was doing. Although both groom Mo Hall and assistant trainer Charlie Bettis had checked Bid, Delp examined him as a precaution. Everything looked good. Hall pinned protective bandages around his legs and fed him his ration of oats. Bid was expecting a doughnut, which was his usual treat, but on race day, Delp would make him wait until after he had won, rewarding him with a chocolate one. Instead, he held out his hand for Bid to nuzzle. No doughnut? Bid grew irritated. As he always did, he hid some oats in the corner of his stall, saving them for later.

Delp thought about having Bid do some light jogging that morning but decided against it. He figured the adrenaline from the crowd would be enough to put him on edge. Instead, he walked Bid for forty minutes. *Just keep him healthy for another twelve hours,* he told himself.

For most of the day, Delp was busy talking to reporters. He made his debut on national television, talking to Howard Cosell of ABC Sports about the Bid-Paster rivalry. "I've been saying that it could be a two-horse race because I don't want the glory or the glamor or the fun to be taken away from it, but I honestly believe it's a one-horse race," he said with a straight face. "I think my horse is a superhorse. I really mean that honestly, and if Flying Paster is as good as Secretariat, he'll make a race out of it."

When Cosell asked Gordon Campbell the same question, predict-ably, he disagreed. "I think Spectacular Bid and Flying Paster are def-initely the two tough colts in the race. They're the ones to beat, but General Assembly, I believe, is . . . capable of running a much better race than he did in the Wood. Golden Act has run very well. He's a much-improved colt since the last time I ran against him, and Screen King turned in a tremendous work here the other day and indicates that he can be awful tough. So it's by no means a one-horse race or a two-horse race. There's others to be considered in there too." There was no mention of Flying Paster's injury; he seemed to be sound and ready to go.

Delp was worried about his jockey. Franklin had ridden a few races during the week to get used to the track and to gauge where the finish line was. But the establishment had not cooperated; trainers at Churchill Downs had refused to use Franklin, so his experience was limited. To calm Franklin's nerves and get him used to the track, Delp had him ride Seethreepeo, one of the other colts the Meyerhoffs had bought with Spectacular Bid, in the seventh race of the day, the one right before the Kentucky Derby. Franklin dueled it out with his nemesis Angel Cordero Jr. but prevailed in the stretch, pulling away for the win. It was a huge confidence boost for the young jockey.

As race time drew nearer, Spectacular Bid got more and more agitated. Delp's anxiety also increased, so he smoked a cigarette and drank a beer to calm his nerves.

When the bugle call finally came at about 5:20 p.m., Bid was in a lather, despite the cool temperature, his dark gray coat almost black with sweat. In the jockeys' room, Franklin got his helmet with his lucky nickel, rubbed Kiwi clear shoe polish on his hands (a prerace ritual since he had started to win with Bid), and strolled down to the paddock with the other jockeys. Knowing that Bid hated crowds, Delp kept him in the stables as long as he could until an official shouted, "Let's make it fast. Hurry up." Then Delp and Hall walked Bid out of the barn and over toward the paddock, right outside the grandstand, where the horses were gathered before being saddled, mounted, and paraded onto the track.

Delp had seen nothing like it: more than 100,000 fans cheering for the horses and their trainers. A year ago, he and Ron Franklin had watched all this unfold on television in his living room. Spectacular Bid had been only a hope, a horse full of potential who had yet to run his first race. Now, one year later, Grover "Bud" Delp of Creswell, Maryland, and his very special colt were part of the Derby experience.

Delp walked by some of the fans, many of whom had already had their fair share of alcohol. Someone yelled, "Hey, Bud, I got $200,000 on your horse. On the nose." Delp stopped, grinned, and threw his right arm up into the air. His confidence growing, he pointed toward the betting machines and shouted, "Go bet! Go bet!" Another spectator said, "You ain't gonna get nothing, Delp—NOTHING!" In an almost surreal moment, Delp turned to Hall and said, "Whisper in [Bid's] ear, now—tell him you love him." Despite Delp's contention that horses were only animals, he felt the need to soothe Bid after the nasty remark, as if it might have knocked his confidence somewhat.

Once they arrived at the paddock, they were met by the Meyerhoffs—Harry and Tom in suits and ties, and Teresa in a red dress and high heels. The large crowd surrounding Bid worked him into a frenzy—so much so that the TV commentators noticed it. "He was geared up coming to the paddock," said former jockey and color commentator Eddie Arcaro. Delp and Hall put a blanket over the paddock fence so Bid could not see the throngs of people, but it did not help. Bid bucked, reared up on his hind legs, and kicked dirt up on the Meyerhoffs and Delp. "He's never been quite this bad," said Teresa Meyerhoff. "He's ready to run." Delp hoped Bid was not headed for the same fate as Damascus, the 1967 favorite who got so worked up before the race that he used up all his energy and finished a disappointing third.

An official from Churchill Downs came by to check the tattoo on the inside of Spectacular Bid's upper lip, a number that corresponded to the horse's registration with the Jockey Club. This prevented owners and trainers from switching a good horse for a bad one at the last minute, or vice versa, and making a killing at the betting window. As the official moved on to the next horse, Bid continued to snort and kick, his muscles tight and bulging, his coat glistening with sweat. He wanted to run.

When the call "Riders up!" was announced, Delp helped Franklin up on Bid and told him, "Get you a position and put his face where he can see daylight. Then ride your race." His final words of instruction were ones he had been repeating to Franklin all week: "Don't misjudge the finish line."

Once Franklin got on Bid's back and the horses moved onto the track, Bid settled down a little as his stablemate, a pony named Rocky, trotted by his side. The University of Kentucky band played the traditional "My Old Kentucky Home." The crowd of 128,488—the fourth largest ever—sang along, and Delp got a lump in his throat. The women sported their fancy hats, and thousands in the crowd drank their mint juleps. More than half of those in attendance had settled in tents and chairs and blankets in the infield, their supply of beer and bourbon almost gone. As the sun went down, the temperature fell. In the grandstand, celebrities such as Elizabeth Taylor, Jaclyn Smith, Phyllis George, Neil Armstrong, and Anita Madden were enjoying themselves.

Before the race, Cosell had asked Franklin to compare his experience to Don Pierce's. Franklin had handled it like a professional. "I got just as much experience on Bid as he's got on Flying Paster and well, it's going to be a horse race, and I think that Bid's just going to draw away like he usually does." When Cosell asked Franklin about his strategy, the jockey said he expected to settle in second or third position, "but I'm going to send him on away from that gate as quick and as fast as I can and set my position. It's a long way for you to get that position. A mile and a quarter's a pretty long race."

The Meyerhoffs were sitting in their box seats along with Margaret McManus, wife of ABC sportscaster Jim McKay and a reporter for the *Baltimore Sun*. Because of the earlier foul weather, Teresa had brought a raincoat with her. She turned to a friend and said, "Would you mind holding my raincoat, because I really don't want to have to take it to the winner's circle."

McManus gave Teresa a surprised look and said, "Can I quote you on that?"

Teresa replied, "Yeah, sure, what's the problem?"

"You sound pretty confident."

"Yeah, I am pretty confident."

At last, the horses made their way down the homestretch, warmed up on the far turn, and walked back over to the starting gate. The gate was placed at the head of the homestretch, which meant that the horses would cross the finish line once before making their way around the mile-long oval again. Bid went into post number three like a seasoned veteran, his nerves having settled down and his mind seemingly focused on the track in front of him. He knew that when the gate opened and the bell clanged, he was to jump out running, pass the other horses, and not stop until Franklin pulled him up.

General Assembly had a tough time at the starting gate, and several assistant starters finally had to push him in. As the rest of the horses fell into place, Franklin's nerves got the best of him. "Sitting in the starting gate, I could hear my knees shaking," he said. Sandy Hawley, Golden Act's jockey, was also riding in his first Derby and was right beside Franklin. He noticed that Franklin was visibly nervous and said, "When the gates open, Ron, it'll be okay. You'll know what to do."

"One horse in," an assistant starter said as Lot o' Gold was being readied to enter the gate. He did so, and someone yelled, "Last horse in!" As soon as Lot o' Gold was in place, the gates opened. The crowd roared.

The announcer yelled, "And they're off!" The premier race of the Triple Crown was under way.

Bid got out as he usually did—slow and clumsy. He veered a little to the left, then straightened up as he tried to get settled. Franklin let most of the horses go by, and they formed a wall in front of him as they raced past the finish line for the first time and headed for the clubhouse turn. He was already trapped. Teresa Meyerhoff was aghast; her mouth dropped open and she whirled her head several times toward her husband as if to ask, "Can this be happening again?" But this time, Franklin moved Bid to the outside and, despite losing valuable ground, settled into seventh place. It was not the ideal position—not the second or third he had hoped to be in before the race—but he was on the outside and out of trouble.

Up front, General Assembly and Shamgo were the leaders, covering the quarter mile in a slow twenty-four and one-fifth seconds—the slowest opening quarter mile since 1912—which was bad news for Bid. If the pacesetters were going that slowly, they would have enough energy to last the whole race. Unless someone challenged him for the lead, General Assembly was in this race to stay. Spectacular Bid seemed to be holding his own. "He wanted to be where he wanted to be, so I kept him there. He had his feet under him real good, and I let him do his own thing early," Franklin said. He knew he had a smart horse, so he let Bid dictate the race.

Rounding the first turn, General Assembly held a slight lead over Shamgo, Flying Paster, and Lot o' Gold. Then Shamgo, a long shot who had lost his last nine starts by a total of seventy lengths, took the lead. By the half-mile mark, Shamgo and General Assembly were five lengths in front of Flying Paster, who seemed to be having difficulty managing the cuppy surface, and Lot o' Gold. Surprisingly, Great Redeemer, who was showing some early speed, was fifth. Another long shot, King Celebrity, was sixth, followed by Spectacular Bid (ten lengths behind Shamgo), Screen King, Golden Act, and Sir Ivor Again.

About halfway down the backstretch, Franklin whispered into Bid's ear, "It's time, Big Daddy!" and Bid slowly gained ground. He was still on the outside and was running at his own speed, as if he knew there was a lot of race left to run. He finally settled alongside Flying Paster, who was making his own move on the tiring Shamgo. The two raced as one, hitting the far turn and chasing General Assembly, who stubbornly held on to the lead and seemed to have conserved his energy, based on the slow initial fractions. The Paster was on the inside; Bid was on the outside. The crowd roared as they saw the rivalry develop, recalling Affirmed and Alydar the year before. These two colts were supposed to battle it out for the Kentucky Derby, East versus West, neck and neck, gunning for the lead. And with them was General Assembly, trying to repeat what his legendary sire had done six years earlier. It was a setup for a perfect ending.

General Assembly drifted a little wide on the far turn, taking the Paster with him, and the Paster bumped Bid a few times. "That just made my horse madder," Franklin said. In a second, Bid moved past the Paster and in front of General Assembly, as Franklin hit the colt on the right side entering the homestretch. "My horse looked Paster in the eye, and the other horse spit the bit right out," Franklin said, meaning that Flying Paster gave up. Don Pierce felt the reins slacken in his hands and knew it was over. "I was beat going into the final turn," Pierce said. "There'd been some bumping, and we got caught in the middle. But that didn't cost us the race. What did cost us the race? The surface of the track? I don't know. I guess maybe it was Spectacular Bid."

Golden Act's jockey, Sandy Hawley, saw the same thing from the back as his horse made a move from off the pace. "It really did surprise me to see Flying Paster stop dead. He usually looks you right in the eye and picks up the bit. But this time, when Spectacular Bid collared him, he couldn't respond and he was gone."

As the pack entered the homestretch, Franklin whipped Bid five times, urging him on. With each stride, Bid lengthened his lead over General Assembly, digging into the sandy surface and throwing it behind him, moving down the track with ease. His upright posture and smooth stride made it seem as if he were floating down the homestretch. Flying Paster dropped back, and Golden Act took his place with a furious closing kick, coming from ninth place.

But Bid was not to be denied. Franklin judged the finish line correctly, and when he crossed it, the margin of victory was two and three-quarters lengths. General Assembly was second, turning in a valiant but losing effort, and Golden Act was third, three lengths behind General Assembly. Flying Paster finished fifth, ten lengths behind, tired and

Spectacular Bid takes the Kentucky Derby. General Assembly is behind him in second, and Golden Act is behind him on the right. (Photograph by Jerry Cooke © 2018, Jerry Cooke Archives, Inc.)

blowing hard. The final time was 2:02²/₅—not a fast Derby, but considering the track conditions, it was fast enough. However, Bid's margin of victory was greater than that of the last three Triple Crown winners— including Secretariat.

Spectacular Bid, purchased by three Marylanders for $37,000 and trained by a small-time horse claimer, had just won the most prestigious horse race in North America. The victory was Bid's eleventh straight and his thirteenth in fifteen starts. The prize of $228,650 increased his career earnings to $964,787. He was also the third gray horse to finish first in the Derby.

As the horses crossed the finish line, photographers leaped onto the track to get a rearview shot of them. But they forgot about Great Redeemer. Once fourth, the last-minute entry had slowed almost to a trot; he finished forty-seven and one-quarter lengths behind Bid and twenty-five lengths behind Lot o' Gold, the next-to-last-place horse. Jockey Richard DePass had to weave around the photographers who had rushed out onto the track and almost collided with a few of them. Before the race, Delp had said of Great Redeemer, "I was afraid Ronnie would look up coming into the stretch, see that horse thirty lengths in front of him and panic thinking somebody was ahead of him, and not realize he had lapped that horse." "He was running good for about the first six furlongs," DePass said. "Then [Spectacular Bid] came by like a blur. Then everything came by like a blur."

The ushers arrived to escort the Meyerhoffs to the winner's circle, which was enveloped by a crowd of Marylanders. Delp ran down to the winner's circle with Pimlico's general manager Chick Lang, as Franklin guided Bid toward them, patting the horse's neck in appreciation for a fantastic race. Delp reached up, grabbed Franklin's hand, and paid the ultimate compliment to the nineteen-year-old jockey: "You is a pro. You is a pro."

Franklin was overjoyed but relieved that the race was over. "No problems, no problems," he told reporters after the race. "It was a very easy race, just like the Florida races." One reporter could not help himself and asked, "Like the Florida Derby?" Franklin ignored the question.

At the awards ceremony, with Bid adorned in a blanket of roses, Harry Meyerhoff limited his words to thanks and gratitude. "He handled [the horse] like a veteran," Harry said of Franklin. "We're glad to come home a winner." Teresa Meyerhoff was just as ecstatic. "I can't believe it," she said. "There's always a chance of something happening, and we knew we had the best horse, and I think he certainly proved it today." The Meyerhoffs were happy to be going home to Maryland victorious. They had received a lot of publicity in Louisville, not all of it friendly. The Kentucky hardboots had not liked having a Californian and a group of Marylanders fighting it out for the Derby, but now the Kentuckians' feelings were irrelevant.

Madelyn Jason, one of the breeders of Spectacular Bid, attended the race and was beside herself with joy. "It was too much of a thrill for me to see him win," she said. "I just started crying and thinking how proud Dad would have been to have seen this race. He was like any man who races Thoroughbreds. He dreamed of coming here with a good horse."

Some fifteen minutes later, B. J. Ridder, the owner of Flying Paster, sat waiting for a tram to take him back to Barn 42, where he would talk with trainer Gordon Campbell about what had happened to his horse. Less than 200 feet away was the winner's circle, where he was supposed to be accepting the trophy as the owner of the winning horse. Instead, the Paster had finished a disappointing fifth—the first time he had ever finished out of the money. He had also suffered a cut on his right foreleg during the race. Did the alleged injury earlier in the week have something to do with his poor showing? If it did, no one mentioned it. Instead, both Campbell and Luis Barrera, trainer of Screen King, blamed the cuppy track for their horses' poor performances. Both horses were long striders, and Barrera claimed that long-striding colts have a hard time on a cuppy track. "Screen King was the longest striding colt in the race," he added.

Also at Barn 42 was Smiley Adams; he sat alone in a tack room and was in a foul mood. His colt Lot o' Gold, who had finished second to Bid so often in Florida, had faded to ninth in the Derby, beating only Great Redeemer. "He ran like a $5,000 claimer," he grumbled. "I know he's a better horse than that. He just couldn't get hold of the track; he was bouncing up and down the whole way. I don't know where we're going to go with him, but it won't be Baltimore [for the Preakness]."

As Delp was getting ready to leave the track, still beaming from his victory, he heard a woman yell, "You didn't lie to us."

Delp smiled and said, "I never lie. I B.S. a lot. But I never lie."

Back at Barn 41, Gerald Delp and Mo Hall cooled the champion, walking him around and whispering words of congratulations and encouragement in his ear as the horse looked up at the dozens of spectators who had come to see him. "He's got a mind of his own," the younger Delp said. "He's the smartest horse my dad ever had." After Bid had cooled down, Hall sponged him down with warm water, the steam rising from his back and neck. Bid returned to his stall, and Gerald handed him his prize: the chocolate doughnut he had been denied earlier. The colt devoured it, as well as his dinner of eight quarts of oats.

The Meyerhoffs celebrated in a private room at Churchill Downs with friends and family. Harry sipped champagne as he recounted the race, admitting that he had been a little nervous as Bid entered the first turn boxed in. "But when he came to the outside and was free, I knew no one behind him would pass him and all we had to worry about were the ones ahead," he said.

Delp was his usual effusive, cocky self. "Those other horses won't even be out walking tomorrow," he said. "My horse will be tearing the barn down. If I had to, I bet I could run him again Wednesday." Then he suddenly got serious. "I'm just thinking that Spectacular Bid is a once-in-a-lifetime thing. The chances that I will ever be back here in this position again are remote at best. I guess that should make me sad. It doesn't." And with that, he got into a van and rode away.

In the jockeys' quarters, Franklin changed into his street clothes, staring at the silks he had just worn to win the Kentucky Derby. Don Pierce patted Franklin on the back and said, "Your horse done real good." Franklin thanked him for the kind words. As he was about to leave the room, he heard a voice call out to him and turned around. It was Angel Cordero. Cordero walked over to Franklin and stared at him, unsmiling. You could have heard a pin drop in the room. Then Cordero grinned and said, "You made, huh?"—jockey-speak for congratulations. It was a great compliment from a great rival. "Thanks, Angel," Franklin said, returning the smile. Then he turned and left with the police officer who would escort him through the crowds.

A few days later, the Meyerhoffs were in bed, when Teresa elbowed Harry during the night. Thinking there might be a burglar in the house, Harry immediately thought about calling the police. Instead, Teresa whispered, "Harry, we won the Kentucky Derby. Do you understand that? Do you realize that? *We won the Kentucky Derby.*"

6

Home Again

Cordero has to realize that [Ron] Franklin is a race rider just like he is.

—Bud Delp

AFTER TRIPS TO Gulfstream, Hialeah, Keeneland, and Churchill Downs, Spectacular Bid was finally heading home to Maryland for the Preakness Stakes, the second jewel in the Triple Crown. It would be run on May 19, two weeks after the Kentucky Derby. Although he had been born in Kentucky, Bid's first wins had come in Maryland, and when he was not on the road traveling to different racetracks, he was stabled at Pimlico. Maryland was also home to Bud Delp, the Meyerhoffs, and Ron Franklin.

On May 7, the Monday after the Derby, Bid boarded a flight from Louisville to Baltimore, accompanied by Delp and Dr. Alex Harthill. Fans greeted them at the airport, and at Pimlico, Zim Zemarel's Dixieland jazz band played "Maryland, My Maryland" and "My Old Kentucky Home" as Delp led Bid off the van. A sign hanging over Bid's stall read, "Welcome Home, Bid, Welcome Home." Franklin and Delp's two sons drove home from Kentucky. The Meyerhoffs flew into Easton Municipal Airport at about 12:15 a.m. They were met by a crowd of well-wishers throwing confetti and fire trucks blaring their sirens and horns. Harry, his necktie untied around his neck, got off the plane with Teresa, who was still wearing the blanket of roses that had covered Bid in the winner's circle.

General Assembly, Golden Act, and Flying Paster (who showed no signs of lameness after the Derby), followed Bid to Pimlico later that day; they would be running in the Preakness as well. Screen King would arrive on Thursday. The rest of the field had seen enough of Spectacular Bid.

"He doesn't know he's at Pimlico," Delp said of Bid. "He doesn't know he won two races here. He doesn't know he's going to be three-for-three after the Preakness is over. Horses could care less where they are. I think they're pretty stupid animals and as long as they have hay in one corner, water in another and the same groom it's all the same." There was no mention of his pre-Derby words with Mo Hall, encouraging him to talk to the horse as if he were a person.

The press was enthralled with Spectacular Bid and heaped adoration and praise upon him. "Spectacular Bid proved today what his trainer, Bud Delp, has been trying to tell the world for months: that he is an indisputably great racehorse, maybe one of the greatest of all time," said Andrew Beyer of the *Washington Post.* Even New York writers were kind to Bid, if not to Delp. "[Bid] can run as fast as trainer Buddy Delp talks, and that was plenty good enough for the gray-coated Kentucky-bred to indicate that he could well become the third consecutive winner of the once-elusive Triple Crown," wrote Russ Harris of the *Daily News.* Will Grimsley, recognizing the rarity of a group of Marylanders coming to Kentucky and stealing the Derby, called it a win for the common man. "It was a great day for kids with pimply faces and lofty ambitions, hot-walkers, and trainers who spend a lifetime medicating and nursing cheap claimers, the little guys in the tough, competitive world of Thoroughbred horse racing."

Most reporters, though, heaped their praise on Franklin. "The ride was superb, a cool, patient ride that kept the favorite within striking distance without rushing him into too much hard early running," wrote Steve Cady of the *New York Times.* "The doubters have been at last hobbled," wrote Ken Denlinger of the *Washington Post.* "At nineteen, Franklin hardly can be called great after winning the Kentucky Derby. But all he needed was to be competent, to keep a skittish horse and himself from cracking under perhaps the most intense pressure in sport. Delp was right. Franklin became a pro today." Will Grimsley of the Associated Press noted, "Saturday, [Franklin] guided his iron-gray speedster around the one-and-a-quarter-mile track with the hand of a genius and drew the ultimate accolade from his boss, Delp: 'You can put your head in the air now.'" Dan Mearns of the *Thoroughbred Record* mentioned Franklin's improved riding. "Franklin truly has matured over recent weeks; he seems much more self-assured now, far less the shy awkward boy of his pre-Derby days."

Only Andrew Beyer was less than congratulatory, claiming that Franklin's performance "could have cost a less-superior horse the race. A more experienced jockey would have sat patiently in the middle of the pack," he said of Franklin's decision to head outside at the clubhouse turn. "Instead, he played it safe; he steered his mount to the outside of the pack, losing valuable ground on the turn but also avoiding the chance of disaster." After running some numbers, however, Beyer proclaimed the next day that Secretariat was "probably the only Derby winner of the decade who could have defeated Spectacular Bid on Saturday." Employing a formula similar to the one he used in evaluating individual performances at the Laurel Futurity in 1978, he calculated that if the times of the last six Derby winners were adjusted for track conditions, Spectacular Bid would have run a 2:01^{1}/$_5$ Derby, third only to Secretariat and Affirmed.

In the wake of the Derby, Gordon Campbell, Flying Paster's trainer, reiterated the reasons for his horse's failure at Churchill Downs. "It looked like he was struggling," he said. "He couldn't get hold of the track. It was cuppy or something. He had never raced on a track like this. . . . I could tell when he was on the backside that he didn't like the track. But he started moving up and got close to the lead. Then he started folding up. That's the way a horse does when he's fighting the track. When it happens, that's it. . . . These long smooth strides he takes weren't there. He was struggling. I'm very disappointed." There was still no mention of the alleged injury the Paster had sustained during his warm-up for the Derby. If anything was wrong with the colt, now would have been the time to come forward. Instead, Campbell merely acknowledged that Flying Paster had lost about 50 to 100 pounds after the taxing Derby and was "sore all over." Both the Paster and Screen King would race in the Preakness on Butazolidin, an analgesic. If Preakness Day turned out to be wet and sloppy, Campbell planned to scratch his horse. However, he preferred the Pimlico surface to the one at Churchill Downs. At the Pimlico track, the

Paster was grabbing clay in workouts, giving him sounder footing. It was more like the surface he was used to in California.

According to Delp, Bid had come out of the Derby "as good and fresh as he ever came out of a race." He galloped two miles on Tuesday—his usual workout—and he would continue to do that until a serious test on Sunday, six days before the Preakness. On Friday, Bid managed to ignore a rearing horse that threw his rider on the track, and for that, Delp gave him a sugar-glazed doughnut. But deep inside, Delp was scared that something crazy might happen on the racetrack—something he could not control.

It rained on Sunday for Bid's serious workout, but it did not matter. About 2,500 fans showed up on Mother's Day to watch Bid cover five furlongs in fifty-nine and two-fifths seconds over a sloppy track. The problems he had encountered in the Tyro Stakes were a thing of the past; he could now run over any surface, any time. "He needed just what he got," Delp said. "It was a mental trial. He needed something to sharpen him up mentally. He's a dead fit colt." The other colts' numbers were not as good as Bid's. Flying Paster went five furlongs in 1:01²/₅ on the sloppy track, galloping out six furlongs in 1:15. Golden Act went six furlongs in a slow 1:16²/₅, galloping out seven furlongs in 1:32—sixteen seconds for the final furlong.

Harry Meyerhoff responded to the track conditions with Delp-like hyperbole, noting that Bid had raced on eleven different tracks while the Paster had raced on only three. "The significance is our horse doesn't care what kind of track it is," he said. "He can run on sand, concrete, a racetrack, the back of my car. He does not carry the racetrack with him."

Flying Paster did not worry Delp as much as General Assembly did. The horse had turned in an impressive effort in the Kentucky Derby. This time, the front-runner would have a shorter track and would not tire as much as he had in the Derby. General Assembly proved that when he ran a sharp five furlongs in fifty-eight and two-fifths seconds on Wednesday. If Bid got off to a slow start, as he had in the Derby, he might not have enough track to catch General Assembly.

Screen King also turned in a superb performance on Tuesday, May 15, running five furlongs in fifty-eight and four-fifths seconds. Bid topped them all on May 17, however, speeding three furlongs in an astounding thirty-four seconds. "That's about as fast as a Thoroughbred can go without becoming airborne, yet Spectacular Bid was still feeling frisky when he returned to the barn," wrote Steve Cady of the *New York Times*. Trainers usually prescribed a quick, short workout a few days before the race to put the horse on "edge," giving him the speed he would need to burst from the gate and use those fast-twitch muscles to power him to victory. "I wanted him to be sharp because the Preakness is oriented to speed. We've got the speed into him now if we need to use it," Delp said.

Once again, Delp was asked whether he was training Bid too hard, putting him through unnecessary two-mile workouts. Andrew Beyer thought it took the speed out of the horse; others thought Delp had not only squeezed the lemon too hard but "put it through the blender." As before, Delp claimed he was probably not working Bid hard enough. "Oh, they've criticized me. I trained him too hard in Florida. I didn't train him enough in Louisville. I did everything wrong. I've read all that. But I believe in doing it my way. I know my horse, and I've got the freshest horse that has ever come out of the Derby." He would rest Bid after the Belmont, then send him to the Jim Dandy Stakes in July and the Travers Stakes in August, both in Saratoga, New York.

In Maryland, the Spectacular Bid crew reveled in the laud and honor of the hometown crowd. The Meyerhoffs attended numerous parties thrown for them. Delp performed his routine for people who were used to his humor and cockiness. But Franklin received the most fanfare as the hometown boy who had made it big. Neighbors hung signs in their windows that read, "Welcome home, champ!" and "Dundalk is proud of you, Ron!" Marian Franklin's yoga class presented her with a sign that read, "Behind every great boy is a great mother!" The local McDonald's asked him to grill hamburgers for charity. Fans stood in line for three hours at East Point Mall in Baltimore to get Franklin's autograph. In an ironic twist, the principal of Patapsco High School named a day in his honor, some three years after he had dropped out. But most surprising of all was an invitation Franklin's father, Tony, received: the vice president of his employer, American Can, invited him for dinner before the Preakness. Never had he gotten such an invitation.

Ron was happy to be back with his family. Despite his closeness with the Delps, and despite being considered Delp's "adopted" son, he loved his parents, and they had always been supportive of his career as a jockey. Before Franklin got a room at Pimlico, back when he was hot-walking horses, Tony Franklin woke up at 4:30 a.m. to drive Ron to the track; in the evenings, Marian picked him up. When Franklin was at the Middleburg Training Center, feeling homesick, Tony drove 100 miles to bring him home so that he could have Thanksgiving dinner with his family. When Franklin arrived for his autograph session at the mall, about twenty-five members of his family showed up in support, including Franklin's five-year-old nephew Walt Cullum, who sported a T-shirt that read, "Ronnie Franklin. My Uncle."

All of Baltimore was going Bid crazy. Vendors hawked T-shirts and buttons that read, "Flip Your Lid for Spectacular Bid." Jewelers sold gold charms shaped like bridles and stirrups and called them "Spectacular Bits." Baltimore mayor William Donald Schaefer presented Bid with a dozen doughnuts and a proclamation making the horse an honorary citizen of the city. Bid, however, ignored the pomp and circumstance, preferring to focus on eating his oats.

Tom Meyerhoff worked with Pimlico's Chick Lang to print and distribute thousands of bumper stickers, pins, T-shirts, and jackets that read, "Spectacular Bid Is Spectacular!" Proceeds from the sales went to the Baltimore Opera Company, one of Teresa Meyerhoff's great loves. "When the people approached us about [selling] the T-shirts, we didn't want to accept any money," Teresa said. "We didn't need it, we didn't want it. I've been an opera buff for many, many years, so we finally decided to give any money we made off the T-shirts and stuff to the opera. It seemed like a good thing to do." Opera officials predicted an income of between $10,000 and $30,000, depending on how well Bid did in the Triple Crown races.

The Meyerhoffs also upped Bid's insurance from $14 million to $16 million.

Racing officials were expecting five to seven horses to join Bid in the Preakness, but as post time approached, only four dared to face him. The field was the smallest at the Preakness since the great champion Citation had won it in 1948 en route to his Triple Crown. Oddsmakers named Bid the 1 to 2 favorite, followed by General Assembly at 9 to 2, Flying Paster at 5 to 1, Golden Act at 6 to 1, and Screen King at 12 to 1.

On Thursday, May 17, the racing secretary drew post positions. Seconds before the drawing started, Tom Meyerhoff walked into the racing secretary's office and leaped onto a countertop. "Hawksworth Farm doesn't care what post position Spectacular Bid gets," he crowed. "We'll race from anywhere. Ronnie Franklin wants outside." Call it a jinx, but Bid drew the number-two post. The East-West rivalry heated up somewhat when Flying Paster drew the number-one post, which meant that the two would be starting side by side. Golden Act was in the third post, followed by Screen King and General Assembly in the fourth and fifth.

If Bid did not get out front early, he might not have time to make his traditional move to the outside and out of traffic. Pimlico's track was known for its tight turns, and the race was one-sixteenth of a mile shorter than the Derby. Franklin would have less room and less time to decide.

Both Gordon Campbell and Luis Barrera, Screen King's trainer, predicted that their horses would run better than they had in the Derby, thanks to the more favorable track conditions. This time, they warned, it would not be a two-horse race. "You have to throw that race of [Flying Paster's] in the Derby out," said Campbell. "He obviously didn't like the cuppy track there. The Pimlico surface is a lot closer to what he's been running on in California. So you can expect to see Flying Paster run much better." Some, however, blamed the Paster's poor performance on a lack of preparation; Campbell had given the horse three weeks off before the Derby. At the very least, he should have had a fast workout during Derby week over the Churchill Downs surface. Instead, he had run six furlongs in a slow 1:13⁴/5 the Monday before the race.

Andrew Beyer questioned the trainers' honesty in explaining why their horses had not performed as well as expected. "Cuppiness," he claimed, is not a track condition but an excuse for a loss. "In the entire history of the sport, there has never been an occasion when a trainer has said his horse likes a cuppy track," he wrote. "This is strictly a negative concept, employed only after a defeat. The track never seems to 'cup out' for great horses like Spectacular Bid, only for the lesser animals who chase them."

Around town, people were already handing the Preakness to Spectacular Bid. The only question was who would take second and third place. They also predicted a livelier Preakness because of the faster track, despite the rains forecast throughout the week. In Beyer's opinion, a fast

General Assembly was the only way Bid could lose on Saturday. If he opened a big lead, Bid might not be able to catch him. "General Assembly has the speed to take such a lead Saturday if jockey Laffit Pincay permits him," he wrote. "If Pincay does decide that he wants to try to steal an early five-length lead, none of the supporting cast in the Preakness field can stop him." Bid would have to stay close to General Assembly and not let him get a big lead; it could then turn into a speed race, leaving an off-the-pace horse like Golden Act to come from behind and beat the tiring front-runners. Anticipating this, Delp told reporters, "I won't be concerned as long as we're laying second. I want my colt to be on General Assembly's tail."

During one workout before the Preakness, Delp sent Bid through his two-mile gallop, but instead of letting him loose during the final furlong, he told the exercise rider to keep him reined in. Bid bowed his neck, twisted his head to the right, and let everyone know that he wanted to run. "Look at that," Delp said. "I think we've made him mad today. He could gallop three weeks like that. All winter in Florida, I would let him go a little that last eighth and people would wonder why I did and why I said all those things I did. What the hell? He is a great horse, and anyway, what if I had been wrong? I've been wrong before. I would still have been here eating crab cakes."

Preakness Day dawned cool and slightly wet. To the consternation of both Delp and Campbell, it had rained the night before, and dark clouds were gathering again. Delp went through the same routine with Bid as he had before the Kentucky Derby—limiting his meals, watching him grow agitated, and spending as much time in the barn as possible. Bid went for a morning jog to get limber, and he was full of life, bucking and prancing onto the track as Mo Hall, holding on for dear life, told him, "Damn, you're as crazy as the boss," referring to Delp.

Back at Bid's stable, there were two messages on the bulletin board: "6 a.m. trackside" and "5:40 p.m. winner's circle." Delp's confidence showed through, even on his to-do list.

Post time drew near. Thirty minutes before the race, Flying Paster kicked off a shoe in his stall and had to have it replaced. Delp spent the last few minutes calming Bid down in the paddock; then he boosted Ron

Franklin up on Bid at the call for "riders up." His final words to Franklin were the same as they had been before the Derby: "Keep him clear and get him running."

The Baltimore Colts' marching band played "Maryland, My Maryland" as the horses paraded for the 72,000 spectators—a disappointing turnout based on the 90,000 race officials had expected, given that a local horse was the favorite. The poor attendance was partly due to the overnight rain and the dark skies that threatened to unleash even more torrential downpours. But the clouds broke in the morning, and the sun partially dried the racecourse.

Those who made it to the track partied like the skies were blue. Vendors sold black-eyed Susans—drinks made of rum, vodka, and fruit juice—as disco music blared from the infield. Fans shared drinks and drugs; a portable toilet was stolen; a prostitute conducted business from one of the numerous tents set up in the infield; one couple even got married. Delp, who had distributed about seventy-five tickets to friends and family, found that he and his sons had no seats, so they sneaked into the Meyerhoffs' private box to watch the race. Some 700 members of the media were on hand to witness the event.

Spectacular Bid entered the starting gate as the 1 to 9 favorite—the heaviest favorite since Citation in 1948—with no trouble. He was followed into the gate by Golden Act, Screen King (with Angel Cordero aboard again), and General Assembly, who again had trouble taking his post. Flying Paster had already entered the number-one position. This time, Franklin was on his home course, and the butterflies had all but vanished. He was ready to ride. A few seconds passed, the bell rang, and they were off.

From the beginning, Bid was in trouble. Off to a sluggish start again, he was bumped by Flying Paster. Then Franklin's nemesis, Angel Cordero, tried to cut him off, moving Screen King toward him and forcing Bid to the rail. "Cordero seemed to be looking for Franklin," Andrew Beyer wrote later. Franklin first accepted the assignment to the rail to get away from Cordero, then looked for his chance to go outside. However, Cordero anticipated this response and moved Screen King in front of Bid, almost inviting him to check his speed and go around him. When Bid fell back to fourth place, Teresa Meyerhoff shook her head, clenched her fist, and said, "No."

General Assembly and Flying Paster were setting a quick pace, running the first quarter mile in twenty-three and two-fifths seconds. Screen King was comfortably in third; Bid was in fourth, five lengths behind; and Golden Act trailed the pack. Don Pierce did not want to play front-runner with General Assembly, but from the inside position, he had no choice; he did not want to lose his place around the shortest part of the track and risk getting boxed in. Both the Paster and General Assembly slowed down; when the Paster sped up, General Assembly matched him stride for stride. They reached the backstretch neck and neck, with a three-length lead on the rest of the horses. Cordero swung Screen King to the outside and almost dared Bid to go inside. Cordero was aware of Franklin's hesitancy to go to the inside—Cordero had created that fear in the Florida Derby. But Franklin was a different rider than he had been several months ago at the Florida Derby. He resisted staying on the inside and swung Bid all the way to the middle of the track—a place where few horses travel. He moved to the outside of Screen King as the two began to catch up to General Assembly, who had a small lead. In the stands, Teresa burst into tears and pumped her fist in the air. The crowd of 72,000 roared.

Heading into the far turn, Franklin let Bid go, and Bid responded. He blew past Screen King, moved directly in front of him, and forced him to slow down. Cordero stood up in his stirrups, in an act that seemed to plead "Foul!" to the stewards. He thought Bid had impeded his progress. Cordero's action cost Screen King valuable seconds; the horse was soon out of contention, with cuts on his forelegs. By this time, Flying Paster had passed General Assembly, and the fans got what they were looking for: a duel between East and West, Bid versus the Paster on a decent track, and no excuses.

Bid stayed wide, and if you blinked, you missed the contest. Within a few seconds, Bid blew past the Paster, leading by one length, then two. The margin doubled to four lengths as the horses entered the home-stretch, Franklin using the whip liberally on both sides of the horse. Golden Act made a late move, but Bid was too far ahead. The Paster faded as Bid increased his lead to six lengths. Screen King was roaming all over the track, bumping hard into Flying Paster, almost running into Golden Act, then moving inexplicably toward the middle of the

A victorious Ron Franklin aboard Spectacular Bid, with groom Mo Hall leading him, moments after the Preakness Stakes. (Jim McCue)

track. As Bid went under the wire, finally reined in by Franklin to save the horse's stamina, he was five and a half lengths ahead of Golden Act. Screen King somehow managed third place; Flying Paster was fourth; and General Assembly, fading badly, finished last. The time was 1:54¹/₅, the second-fastest Preakness in history and just a fifth of a second slower than the record set by Cañonero II in 1971.[1] It remains the fastest Preakness ever run on a wet track. If Franklin had not pulled Bid up toward the end, or if he had had better competition to push him, the record would have been his.

Former jockey and ABC commentator Eddie Arcaro was impressed at Bid's kick to go to the front. "In all his races, I never saw him explode like that," he said. CBS Radio commentator Win Elliot proclaimed that Bid "won with resolution."

For the win, Bid earned $165,300, which brought his career earnings to over $1.1 million. He had now won twelve races in a row and fourteen of sixteen in his career. The Meyerhoffs exchanged congratulations and kisses and exploded in screams as they began their frantic rush down to the winner's circle.

Back at the Corral Inn, Al Franklin, Ron's uncle, had lit his customary cigar before the race and watched events unfold. When Bid crossed the finish line, Al, who worked as a welder for Bethlehem Steel, broke down and cried. "This is the happiest day of my life," he said. "I can't help it. I love that boy and I love that horse."

Right after the race, several jockeys protested. Franklin accused Cordero of bad sportsmanship in luring him outside. Cordero accused Franklin of impeding his progress by moving in front of him. However, the Pimlico stewards ignored those complaints and focused instead on Cordero's sudden move into Flying Paster with about an eighth of a mile to go, forcing Don Pierce to check his speed and stand up in the saddle. After reviewing the tapes, the stewards saw no foul—to the bafflement of journalists, who supported Pierce's claim that Cordero had bumped him.

Franklin criticized Cordero's ride: "He brought his horse way out . . . and I'm surprised at him," he said. "He did take his horse way out down the backside. He took him clear out to the outside fencing." In an earlier race that day, Franklin had lodged a complaint against Cordero for bumping his horse in the stretch. Were Cordero's tactics revenge or bullying? "What else is new?" Cordero yelled from the jockeys' quarters. "I ride my horse and he rides his horse. If he wants to go outside around twenty horses, that's his problem. But it's a good thing he has a good horse when he does it. I was outside all the way because I want to be there. He can go anywhere he wants. Why did he come around me on the first turn? Ask him. I had nothing to do with it. But all I hear is 'Angel, Angel, what happened?'" Later, Franklin softened his words toward Cordero, but he defended his move in front of Screen King later in the race. "He was doing his job. But I was doing my job when I went past him and pushed him back down there where he belonged."

"Riders with fear don't make that move," wrote Dave Kindred of the *Washington Post,* referring to Franklin's tactic of moving Bid in front of Screen King. "Riders burdened by excess caution don't make that move. Losers don't make that move. Franklin moved over in front of the great jockey who had moved in front of him for three-quarters of a mile. Cordero had to slow down." Delp agreed. "Cordero has to realize that Franklin is a race rider just like he is."

At the very least, Cordero's ride was curious. His mount, Screen King, was all over the track, cutting in and out between horses so much that Kindred called it a "blueprint for spaghetti. Four-year-old urchins making their first ride on a bicycle don't go so crooked as Cordero did today in one of America's premier horse races."

Tom Meyerhoff was overjoyed at Bid's win in front of the hometown crowd, saying that Bid "still has something else to do, but nothing to prove." To Teresa Meyerhoff, the win in Maryland was special. "It's the Preakness. It's home. To me, it's just as wonderful as winning the Derby. I'm as thrilled for Baltimore and Maryland as I am for us."

"Fantastic!" Someone yelled to Tom Meyerhoff as he approached the winner's circle. "It wasn't fantastic," he replied, throwing the fan a Spectacular Bid T-shirt. "It was spectacular."

Delp was—well, Delp. Surrounded by reporters, he stared at each one of them and, with a smug look on his face, asked, "How great is he, fellows?" He then pontificated on a number of topics. About the time of the race, he said: "There's no doubt in my mind that he could have knocked two-fifths off the record." On Cordero: "Ronnie demands respect, and I think he gets it now. I hope Mr. Cordero will see this is a game everyone can play, not just a select few." On the possibility of Bid racing 1978 Triple Crown winner Affirmed: "Three-eighths or three miles, let them pick the distance. Winner take all? That would be all right with me." When asked what would have happened if Franklin had taken Cordero's bait and headed inside, Delp replied, "That's a dumb question." When the reporter smirked and said, "I'm a dummy," Delp said, "I don't talk to dummies."

Franklin was jubilant and confident after the race. "I think we are a cinch" for the Triple Crown, he boasted.

LeRoy Jolley, General Assembly's trainer, had seen enough of Bid and said his horse would not race against him again. "My horse couldn't have beaten him if he had cut through the infield," he said. Luis Barrera, Screen King's trainer, said, "I no chase him anymore. I try him twice, that's enough. He is one bad hombre."

When Franklin walked his horse to the winner's circle, a blanket of daisies with the centers painted black (black-eyed Susans were not in season yet) was placed around Spectacular Bid's neck. Franklin hugged longtime friends, who congratulated him on his victory. As the home crowd screamed, "Ron-nie! Ron-nie!" he grinned. He was on top of the world.

The Meyerhoffs held a victory party for about 130 friends at the Prime Rib, a high-class restaurant in Baltimore. The owners of the restaurant closed on their busiest night for the private party. "I guess it was a good thing we won," said Tom Meyerhoff.

Bud Delp had his own party at his house. Ron Franklin was at Delp's party and celebrated too—with a few lines of cocaine.

7

One More for the Crown

There's no way Bid can lose the Belmont on Saturday, barring
illness or an act of God.
                                                              —Bud Delp

DAVID WHITELEY LOOKED at his stopwatch as Coastal went by
the grandstand. The watch read thirty-four and four-fifths seconds for
three furlongs. Four days earlier, he had worked five furlongs in 1:00¹/₅.
     In the buildup to the Belmont Stakes, a new challenger was rising.
Some six months after ending his convalescence in California from the
eye injury, Coastal—the son of 1969 Kentucky Derby winner Majestic Prince who had won the Tyro Stakes as a two-year-old and finished
fifth to Spectacular Bid in the World's Playground Stakes—was showing signs of competitiveness. Trainer David Whiteley decided to take
Coastal to New York to test his speed. In his first race in the East, a week
before Bid won the Kentucky Derby, Coastal came from off the pace to
win an allowance race at Aqueduct Racetrack by one and three-quarters
lengths. Two weeks later, before Bid's win in the Preakness, he won his
second straight race—a seven-furlong trial—by eight lengths.
     The Peter Pan Stakes (named after the famous turn-of-the-century
racehorse) was a popular Grade 3 stakes race for horses not expected to
qualify for either the Kentucky Derby or the Preakness. A one-and-an-
eighth-mile race for three-year-olds, it was held in the second week in
May at Belmont Park. The favorite had been a horse named Czaravich, a
lightly raced colt that some thought could challenge Bid in the Belmont.
But when Czaravich developed a fever and was withdrawn, Whiteley saw
a chance for his colt and entered him in the Peter Pan.

On May 25 Coastal went off as the 4 to 5 favorite in the race. Despite bumping his head against the starting gate and smashing the protective plastic blinker covering his previously injured left eye, he ran well. The accident at the start did not seem to bother him. He came from behind, as he had done before, embarrassing the field with a thirteen-length victory and covering the distance in 1:47, four-fifths of a second off the stakes record. It was the fastest time at that distance for a three-year-old that year, and it was Coastal's fifth win in eight tries. The blinker came off for future races.

But Coastal was still such an afterthought, such a low-rated weapon in Whiteley's arsenal, that it took several days to convince himself to enter the horse in the Belmont Stakes. After Coastal's workouts of five furlongs in 1:00¹/₅ and three furlongs in thirty-four and four-fifths seconds, Whiteley began to think seriously about the Belmont.

One week after his victory in the Preakness, Spectacular Bid paraded down the homestretch at Pimlico as fans cheered. It was their last chance to see him before he made the trip to New York and the Belmont Stakes. Bob Maisel noticed that, unlike some horses at this point in a Triple Crown campaign, Bid did not look tired; nor had he lost any weight. "If anything, Bid looked better than ever yesterday, before, during, and after his gallop, prancing, bouncing, biting, kicking, apparently asking to run," he wrote. In the winner's circle, exercise rider Robert Smith and groom Mo Hall received special trophies from the Maryland Jockey Club for their contributions to the development of Spectacular Bid.

However, things were not going so well for Ron Franklin; his temper, a problem since childhood, had reared its ugly head again. On May 22, three days after the Preakness, Franklin was fined $100 for whipping a horse on the head and kicking him in the stomach after losing a race at Pimlico. Big Vision, a four-year-old gelding owned by Hawksworth Farm, had run fifth in the race, nine and one-quarter lengths behind the winner. Franklin was not available for comment afterward—he was getting a wisdom tooth extracted—but Richard Delp, Bud's brother, came to his defense. "I didn't see the incident, but I know that the horse gave Ronnie a rough trip the whole race. Ronnie was real mad, he just lost his temper. I never knew him to be that way with any horse before." For a person who loved horses so much, it seemed out of character for Franklin to abuse one. The jockey later apologized for the incident. "I'm sorry I hit him with the whip," he said. "I know I did wrong." Delp said when Big Vision got back to the barn, he kicked the horse in the belly, too. "But it didn't hurt him," he claimed. "You can't hurt a horse by kicking him in the belly."

On May 30 stewards disqualified Franklin's mount, Croatoan, after another jockey accused Franklin of interfering with his horse coming out of the starting gate. The videotape showed Croatoan veering momentarily into the other horse's path, and even though Franklin steered him out of the way, the stewards ruled that interference had occurred. Next, they had to decide whether to suspend Franklin for his part in the incident. If suspended, he would begin serving a seven-day sentence that Sunday, and the Belmont Stakes was the following Saturday. Delp howled at the possibility, calling the stewards' inquiry "another way to show their incompetence." He said he would appeal "to the highest court in the land" if Franklin were suspended. However, that proved unnecessary when the stewards cleared Franklin of any wrongdoing. Although they saw Croatoan break in sharply at the start, they also saw Franklin grab his horse immediately and try to keep him off the other horse. Franklin would ride in the Belmont.

But something was happening to Ron Franklin. The usually quiet, carefree boy was turning into a cocky race rider with a bad temper. "Once a friendly little scrambler who was happy if anybody gave him a second look or a chance for a word in the papers or on television, Ronnie Franklin has become as obnoxious with his mouth as with his stick," wrote Bob Barnet of the *Muncie Star Press*. "It's too bad that a kid like Ronnie could so quickly be turned into an individual who not only appears to dislike horses, but people as well. . . . It didn't take him long to forget his humble beginnings. Gratitude for a rags-to-riches obviously isn't one of his characteristics." Barnet could not resist taking a shot at Delp as well. "Here surely is a case of what instant success and a trainer and mentor who yields to no man in making stupid speeches can do to a nineteen-year-old kid."

Andrew Beyer criticized the decision not to suspend Franklin. "Such misadventures typify Franklin rides," he wrote. "The teenager did not display much aptitude when he launched his career at Pimlico a year ago, but he is riding even worse now. People who watch Franklin on a day-to-day basis at Pimlico have been horrified by his lack of control over the horses he rides." In Beyer's opinion, the only reason Franklin had not embarrassed himself in the Triple Crown races was because of Spectacular Bid's greatness. "[Franklin] was so afraid of getting into trouble that he took Spectacular Bid even farther to the outside. If Cordero had gone into Row A of the parking lot, Franklin would have been in Row B. . . . [Bid] deserves the chance to demonstrate unequivocally how great a horse he is. . . . It will be small consolation to know that he was the best horse when he is eventually beaten because of Franklin's ineptitude."

On June 1 Bid arrived at Belmont Park, and Delp was already talking. He was the victor invading enemy territory, ready to take over the town. He sensed that the New York establishment was watching him, and he loved every minute of it. "Damn right," he said of the establishment's dislike of him. "I'm representing ninety percent of all horsemen. The other ten percent can go pound sand." Earlier, when Triple Crown fever was just beginning, right after the Derby, Delp confided to reporters, "I'm an outcast in New York, and I'm a bad guy down here. They want to see me get beat so they can laugh at me." He added, "Winning a horse race is never a formality, but there's no way [Bid] can lose the Belmont Stakes unless he runs into some terribly bad luck."

After being taken off the moving van, Bid was placed in Barn 13. He was going after his thirteenth straight victory. And Delp's tack-room office, where he worked and kept all his equipment, occupied stall 13. "Hell no, I'm not superstitious," Delp said when asked about the coincidence. "I'd better not be. Listen, thirteen and thirteen make twenty-six, and that's one of my lucky numbers. Three thirteens are thirty-nine, and that's a lucky number."

That day and the next, Delp scheduled two-mile gallops for Bid, followed by a one-mile workout on Monday and a final blowout the day before the Belmont to sharpen him. Backstretchers wondered whether any of the times would have a thirteen in it.

Most of the Preakness entrants, including General Assembly, Golden Act, and Screen King, would be running in the Belmont. Flying Paster had gone home to California to rest. As race day neared, word circulated that Coastal was a possible contender. "The consensus around the barns is that Coastal is the only horse who could be a real threat to the favorite in the so-called 'Test of Champions,'" wrote Steve Cady in the *New York Times*. "At worst, some of the experts are saying, Coastal could probably finish second in the race." Since he had not been nominated for the race several months earlier, his owner would have to pay a $20,000 supplementary entry fee—$5,000 due when the horse was entered, and $15,000 due on the day of the race. Coastal's owner balked at the high fee and considered not entering him.

Meanwhile, Bid was not running his best. On Monday, June 4, five days before the Belmont Stakes, Bid went a mile in a sluggish 1:39. Worse was that, the longer he ran, the slower he got, with fractions of :24, :24²/₅, :25, and :25³/₅. "He went well," Delp said, but even the trainer was not his usual effusive self. "He got a little tired, but it was a tiring track." To be fair, the track was muddy, and track officials had placed cones toward the middle of it to keep the inner surface from becoming any muddier. Still, the progressively slower numbers led critics to wonder whether Delp had finally squeezed the lemon too hard. Ignoring his critics, Delp talked up his horse as if he were the next coming of Secretariat. "There's no way Bid can lose the Belmont on Saturday, barring illness or an act of God. I have no idea what the strategy is going to be against him. I only know he's going to be ready to break Secretariat's track record if necessary. He won't break it, though. He won't be pressed. No three-year-old in the country can come close to him."

About the workouts Bid was getting this week, Delp said, "Because of the longer time between races, I'm now working Bid a little harder. He's eager. Most horses lose weight over the Triple Crown haul. Not Bid—he has picked up weight. He could go two miles Saturday if we asked him. . . . In the barn, he has the best security and the best of care, but he has to go out there on the racetrack in the morning and do his job to get ready. I'm having a good time in New York but I'm still up at 4:30 in the morning and out at Barn 13 seeing that everything is all right with Bid."

So confident was Delp that he talked again about a matchup with Affirmed once Bid took care of the Triple Crown, proposing a match race with a purse of more than $2 million. "Spectacular Bid still hasn't hit his peak," he said. "I'm looking for him to peak the day he runs against

Affirmed." Laz Barrera, Affirmed's trainer, was open to the idea. "Spectacular Bid is a tremendous horse, but when he runs against Affirmed, it won't be like against Golden Act and Screen King. It will be a different horse than he has ever met before."

While Delp was making this challenge, Ron Franklin was in another barn around the corner, talking to several of Delp's lesser-known horses and feeding them doughnuts. "Franklin . . . prefers talking to animals than sports writers," wrote Jack Murray of the *Cincinnati Enquirer,* one of the few to notice Franklin's actions. The jockey never overlooked his prized horse, visiting him every day.

Coastal's team was still undecided about entering him in the race, and time was running out; they would have to decide soon. "Running him against Spectacular Bid might be kind of foolish," said William Haggin Perry, Coastal's owner. Whiteley sang the same tune. "The numbers don't come up well," he said. "He's an unseasoned horse, and we'd probably be pipe-dreaming it." Still, it was a dream, and on the last possible day, Perry paid the $5,000, knowing that he could still scratch the horse if he got cold feet. But things were working out in his mind—things that could lead to a victory for Coastal.

First, Coastal was fresh, having run only three races in the past few months, while Spectacular Bid, Golden Act, Screen King, and General Assembly would be running their third race in five weeks. And despite the steep $20,000 entry fee, the payoff—upward of $160,000—could be tremendous; even second or third place would make it worthwhile. Second, rumors were flying that Bid was not training well at Belmont—his slow mile being a perfect example. Coastal had just worked six furlongs in 1:12 on a sloppy track—the fastest six furlongs of the day by two seconds. The race needed a new challenger, and many New Yorkers behind the scenes were encouraging Perry to enter Coastal.

The Thursday before the Belmont, Franklin was in the starting gate aboard a horse named Lorine in a five-and-a-half-furlong sprint for two-year-old fillies. Right beside him was a horse named Ski Pants, ridden by Angel Cordero Jr. Once the gates opened, Ski Pants' head cocked to the left, and the horse cut across into Lorine. Franklin was forced to stand up in the saddle, slowing his horse, and Lorine dropped to last place. She finished eighth out of ten horses; Ski Pants fared a little better, finishing seventh.

When the race was over, according to eyewitnesses, Franklin walked into the jockey room, set his helmet on a bench, and walked over to Cordero, who was sitting in front of his locker. No one remembers who threw the first punch, but before anyone could react, there was an all-out brawl, fists flying. It took a Pinkerton guard and a valet to separate the two. It was the culmination of several months of tension and feuding, of accusations and arguments, of rough and questionable race riding. In an interview with NBC's Dick Schaap, Franklin said Cordero "jumped across the room at me . . . like a monkey. I got him down on the ground and began busting his head on it. He's chicken. I'd like to get him in the ring and show him what it's all about. I'd knock him on his ass."

The stewards summoned both jockeys to question them about what had happened, review the film of the race, and hand down punishments. The film showed the head of Cordero's filly moving to the left and Cordero's right arm pumping, driving his horse into Franklin's. But in a surprising move, the stewards ruled that Cordero was not guilty of careless riding. No suspensions were handed down, and both jockeys would race in the Belmont. However, they were each fined $250 for fighting.

Delp came to Franklin's defense. "Cordero wanted to bury [Franklin]," he said. "He wanted him on the ground. He made no effort to take the horse off the boy." Dale Austin of the *Baltimore Sun* thought the stewards were colluding to keep Cordero out of trouble because he rode for Dinny Phipps, chairman of the board of trustees of the New York Racing Association. "The New York stewards have continued to allow Cordero to get away with rough riding," Austin wrote, and lately, some notable, fair people have "begun to say unkind things about the New York stewards. . . . Their ability to rise to the important occasion seems questionable."

On Friday, the two jockeys exchanged forced apologies, hugged awkwardly, and shook hands in front of the media in a show of sportsmanship—and public relations. "We have nothing against each other," Cordero said, sounding almost rehearsed, after meeting with stewards a second time. "He's doing his job, I'm doing mine. We're friends." No one believed them.

ॐ

On Thursday, as the racing secretary was ready to draw post positions, he received a $15,000 check from William Haggin Perry. Coastal was in. Whiteley, however, claimed that they could still back out. If the horse was healthy, Coastal would race in the Belmont. "If he had flicked an ear in the wrong direction, we would have scratched," he said.

When Delp learned that Coastal was an entrant in the Belmont, he scoffed, "I beat this horse by seventeen lengths in Jersey. Why is he coming in here?" Also running were King Celebrity, who had finished fourth in the Kentucky Derby; General Assembly; Golden Act, who had finished in the money in the first two Triple Crown races; and Screen King. Other newcomers included Quiet Crossing, Picturesque, Gallant Best, and Mystic Era. Bid had drawn the number-five position; Coastal, the number-eight position. Cordero, aboard General Assembly, was in the second post. That would give Franklin enough time to get to the outside before Cordero could try to do anything to him.

Horse enthusiasts were excited about Coastal's entry into the Belmont. They compared him to Stage Door Johnny, the colt who had won the Peter Pan Stakes in 1968 and then ruined Forward Pass's chance at a Triple Crown. But even though Andrew Beyer admitted that Spectacular Bid was not a lock for the Belmont anymore, he questioned Coastal's ability to go a mile and a half. The colt had never even run a race with two turns in it, he pointed out. Trainer Whiteley also expressed concern about Coastal's inexperience: "If he had had just one more mile-and-one-eighth race, I wouldn't hesitate a second [to run him]," he said.

Trainer Woody Stephens saw Coastal as the one horse that could give Spectacular Bid a run for his money. "The favorite has run big, and he's run fast," he said of Bid on Friday. "He's only got that one horse [Coastal] to beat." Lucien Laurin, who had trained Secretariat, offered some advice to Ron Franklin: "If I was training Spectacular Bid, I'd tell Franklin to put him right on the lead and not fool around."

The day before the race, Spectacular Bid had a final three-furlong blowout timed at an amazing thirty-three and three-fifths seconds. He was ready.

Journalists were all but handing Spectacular Bid the Triple Crown. Odds were 1 to 10 on the colt, and although people were not ready to compare Bid to Secretariat, they were putting him in the same league as Seattle

Slew and Affirmed, the last two winners of the Triple Crown. "The question to be answered at Saturday's Belmont Stakes is not if Spectacular Bid can become the twelfth horse in history to win the Triple Crown, but by how many lengths he can take this third leg," wrote Buddy Martin of the *New York Daily News*. Delp was his usual boastful self, saying, "I've got no worries about any of the other horses in the race. It should be Bid's easiest race." To another reporter, he asked, "How much did Secretariat win by?" When the reporter told him the length of that victory had been thirty-one lengths, Delp said, "Then I'll settle for thirty-one and a half."

The Meyerhoffs were confident as well. When asked who would win the Belmont, Harry Meyerhoff winked and said, "Spectacular Bid." The reporter rephrased the question, and Harry replied, "There are no others in the field that can win." As he had done in Maryland for the Preakness, Tom rented out a bar for the planned victory party on Saturday night.

Reporters also hypothesized about why there had been so many Triple Crown winners in the 1970s after a twenty-five-year drought. Jimmy Jones, who had helped train Citation, said, "I'd say it was just a fluke, an unusual run of luck for four very talented horses. . . . All of them stayed sharp and stayed sound until they had won the Kentucky Derby and the Preakness and the Belmont Stakes. That takes a lot of luck." Former jockey Eddie Arcaro, winner of two Triple Crowns, was more spiritual: "It's not hard to win the Triple Crown. All you need is the fastest horse and the strongest horse and the healthiest horse. Then you need tons of luck and a jockey who has been kissed on the forehead by the Man Upstairs."

Delp refused to elaborate on the reason for so many recent Triple Crown winners, but he was cautious. "You can lose one [race] if you don't pay close attention to every small detail. One little rock that the horse can step on as he goes from the stable to the track, one mouthful of bad food, one workout that just isn't right—any one of them can beat you. People can call me nuts if they want to, the way I handle Bid, but I know it's the right way. I check over the ground he's going to be walking on, pick up the rocks he might step on. Hell, I'd even personally test his water and his grain if I thought anything wasn't just right."

❧

Race day, June 9, 1979. The sun rose on a glorious Belmont track, its rays glistening off the dew on the finely manicured lawn. Some 900 workers were already at their jobs, tending to the horses, putting fresh hay in the stalls, and making everything look perfect for the most important day of racing at Belmont. Nearby, a seamstress was putting the finishing touches on the blanket of red carnations that would cover the winner of the 111th Belmont Stakes. It was a special day at Belmont because yet another Triple Crown winner might be named—the fourth in a decade and the third in a row.

Groom Mo Hall checked on Bid at 4:00 a.m., as he did every morning. It was his job to clean out Bid's stall and give him his ration of hay and oats in preparation for the race. He would also get him ready for his morning workout, which would consist of a jog or a light trot.

The minute he arrived at the stall, Hall noticed something was wrong. The colt was holding up his left foreleg and would not put any weight on it. At about the same time, Bud Delp, his brother Richard, and assistant trainer Charlie Bettis arrived in a limousine. Before Delp even got out of the car, Hall approached him and said, "Hey boss, this horse is lame."

Those are words no trainer ever wants to hear, especially on the day of the most important race in his horse's career. Delp rushed into Bid's stall, looked at the left hoof, and found a large safety pin lodged in it. Bid had stepped on it with the full weight of his 1,000 pounds and pushed it in about an inch deep. "It was stuck in there as hard as cement," Delp said later. He slowly and gingerly pulled the safety pin out—it took some strength even to get it to move. A thin, brownish liquid ran out of the puncture wound, and "it sealed off like a sponge; you couldn't even see where it came in."

Horses can do crazy things in their stalls, stuck in there for twenty hours a day. They bang their hooves and bodies against the stable walls, injuring themselves; they get their heads and necks caught in nets or ropes on rare occasions. So every night, grooms wrap bandages around the horses' fragile legs to protect them from injury. When Hall bandaged Bid's legs, he normally sprinkled red pepper on the wraps to keep Bid from chewing on them, and then put adhesive tape around the bandages. Bid was what horse experts called a "pin-picker," meaning that he often attempted to unravel his bandages by picking at the safety pins with his mouth. With red pepper on the wraps, "he would never bother it," Delp said. But Hall had not added red pepper when bandaging Bid the day before. It was a recipe for disaster: Bid had loosened the tape and then unfastened one of the pins with his teeth. It fell in the straw sharp side up, and Bid stepped on it. The odds of that happening were astronomical—but the impossible had happened.

Delp looked at Bettis and said, "The ballgame is over." But when Delp walked Bid out of his stall, leading him around the barn, the horse seemed sound. Delp packed the hoof in Bowie mud, a concoction of Maryland mud, vinegar, and Epsom salts that was supposed to draw out any infection. He walked the colt again, then jogged him for a few moments. Still nothing.

Delp's own words were coming back to haunt him:

What could happen is an act of God, but every realistic precaution is being taken to ensure his safety and well-being.

I think only an act of God will stop Spectacular Bid from winning the Triple Crown next year.

There's no way he can lose the Belmont Stakes unless he runs into some terribly bad luck.

This horse would never get hurt in his stall. He's smart; I never worry about him in there.

Later that morning, Delp consulted with Harry Meyerhoff, waking him at his hotel. Delp said that Bid would probably be okay, but if things got worse, they might have to scratch him. "We asked Bud what he thought, how serious is it, is it something that could be debilitating, or something that frankly was no big deal," Teresa Meyerhoff said. "It was a really, really hard decision. We had won two races of the Triple Crown, and now we've got a real shot at the third. If Bud had said he was going to be crippled, we would have said okay, never mind. Let's get him healthy again and see what happens. But you know, Bud didn't think it would be that bad. His indication to us was that ultimately it was our decision, that it was a pin prick, and it would probably be fine."

Delp assured them that the colt could still win. The Meyerhoffs agreed to let him run.

Delp then sped back to Franklin's hotel to let him know what had happened, warning him not to tell a soul about the injury. Franklin's stomach turned when he heard the news; this would not be an easy ride after all. His mind raced as he considered how the horse's condition would change his strategy. Would the horse show any symptoms of pain? Should he pull him up at any sign of distress? Would he last a mile and a half with the injury?

The Meyerhoffs rented two limousines to take them and their entourage to Belmont. During the trip, one limousine got a flat tire. Tom, already skittish because of Bid's injury, wondered if it was a bad omen.

In an attempt to modernize the TV coverage of the Belmont Stakes, CBS had persuaded Delp to wear a wireless microphone before and during the race to capture his thoughts and reactions. He would not be censored but had the ability to turn the mic off. "If he curses, so be it. That's our problem, not his," said Bob Fishman, director of the show. "We want him to be natural. We don't want him to be toned down. We want him to be Buddy Delp."

Delp thought about the situation. Should he inform track officials of Bid's injury? They had checked his condition earlier, flexing his leg joints and watching him jog. Finding nothing out of the ordinary, track officials had cleared him to run. Was this a simple wound that would disappear after a few hours, like a paper cut? Nothing seemed to affect the horse—he had done everything asked of him—but Delp had always babied this horse. He knew that Bid was special, the kind of horse a trainer came across only once in a career—or a lifetime. Now he had a decision to make: scratch the horse as a precaution, drawing the ire of millions of fans throughout the country who wanted to see a Triple Crown winner, or race him and risk further injury?

At about 3:30 p.m., Delp picked the Bowie mud out of Bid's hoof and felt the area around the puncture wound. There was no heat, which could be a sign of infection, but it was still too early for an infection to develop. What mattered was whether Bid could walk and jog without pain, and so far, he could. Delp decided to run him. A horse had only one shot at the Triple Crown—the three races were open only to three-year-olds.

All the walking and jogging to assess the injury were not part of the usual prerace routine, and Bid sensed it. As he waited in the paddock for the "riders up" call and people flocked toward the horses, he grew increasingly irritated. He was what equestrians call "rank"—refusing to relax or settle down, fighting the rider, and thrashing about in the stall in defiance. His behavior was worse than it had ever been before a race—even worse than at the Kentucky Derby—and the Meyerhoffs became worried as they watched their prized possession acting up. But they could do nothing except watch.

The situation was also out of Delp's hands. As the "riders up" call was announced, he hugged Franklin before boosting him up on Bid, reminding him again to be aware of the long homestretch that would greet him toward the finish. Franklin looked concerned, even afraid, clutching his whip with both hands.

"Spectacular Bid seems to be on his toes, sweating a little bit," outrider Jim Dailey acknowledged on live television during the post parade. As he accompanied Bid to the starting gate, he noted, "This crowd's got him a little excited. . . . He's doing a little jig on the way to the post here, and the jock's getting tied on, fixing his stirrups. The rest of the field seems to be going perfect. . . . Looks like the Bid is the only horse shook up."

The horses went down the homestretch to the song "The Sidewalks of New York."[1] The fans sipped their white carnation drinks and prepared to witness history in the making. Only a handful of people knew what was going on with Bid's foot. Delp, too nervous to say anything, had turned off his microphone, to the consternation of Bob Fishman.

King Celebrity, a 90 to 1 long shot, was the first horse in; the Kentucky Derby entrant was not expected to make a splash in this race. General Assembly, this time ridden by Angel Cordero, went into the number-three gate at 12 to 1, bucking a little and causing trouble as usual. As luck would have it, Bid and Franklin went in right beside General Assembly and Cordero; Picturesque and Quiet Crossing, the two horses between them, had been scratched. Franklin wondered whether he would have any trouble with Cordero, and his stomach knotted even more. Despite his rankness earlier, Bid went easily into the number-four post; he was the 1 to 5 favorite. Screen King, at 20 to 1, was next to Bid in the starting gate; beside him was Gallant Best, an 80 to 1 long shot that usually went to the front to set the pace. Golden Act went in next at 10 to 1, followed by Coastal, who was the second choice in betting at 4 to 1. Mystic Era was the last horse in, at 90 to 1.

As Bid was being loaded into the starting gate, Franklin continued to overanalyze things. Would Bid come up lame? Would he favor his left foot? Was he tired from all the rankness? Other than being nervous, Bid had seemed okay in the post parade—no lameness, no favoring of the foot, no discomfort. To Franklin, everything seemed to be happening in slow motion—the assistant starters checking all the horses and yelling instructions to one another, an occasional horse lifting his head, seen out of the corner of Franklin's eye—and it seemed to take an eternity for the bell to ring. Finally, when all the horses were settled and facing the track, the bell clanged, the gates opened, and the eight horses faced one and a half miles of track—the longest distance Spectacular Bid had ever raced.

Gallant Best broke first and took the early lead, followed by Bid, who had a good start. Coastal was third, then Mystic Era. Heading into the backstretch, Gallant Best increased his lead to four lengths, hoping to get so far ahead that the others would be unable to catch him. Bid was trailing in second, a length ahead of General Assembly. Coastal dropped back to fourth, a half-length back.

Bid was running just off the rail and was clear of the trailing field, with no possibility of getting boxed in. It appeared that Franklin had him perfectly positioned to win the Belmont, but all was not perfect: Bid was refusing to change his lead. A galloping horse runs in patterns called *leads*. When running on the left lead, the horse's first step is with the right hind foot, followed by the left hind foot, then the right fore-foot, and finally the left forefoot. The right feet support the brunt of the horse's weight when landing, and the left feet push off. Briefly, all four feet are off the ground. When a horse is on his left lead, he should have more weight distributed on the right side of his body. Racehorses in North America, who run counterclockwise around the track, typi-cally take turns on their left lead because they are more balanced when they lead with the leg corresponding to the direction of the turn. When they reach the straightaways, they switch—sometimes in midair—to their right lead, stepping first with the left hind foot, followed by the right hind foot, then the left forefoot, and finally the right forefoot. By switching leads on the backstretch and homestretch, horses can conserve energy because they are not leading with the same foot on every stride.

Jockeys often give horses a cue to change leads (often with a flick of the wrist or a shifting of weight) on the backstretch; then they switch back on the far turn and once again on the homestretch. Many horses learn to change leads automatically. If they stay on one lead for too long, they will get tired. West Point Thoroughbreds, a racing stable, likens running on one lead to a person carrying a suitcase in the same hand when traveling through an airport. That person has to switch hands occasionally, or else one arm will get too tired. Alydar was well known for refusing to change leads, and many horse racing experts believe that his many close losses to Affirmed could have been reversed if he had just learned to change leads when asked.

Bid switched to his left lead heading into the clubhouse turn, as he had been trained to do at Middleburg. Heading into the straightaway, he switched to his right lead, then switched back to the left, as if something was bothering his left foot. He landed with his right foot first and kept most of his weight on the right side of his body, not wanting to land on his left forefoot. Franklin tried to switch him to the right lead; he even tried to turn Bid's head to the right to get him to change, but nothing worked. Then Franklin—perhaps like the traveler who wants to get through the airport quickly because he is carrying his suitcase in one hand and tiring his arm—did something that, in hindsight, many critics said made no sense: he relaxed the reins on Spectacular Bid, pumped his arms, and let him loose on Gallant Best.

At that same time, Tom Meyerhoff, watching from his box in the stands, snapped his fingers and said, "Now." Bid reacted like lightning in an attempt to catch up to the pacesetter, who had blazed through two furlongs in twenty-three and two-fifths seconds, the fastest quarter mile in the Belmont since 1967. There was no way any horse could keep up that pace. Bid made up four lengths in less than a furlong and pulled in front by a head; he increased his lead to a full length, then three. General Assembly made a move on the inside, Coastal was still stalking the leaders in fourth place, and Golden Act had moved up to fifth. They finished a half mile in forty-seven and three-fifths seconds—still much too fast. Bid ran six furlongs in 1:11$\frac{1}{5}$ and a mile in 1:36. In the 110 runnings of the Belmont Stakes to that point, only four other horses had ever run a mile as fast as Bid did—and one of them was Secretariat. Two of those horses ended up winning the Belmont, and two lost steam and finished out of the running.

As the horses headed into the far turn, Bid—still on his left lead and refusing to switch—held a two-length lead. General Assembly, in second, was trying to gain ground. The Meyerhoffs tentatively began to congratulate themselves, slapping one another on the back. Their horse was in command, with only the long homestretch looming between him and immortality. Gallant Best was tiring but still hung on to third place, and Golden Act moved up to fourth.

Whiteley thought he had a dead horse on the backstretch. Coastal seemed to be fading—or was he? Coming into the homestretch, Coastal's jockey, Ruben Hernandez, saw Spectacular Bid drifting to the right— a sign of a tired horse—which created daylight on the rail. Hernandez went for it, passing Golden Act, Gallant Best, and General Assembly with relative ease. Bid was two lengths ahead of him. Bud Delp turned to the Meyerhoffs and said, "We're gonna get beat." The three looked at him in surprise.

Bid was tired—something he had never experienced before, not even during his long two-mile training runs. Coastal and Bid fought it out for about fifty yards, and then Coastal passed Bid with ease. Bid had nothing left in his reserves and could not run any faster, the way he usually responded when challenged by another horse. His foot hurt; the suitcase was too heavy. Coastal lengthened his lead to two, then three lengths. Then, adding further insult, Golden Act came on the outside of Spectacular Bid at the sixteenth pole. As they went under the wire, it was Coastal by three and one-quarter lengths over Golden Act. Spectacular Bid was third by a nose.

Teresa Meyerhoff sat down and turned her head to hide her tears. Harry asked her if she was okay but got no response. "I had no idea this would happen," Delp told the Meyerhoffs. "I just hope the colt is all right," he said, privately alluding to the injury. And the CBS camera missed it all, a broken cable causing the network to miss the owners' reactions. "There are no quotes this time," Tom Meyerhoff said, in shock at what had just happened. "We are speechless."

The crowd was equally stunned by Bid's loss. "Well, if it were an

Coastal, on the rail, makes his move on a tiring Spectacular Bid in the Belmont Stakes. Golden Act is on the outside of Bid. (Associated Press)

upset, [Coastal] was obviously the horse," said race announcer Marshall Cassidy. "He was the only one that had not been defeated by Spectacular Bid. . . . I don't want to be the one to point a finger, the Achilles' heel. They felt that if Franklin pushed the button too early, moved too soon, it might compromise him. I think Coastal beat him fair and square, but [Bid] did commit himself a mile away from home."

The disbelief of the New York crowd turned to boos and catcalls as Bid walked back to his stable—the first time in thirteen races he had not gone straight to the winner's circle. But Bid was tired, blowing hard, as he slowly made his way past the crowd. As Franklin walked back to the jockeys' room, he was pelted by paper bags and programs. "In a way, I felt worthless. Man, how could I blow that?" he said. "When I come back with the horse, everybody was booing me. I just covered my head and just wanted to crawl in a hole somewhere."

When Delp walked to the barn where Bid was getting his routine tests for performance-enhancing drugs, a groom cracked, "Hey Delp, the best horse won." Delp's face reddened, but he kept his cool. "Yeah, yeah, the best horse won." He confirmed it later at the barn, calmly drinking a bottle of Heineken. His stoicism in the face of defeat was unheard of for Delp, a rare and remarkable exhibition. "The best horse won it. [Bid] had no excuse. I didn't think he ran his race because that second horse beat him. But the best horse won the race, and that's usually the way it is. . . . Hey, I thought he could run two miles. I was wrong. He might not be a genuine mile-and-a-half horse. Some horses are exceptional who can't go a mile and a half. He was trained fit. He just got outrun, that's all." There was no mention of the safety pin.

For many in New York, the loss was sweet revenge for all the bragging Delp had done during the previous two Triple Crown races. Delp had the best explanation in the world for the loss but chose not to use it. Why? Later, Delp would say that he did not want to appear to be making excuses in front of everyone and take away from Coastal's victory. Pin or no pin, Coastal had won, even though he did not defeat a healthy Bid.

There would be no Triple Crown. Spectacular Bid became the ninth horse to miss a Triple Crown because of a loss in the Belmont. Coastal, however, avenged his sire, Majestic Prince, who had headed to the Belmont Stakes in 1969 with a Triple Crown on the line but finished second—after injuring himself. Back in his barn, Coastal was oblivious to all the buzz. Whiteley said the horse was very tired but would not need a long rest. The trainer did not plan to race him again for at least three weeks.

What had happened? Steve Cady of the *New York Times* discussed Franklin's early move. "Second-guessers immediately blamed [Franklin] of having permitted his mount to run too fast too soon. . . . Yesterday, the teenager stalked a fast early pace and put the favorite on the lead with almost a mile to go." Sportswriter William Nack agreed. "I just think he went way too fast and he tried to run after that horse. And it was just a terrible ride. I mean, the young kid panicked. He had all the world looking at him and the weight of the world on his shoulders. Why Buddy Delp kept with that kid after the Florida Derby on what was clearly a horse of history bewildered me. Most any other trainer would have taken that kid off immediately and said, 'You know, we've got a horse of history here, and we can't be messing around. We need an older, more experienced jockey with steady hands and a functioning brain in terms of times of crisis in a race.' The young man didn't have that. And it's not his fault. He was very, very young. I never understood why Buddy kept with him. It made absolutely no sense whatsoever."

Even the other jockeys piled on. "I was surprised when Spectacular Bid went by me so early," said George Martens, rider of the early pacesetter Gallant Best. "He was really rolling—no horse can be pumped for a mile and a half and wind up winning," he said, even though Gallant Best had set the fast pace and had recently won a mile-and-a-half race. The writer who quoted Martens noted that most of the criticism of Franklin came from New York–based riders, "a tightly-knit clan often resentful of outsiders, especially the outspoken Maryland crew surrounding Bid." They took the opportunity to kick the Marylanders while they were down.

But not all jockeys were part of that clan. Sandy Hawley, who had reassured Franklin before the start of the Kentucky Derby, came to his defense. "I don't think you can say Franklin moved too soon," he said. "It has been a tough campaign for Bid and the other horses who have been shipped around the country for the Triple Crown."

Asked whether he had ridden a bad race, and whether Delp had chastised him for going to the front so early, Franklin said, "No, he didn't say a word to me. If I had messed up the race, he would have been on my back. I figure I did a good job." He explained that he had taken Bid to the lead because he mistakenly felt the pace was slow.

Andrew Beyer was the most sympathetic toward Franklin, noting that the jockey "will be criticized for his performance today, because riders always are blamed when a 1-to-5 shot is upset. But Spectacular Bid lost either because he was tired from the rigors of the Triple Crown campaign or because he could not handle the Belmont's demanding one-and-a-half-mile distance." Later, he wrote, "The notion that his jockey caused [the defeat] is idiotic. Any time a front-running horse is beaten, second-guessers can (and will) say that the rider moved too soon. Whenever a stretch-runner is beaten, they will say that the jockey moved too late. . . . They are usually wrong. Franklin gave Spectacular Bid a ride on Saturday that was intelligent and tactically sound. . . . The fact that Spectacular Bid turned in one subpar effort after twelve straight brilliant victories hardly mars his reputation permanently. He has already proved his greatness, and he can be forgiven one defeat even if he doesn't have a legitimate alibi."

Jockey Don Pierce was also sympathetic toward Franklin. "He was under so much pressure when he rode [Bid] in the Belmont. Shoemaker and everybody's trying to ride him, and here's the kid—you're going to make mistakes. If they had just left him alone, he wouldn't have made no mistakes."

What was unusual was the criticism Franklin received for going after the lead too early. Triple Crown winners Secretariat, Seattle Slew, Affirmed, American Pharoah, and Justify all grabbed early leads in the Belmont and then hung on to win the grueling one-and-a-half-mile race. Bid's move in the backstretch may have been too strong, but taking the early lead is a popular tactic for the Belmont. Set the right pace, and you are home free. In fact, Lucien Laurin had advised Franklin to do just that before the race.

In the jockeys' room right after the race, reporters surrounded Franklin, asking him what had happened. There was no mention of the safety pin, no mention of Bid not changing leads. Instead, the jockey offered a bizarre explanation: "I noticed something wrong at the three-eighths pole," Franklin said. "Before, when I'd ask him [for a burst of speed] he'd give it. Not today. And when I pulled him up, I heard him gargle a little bit, like he wasn't getting breath right. He never choked up before." To another reporter, he lamented, "I kept asking him and he didn't give it to me. He just didn't give it to me. Every time before when I have asked him for something, he has always given it to me. Today, he didn't have it. He just didn't have it." Franklin kept repeating himself. "I still can't believe it. I just can't believe it. . . . But I guess it happened."

Not too far away, Angel Cordero laughed and smiled as he had his fun with reporters. "You guys say [Bid] was unbeatable. What is the excuse today? I told you there's no horse [that is] unbeatable. Every turkey has his Thanksgiving." He later got on the public-address system in the jockeys' room and told Coastal's jockey, "Ruben, you make all the spics very happy today," referring to Franklin's racial slur after the Florida Derby. "Everybody happy. You guys was the one that say he was unbeatable. I told you. Every time he run, he put the opponents away early, but he cannot do that over here going a mile and a half. That's what he does all throughout Triple Crown—make a move on the backside, he makes the lead and nobody comes to him. Now when you go a mile and a half, you cannot do that." Cordero was on a roll. "Look at your super horse, guys. Your super horse, he ain't that super like you guys thought.

I hope you write that down. You brag all month, all Triple Crown, that he was a superhorse. Super shit."

Cordero finished seventh on General Assembly.

About Franklin's ride, Delp was complimentary. "He rode him good. He rode him just like I would have if I had been a rider." A bystander couldn't help himself and said to Delp, "So your horse won't be remembered with Secretariat." "No," Delp said. "He sure won't be, but I'll remember him pretty good."

Waiting for Franklin to return from the jockeys' room, Delp waxed nostalgic about the race. "I'll have a beautiful remembrance of all, a good feeling about it. I feel bad not winning the Triple Crown, but we're gonna throw this race out and freshen him up. He's had a hard campaign. It's not the end; he's not the only one who ever had this happen to him."

When asked whether he was shocked at the result, Delp was even more laid back. "I'm not shocked, but I'm disappointed," he said. "I understand horse racing. I'm prepared to lose . . . I've always been a good loser. I've lost a lot more than anybody here, but I've won some, too. If you're not prepared to lose, then you better take up another profession."

As Delp and Franklin entered the blue limousine waiting for them, a woman asked for their autographs. Delp signed the scrap of paper, then let Franklin sign it. Delp muttered, "There, lady, you got the losers." They disappeared into the limo and exited Belmont Park, just as the sun was starting to dip behind the grandstand.

8

Growing Pains

How'm I gonna not think about it? I been thinking about it
ever since the Preakness. This is the biggie. Anyone got eyes
can see that.

—Bud Delp

The day after the Belmont, Delp told the press about the safety pin,
and reporters smelled a rat. Franklin, too, admitted that he had lied
about Bid choking and gargling, and he revealed to the media that the
horse had refused to change leads. Franklin claimed that he had panicked on live television and felt compelled to give them some reason for
Bid's failure to perform up to expectations. There had been an agreement
between Franklin and Delp not to mention the safety pin to the media,
and they kept their promise—for twenty-four hours.

The racing establishment was skeptical and thought the two were
trying to fabricate some reason for Bid's loss in the Belmont. "They
found a needle in a haystack," one backstretch worker quipped. Another
said, "If that pin went in an inch, Bud Delp never would have let the
horse run." But former jockey Sam Renick defended Delp, saying, "Bud
Delp may talk a lot, but there's one thing about him you can count on.
He tells the truth." Richard Delp corroborated his brother's story about
the safety pin. "That horse had a pin in his foot. I was there," he said. He
also saw that Bid was not 100 percent coming out of the race. "I know
when he came back from [the racetrack], he was a little bit sore on it,"
he said.

Adding to the conspiracy theory was the testimony of the veterinarian who had examined all the horses before and after the race. Dr. Man-

uel Gilman, the Belmont Park veterinarian, saw Bid three hours after the alleged injury. "Nothing was mentioned to me. He was sound then, he was sound going into the race, he was sound coming out of the race, and he was sound when he left here this morning," Gilman said. He admitted that he had not seen the pin in Bid's hoof but weighed in on the possibilities anyway: "It's not impossible [to step on a safety pin], but it's pretty hard to do."

The day after the race, several stable hands tested that theory. They threw a safety pin up in the air and watched as it landed in a small pile of straw. Not once did it fall sharp side up in a position to hurt a horse, wrote Jenny Kellner of United Press International, "unless the animal had the dexterity of Baryshnikov and could twist his foot sideways, slide it along the ground and jam it into the pin. . . . Not only is the excuse poorly timed and full of holes, but it detracts from Coastal's impressive three and one-fourths [length] victory over Golden Act." She considered the excuse an insult to Coastal and his entire entourage. To this, Delp responded, "I don't alibi when I get beat. Besides, this one's too bizarre for me to make up."

Joe Piscione of the *Trenton Evening Times* wrote that although he could not imagine Delp making up such a story, Bid had not favored the leg or limped during or after the race. He put the blame squarely on the shoulders of Franklin. "The people who knew racing spotted it before the race was a half mile old. They saw it in Franklin's arms as he pumped Spectacular Bid down the backstretch. While the other jockeys were easing their horses into smooth, relaxed strides, Franklin was urging Spectacular Bid in the suicidal pursuit of an outclassed pacesetter."

Russ Harris of the *New York Daily News* estimated that, given the number of bandages applied to the horses stabled at Belmont, the odds were 3.6 million to 1 that a horse would step on a safety pin in any given year. One New York–based trainer had trouble believing Delp's story. "I've been working here at Belmont nine years," he said. "I ain't yet seen or heard of a horse stepping on a safety pin that had been removed from a standing bandage. That is, not until last Saturday." However, Harris soon discovered another incident involving a safety pin. A stakes winner named Ferrous had stepped on a pin in his stall at Aqueduct on May 10 and had been lame ever since. Lightning, it seemed, had struck twice. Howie Tesher, Ferrous's agent, said the infection had spread so badly that it looked like the horse might have to be put down. So much for astronomical odds.

Other theories were floating around the racing community about Spectacular Bid's loss. One was that Delp wanted to break Secretariat's thirty-one-length record in 1973 and had told Franklin to take Bid out of the starting gate quickly. He had been quoted as predicting that Bid would win by thirty-one and a half lengths. And Harry Meyerhoff had been overheard asking Delp jokingly, "Can Spectacular Bid sprint a mile and a half?"

Another explanation for Franklin's sudden move on the backstretch was that he was trying to get away from Angel Cordero and General Assembly. The showdown with Cordero had rattled him, and he was trying to flee the usual front-runner to keep Cordero from sabotaging the race. But Bid had broken well and was ahead of General Assembly entering the backstretch; there was no reason to lengthen the lead unless General Assembly made a move on him. Years later, Franklin admitted that he rushed the down the backstretch. "I shouldn't have chased that horse," he said. "I know I made a mistake. . . . You don't realize that extra quarter of a mile you're going—it's like an extra mile, it seems. And I used him up too early." However, he thought that, if not for the injury, Bid would have won, despite his early move on Gallant Best.

Among those who accepted the safety pin story, many thought Delp should have made the injury public. "If not actually unethical, it was certainly indiscreet to hide the injury," Will Grimsley wrote. "It is an injustice to the millions who trust the [betting] industry to give them a fair shake when they put up their hard-earned dough." Adding to the criticism of Delp was one of Bid's regular veterinarians, Dr. D. Robert Vallance, who did not believe the injury had anything to do with Bid's loss. "Some horses win and some horses lose after an injury like that," Vallance said. "In my opinion, it was the combination of a long campaign and a fresh horse. Personally, I think what happened was just a case of the best horse winning."

Skip Bayless of the *Dallas Morning News* was more forgiving. Racing for the Triple Crown is a stressful situation, he observed, and horses are fragile, destruction-prone creatures. "Backstretchers say there are a thousand ways to lose a race. Ten thousand might be closer. A trainer bets his livelihood . . . on a beast which doesn't have the sense not to kick his own legs at night. On a mighty looking two-ton creature which breaks like kindling. On a moody quadruped which, for no logical reason, may not run fast tomorrow."

One handicapper accused track officials of scraping the inside of the track to favor horses running on the rail. Coastal had made his move from the rail when Spectacular Bid drifted wide in the homestretch, as had several horses that day. "The track bias at Belmont favors the rail tremendously," he said. "So they scraped the rail Saturday, really gouged it and pushed a lot of loam out to the middle of the track where Bid likes to run. The other riders knew the strength of the rail, but Franklin didn't." New York Racing Association officials vehemently denied those claims. In a letter to the *New York Times,* they wrote, "Nothing different was done to the racing strip on Belmont Stakes Day than on any other day. Elaborate measures are taken daily to ensure that the track will be level from the rail out. Surely, on the biggest day of the year, we would not do less."

Back at Hawksworth Farm, the Meyerhoffs were trying to deal with the upset. Harry took it better than Teresa and remained stoic. "I think we were prepared (for the defeat)," he said. "I think we dealt with it well." Teresa, however, admitted that she was down. "First, it was [a] shock, but I still haven't been able to accept it, something so fluky. I have difficulty dealing with the freakiness of it. It just doesn't seem fair."

On Sunday, the day after the race, Franklin, Delp, and Bid returned to Pimlico. As Franklin was leading Bid off the van, he noticed that the horse was limping. When they removed the horseshoe from the left front foot—the one injured by the safety pin—they found that it was badly bruised, discolored, and tender to the touch. Dr. Vallance was at the barn and gave Bid a tetanus shot, Butazolidin to relieve inflammation, and antibiotics. He also placed Bid's hoof in a tub of warm water and Epsom salts to draw out any possible infection. Vallance said the pin had gone into the hoof at a forty-five-degree angle.

By Monday, Bid had a fever of 101 degrees.[1] The drugs were not working. Bid even refused to eat his daily doughnut. Alarmed, Delp called Dr. Alex Harthill to come and examine Bid. He recommended immediate action, warning that Bid may have developed a serious infection. To find the source of the infection, Harthill used a tiny plane to shave about three-eighths of an inch from Bid's hoof, revealing a dark spot. He then drilled into that spot, "and pretty soon the thick, dark contents came out of there like a fountain," Delp said. "And he looked up at me and said, 'Hey, Bud, where are all those sons of bitches who called you a liar?'"

The pin had gone all the way into the laminae, the sensitive vascular tissue that provides the foot with nutrients. Harthill speculated that the puncture had caused a hematoma, or blood clot, within hours after the injury, which had been aggravated by running on the hard surface of the racetrack. "I think he ran with pain," he said. No wonder Bid would not switch leads. Harthill elaborated:

> A lot of skeptics say that the pin prick couldn't have influenced the way the horse ran because an infection doesn't set up that fast, and they are right—to a point. The infection probably wouldn't be a problem a few hours after the injury, but what they don't understand is that there also was a hematoma associated with the injury, and that could have caused Spectacular Bid problems the same day.
>
> I suspect the hematoma wasn't very big just after the injury, maybe just a drop or two of blood, but as the day progressed, it could have gotten a little bigger. Then running in the Belmont really compounded the injury, making the hematoma much larger, and much more painful . . . I suspect he had a very serious injury.

It was like a blood blister under a fingernail, which "hurts like the devil until you can relieve the pressure, and that is what we had to do with Spectacular Bid."

When he heard this, Franklin had to admire Bid's guts and determination to not only finish the race but also to finish third, despite the injury. "Most horses would have probably been pulled up. But he still hung in there and finished," he said.

Robin Richards, a former trainer for Middleburg Training Center, believed that the blood pressure in the hooves built up from the incessant pounding during the race, pushing blood to the wound and exacerbating any minor injury. It would be like running with a bruise on your heel, she explained; running on it will not make it any better, and running a long distance might aggravate it. And that kind of injury hurts, affects your gait, and causes you to slow down to alleviate the pain.

"The Belmont knocked the hell out of [Bid]," Delp said later. "The first four days after the race he lost thirty pounds." But the doubters remained. The New York State Racing and Wagering Board sent investigators to Pimlico to look into the safety pin incident. After talking with the veterinarian, the Meyerhoffs, and Delp, they assured everyone that this was no formal inquiry. Delp said he did not tell Belmont officials about the incident because he did not trust them. "My experience with Doc Gilman is bad," he said. "He scratched a horse of mine last week and didn't have the common decency to notify me. . . . Why would I go to Doc Gilman [about the safety pin]? I can't trust Gilman if he can't trust me." Delp wondered whether there would have been an inquiry if the horse were from New York or Kentucky. "Who do I trust? I'm a country boy come to the city with a great horse."

After numerous interviews, the board concluded that Bid had been sound on the day of the Belmont and had "sustained no injury that would affect his racing performance." At least that would satisfy the bettors who had put money on Bid that day—the group the New York Racing Association was most concerned about. Instead of blaming the safety pin, the board hinted that Franklin's ride had been the cause of the poor performance.

The media, quick to kick someone while he's down, relegated Bid to obscurity; he was just another horse that had come close but could not pull it off, a good horse that had faded in the stretch. One journalist wrote, "Never again will Spectacular Bid be mentioned in the same breath with Secretariat, Seattle Slew, or Affirmed."

The loss was a financial punch in the gut for the Meyerhoffs. Representatives of Caesar's Palace had been on hand at the Belmont to offer the owners of Spectacular Bid and Affirmed $5.5 million for a match race between the two. Now that offer had been withdrawn. Experts estimated that Spectacular Bid's value had decreased by $8 million with the Belmont loss.

For Ron Franklin, the Belmont Stakes marked the start of a downward spiral. The week of the Belmont, he was hit with a paternity suit by an eighteen-year-old Maryland woman who worked at the concession stand at Pimlico. According to the suit, she claimed that Franklin was the father of her five-month-old son. The two had met in January 1978 on a blind date, but Franklin had stopped seeing her in July after he learned she was pregnant. Franklin denied the charges. "I wasn't slapped with no papers or anything. I wasn't took into court or nothin'." The woman's attorney corroborated Franklin's story, saying that when she failed to contact him, he withdrew the case; Franklin was never formally served.

On June 16 Franklin was fined $25 for being rude to a guard at Pimlico who did not recognize him and asked to see his identification. Delp, who was in the car with Franklin, faced similar charges because he also said something offensive to the guard.

Three days later, Franklin was in California for an all-star jockey race at Hollywood Park. After the race, at about 1:30 p.m., he was in a Disneyland parking lot with some friends and relatives when a security guard discovered Franklin in his car cutting a white substance with a razor blade. He was arrested and charged with possession of cocaine. After he posted a $1,500 bond, he was released and ordered to appear for arraignment at North Orange Municipal Court within ten days. If convicted, he could face up to ten years in prison. The three others with Franklin were not charged.

This trip to California was the first Franklin had made by himself, without Delp. Delp had always treated Franklin like a son, accompanying him to all his races and watching out for his well-being. But after Franklin's latest antics in California, Delp had had enough; he ordered Franklin off all his horses effective immediately and relegated him to cleaning stalls, hot-walking, and holding horses' legs as they were being shoed—back to the bottom again. "I'm glad they caught him," Delp said. "The world's going to know about it. It might do him some good. And I'm going to do anything I can that might pick his head up."

According to Delp, when Franklin informed him that he would be returning to Maryland, he "didn't say a damn word about being busted." Delp learned about the arrest from reporters. It was clear that he was angry—in truth, probably more disappointed than angry. The warning signs had been there: kicking the horse at Pimlico, the well-publicized fight with Cordero, the criticism for the Belmont ride, the fine for yelling at the security guard. The cocaine bust was the culmination of everything that had been building up inside Franklin. The pressure of being in the spotlight was taking its toll on the nineteen-year-old. Just three years earlier, he had been in high school and had never ridden a horse. It had been a whirlwind ride to the top, from hot walker to apprentice jockey to rider of one of the best horses of 1979. Now, the way down promised to be just as precipitous and meteoric as his rise.

Franklin came back home to Maryland a "whipped puppy," according to Delp. But after hearing Franklin's description of events in California, Delp reinstated him as his jockey. "I heard his story and I believe him," Delp said. "He's a nineteen-year-old boy and he's susceptible to temptation like any other boy that age. He was with his cousins and a friend and someone pulled out some cocaine." They asked Franklin to cut the cocaine. "I don't condone using it, but Ronnie is certainly entitled to a mistake," Delp said. Like a father, he believed Ron's story and lashed out at police for targeting him. "The cousin and his girlfriend told the police it was their cocaine," Delp said. "But they arrested Ronnie. They recognized him, and that's the price he pays for being sort of a celebrity. If he were just another nineteen-year-old teenager, Ronnie Franklin wouldn't have been busted. They put him behind bars for four or five hours." Delp admitted that the pressure might have gotten to Franklin. "[I told him] 'Ronnie, this has got to be a lesson to you. You can't get away with things like this.' Maybe too much came to this kid early, and with the Cordero business and all of that, there was too much weight on the kid. Could have been my fault."

Andrew Beyer agreed and was livid. "The kid from Dundalk, Maryland lacks the savvy and sophistication of last year's superstar teenage jockey, Steve Cauthen," he wrote. "More important, he lacks any semblance of the ability that bred in Cauthen an air of mature self-confidence. Franklin had been thrust into a role for which he was completely ill-equipped." Delp had been a poor surrogate father and role model, according to Beyer, and he cited Delp's own bad behavior, which included hitting an exercise boy, believing in a "Latin conspiracy" among the jockeys, not telling veterinarians about Bid's injury, and berating a security guard along with Franklin. "Franklin was so poorly prepared to cope with life at the top of his profession that he probably doesn't deserve full blame for his present woes. If a child is thrown in the deep end of a pool and drowns, do you blame him for not knowing how to swim? Or do you blame the person who threw him in?"

Despite Delp's promise that Franklin had been reinstated, on June 21 a substitute jockey was riding his horses. The reason would become apparent soon enough: Bid was getting a new rider. On June 23 the official announcement was made: forty-seven-year-old Hall of Fame jockey Bill Shoemaker, winner of more than 7,700 races amounting to more than $80 million in purses, would be Bid's new jockey. Delp had told the Meyerhoffs he wanted to make a change when they returned from a sailing trip to Bermuda, and he had given them a list of possible replacements. Delp favored Shoemaker, whose gifted hands and touch would best benefit Bid. The Meyerhoffs agreed.

In explaining the change, Delp said he wanted "to take the pressure off Ronnie. He's all mixed up, and we want to let him go back to being a teenage kid." However, Tom Meyerhoff said later that Franklin's performance in the Belmont Stakes, not his off-track antics, was the main reason for replacing him. "Ronnie had done such an amazing job," said Teresa Meyerhoff. "It was a very hard decision. He was a good kid. But we just felt that was the right way to go. I think that our thinking was, maybe we're not doing him a favor by keeping him on. Maybe the pressure was going to be too much for him and he was going to fold or be more intimidated. Maybe something else could help."

Shoemaker, of course, had been an option back in March after Franklin's disastrous ride in the Florida Derby. At age forty-seven, he was riding better than he had in years, partly due to a new marriage and a new outlook on life. He had demonstrated strength and determination his whole life. When he was born one month premature on August 19, 1931, weighing just two and a half pounds, his parents were told he would not live through the night. But his grandmother took the baby into the kitchen, opened the oven, and put the baby beside it, creating a homemade incubator. He got on his first horse at age five, riding the family pony bareback. At age eight, while working in the fields one day and sweating profusely, Shoemaker threw down his hoe and said to his grandfather, "I'll never pick up another hoe. There's got to be a better way to make a living, and I'm gonna find it."

Shoemaker found it by riding horses. He got his first win aboard

Bill Shoemaker.
(Keeneland Library
Featherston Collection)

Shafter V on April 20, 1949, in the second race at Golden Gate Fields. He was only seventeen. Later that year, he won his first stakes race at Bay Meadows on a horse named Al. He quickly gained fame as a superb rider, winning his first riding championship in only his second year as a jockey. In 1954 he won an astounding 30 percent of his races—a record for a rider in the twentieth century. Soon he was the heir apparent to Eddie Arcaro and Johnny Longden, legends in the sport. He won the 1955 Kentucky Derby aboard Swaps and almost won the 1957 Derby on Gallant Man, but he misjudged the finish line and stood up in the stirrups too early. Gallant Man was beaten by a nose by Iron Liege. Shoemaker got revenge in 1959, winning the Derby again with Tomy Lee, and again in 1965 with Lucky Debonair.

Then bad luck hit. On January 23, 1968, Shoemaker was part of a three-horse accident at Santa Anita Park and broke his right femur, forcing him to convalesce for thirteen months. Once doctors cleared him to ride again, he returned to racing and rode three winners in three attempts at Santa Anita on his first day back. Not one horse was a betting favorite.

Two months later, he was on a three-year-old filly named Poona's Day when she reared, unseating Shoemaker; the horse then fell on him, shattering his pelvis and injuring his bladder. It was back to rehabilitation. Several years of depression and malaise followed, and he got a divorce. In 1978, the same year he remarried, Shoemaker found new motivation, and his mounts' winnings hit a personal high. He had never grown beyond his four-foot-eleven, ninety-five-pound frame, and he boasted that he was still at his teenage weight thirty years after the fact.

"Shoemaker brought that unflappable calm—and that knack for getting out of trouble—to every racetrack he rode on," William Nack wrote. "Few jockeys, if any, have ridden neater on a horse—hands back with a long hold, sitting ever so still. And few have had his ability to keep a horse out of trouble, to find the surest way home, to rate a horse, to control him with the subtlest flick of his wrist and hands, to slip-slide out of traffic and hold a horse together in a drive. Eddie Arcaro used to say that Shoemaker could ride a horse with silken threads for reins."

Columnist Jim Murray wrote, "No one ever rode a running horse the way Willie Lee Shoemaker does. Not Geronimo, the James brothers, the Pony Expressers, the buffalo hunters, the Lone Ranger, Paul Revere or the Headless Horseman of Sleepy Hollow. He is history's all-time cavalryman."

A new jockey was not the only change Bid experienced after the Belmont. Perhaps because of the safety pin incident, but more likely because of the increasing pressure to keep Bid out of trouble in his stall, Mo Hall asked to be relieved of most of his duties, and assistant trainer Charlie Bettis assumed most of the groom's job.

With Bid slowly improving and a new jockey on his back, Delp began to talk about a possible Affirmed–Spectacular Bid match race. Louis Wolfson, Affirmed's owner, was open to a winner-take-all race with a purse of $1 million, although he was generally opposed to match races. The last great match race, in 1975 between Kentucky Derby winner Foolish Pleasure and the undefeated filly Ruffian, had ended in tragedy when Ruffian broke her leg and later had to be destroyed. But Affirmed's trainer, Laz Barrera, had been offended by some remarks Delp made a few weeks earlier, saying that Bid could beat Affirmed by ten lengths at any distance. Barrera wanted to see Affirmed beat Spectacular Bid, and he also offered a personal bet on the side, with the loser donating the money to a charity of the winner's choice.

Soon the Meadowlands wanted in on this match race. General manager Bob Quigley pointed out that the Meadowlands was a prime-time racetrack and a good venue for the race. However, he was concerned about Bid's condition; he wanted to see Bid win a few races to make sure he was in top physical shape before such a race occurred. The Meadowlands also proposed a "Big Three" matchup of the top three finishers in the Belmont Stakes: Coastal, Golden Act, and Spectacular Bid.

Toward the end of June, Delp had farrier Jack Reynolds flown in to replace Bid's regular horseshoe with one that had a rubber cushion and felt pads, as well as extra protection provided by an aluminum extension. Almost three weeks later, though, Bid was not jogging normally and was still favoring his left forefoot. "If I can't get some serious work into him within the next week or two, we're getting to the point where we might not even be able to make the September races," Delp said. To get the hoof to grow back, they fed him gelatin, and every day for a month, they packed cotton and iodine under the cushion to keep the wound from becoming reinfected. "Even with the special shoe, he acts mighty careful when he walks or moves around. The bruise is there and he knows it," he said.

On July 11 Claiborne Farm announced that Spectacular Bid and his rival Coastal would be joining its facility for stud duty after their careers ended. Coastal had been syndicated the previous month to a group of people who had bought the breeding rights to the colt for $5.4 million. Spectacular Bid, whose stock had plummeted some $8 million since his Belmont loss, had not been syndicated yet. Seth Hancock, the thirty-three-year-old owner of Claiborne Farm, was hoping Bid could bounce back from his injury and command a better price. His current value was estimated at $12 million to $15 million.

Bid missed the track. It had been weeks since he had flown past a quarter pole in either a workout or a race, and he grew irritable. He was upset by the care and attention being given to his left foot. His condition went from bad to worse. He developed a corn in his right hoof, probably because he had been favoring it since the injury to his left foot. The road to recuperation would be long.

Then things got a little muddled. On Tuesday, July 24, Delp informed the press that Bid's career was in jeopardy. "I've got a horse with two sore feet," he told the *Fort Lauderdale Sun-Sentinel*. Bid would not run in the August 5 Jim Dandy Stakes or the August 18 Travers Stakes at Saratoga. "I don't tell lies. I may bull some, but he may never race again. I've got a fifteen to twenty million dollar horse there. I'm not going to take him out unless he's one hundred and ten percent. I'm no damn fool." He then took another swipe at New Yorkers. "These other people have been wrong all along," he said. "They're up there trying to say there's nothing wrong with my horse. He developed an infection after the pin lodged in his foot. There was a bruise the size of my thumb. The vet had to core away and get the infection out of there. Now, we're trying to grow the foot back and toughen it. If he was right, we'd have shipped him to Saratoga already. I'd have him ready, and we'd win too. Hell, I don't duck nobody."

Harry Meyerhoff was a little more optimistic: "If this is just a matter of sore hooves, we can let them grow out, skipping the races this fall, and run him next year." Bid might run during the winter in California, he said.

In the meantime, David Whiteley entered Coastal in the Dwyer Stakes at Belmont Park on July 8. The Belmont winner defeated unbeaten Private Account, taking over in the homestretch by four lengths. He earned $63,840 for the victory, raising his career earnings to $305,909. The Belmont had been no fluke.

On August 6 a municipal court judge ordered Ron Franklin to enroll in a drug counseling program. If he finished the program and had no drug offenses for six months, the charges would be dismissed.

Franklin was still riding for Delp. He got up at 5:30 a.m., gave several horses their morning workouts, and went to Delp's home for lunch. Then he went back to the track and rode his races for the day—anywhere from two to seven races. At around 6:30 p.m. he rushed back to Delp's for dinner. He did not go out at night; Delp's curfew would not allow it. "He's a good kid, but he doesn't always tell the truth," Delp said. "He does his share, but he has to be watched." He added, "It's too bad. I let him get too big too quick."

One day, not long after the arrest, Franklin was riding Armada Strike at Pimlico, and a man yelled at him, "Hey, Nose, you give that horse a snort, too? Atta boy, Franklin, things go better with coke. Let's cut a few lines after the races." Those were some of the kindest remarks thrown at the boy. Every time he failed on a favorite, the crowd let him have it with a barrage of jeers and epithets. Even his hometown, which had greeted him with signs and celebrations just two months ago, had turned on him.

Meanwhile, Delp was bringing Bid along slowly, steadily upping the speed of his workouts while the horse continued to rehabilitate. On July 23 he ran three furlongs in thirty-five and four-fifths seconds, galloping a half mile in forty-nine seconds. Delp and Bettis took the protective horseshoe off on July 25; a day later, Bid went on his normal two-mile gallop, and on July 29 and 31 he repeated his half-mile run in forty-nine seconds. He breezed five furlongs in 1:01²/₅ on August 4 under conditions so foggy that the exercise boy had to shout when he got to the five-furlong pole. Then Bid turned it on. He worked six furlongs in 1:13²/₅ on August 11, four furlongs in forty-eight seconds flat on August 13, and seven furlongs in 1:24⁴/₅ on August 14. Although he would not be ready for the Travers Stakes on August 18, Delp started looking for a good race where Bid could make his comeback. On August 21 Bid covered five furlongs in an amazing fifty-eight and two-fifths seconds. That was it. Delp pronounced the horse 110 percent healthy. He entered Bid in a mile-and-one-sixteenth allowance race in Dover on August 26, ending an almost three-month absence from the track. It would also be Shoemaker's first ride on the horse.

When race day arrived, Bid seemed crabby, refusing to let Delp and Hall put the saddle on him. The horse was muscle-bound, almost too tight to move, his coat glistening with sweat. Once he was on Bid's back, Shoemaker could not get the horse to do anything he asked—it was as if Bid had a mind of his own, and no one was going to change it. Shoemaker thought to himself, "Bill, what have you got yourself into? This horse has had it." A few moments later, Bid broke well from the starting gate, and Shoemaker felt the rush as the horse strained against the reins, the jockey pulling back with all his might. "Jesus, Bill, hang on! You're in for a ride now," he said to himself.

Carrying 122 pounds, Bid settled into third place heading into the clubhouse turn. He stalked the front-runner, Pity the Sea, whose 15-pound advantage over Bid had allowed him to open a three-length lead on the field. But Bid bided his time and made his move on the backstretch. Entering the homestretch, he passed Pity the Sea effortlessly and did not look back, accelerating in his own machinelike style, putting away all challengers, and winning by *seventeen lengths*. All Shoemaker had to do was wave his whip occasionally to keep Bid's mind on the race. Armada Strike, another Delp-trained colt, finished second, and Not So Proud was third. Bid had traveled the one and one-sixteenth miles in 1:41³/₅, setting a new track record for the distance. Bid was back.

"He did it on his own," Shoemaker said. "All I wanted to do was get a good race into him for the Marlboro [Cup]. I didn't start riding him until the stretch and by then he was too far ahead to matter." After his first ride on Spectacular Bid, Shoemaker was already comparing him to some of the best horses ever. The jockey had ridden Kelso, Swaps, Round Table, Northern Dancer, Buckpasser, Damascus, and Forego, and he said, "Spectacular Bid is as great as any horse that I've ever ridden, and I've ridden some of the great ones in the world."

Bid's next appearance? The Marlboro Cup on September 8. Two of the other entrants? Affirmed and Coastal.

The Marlboro Cup was a handicap, meaning that racing secretaries assign weights to the horses based on past performance. The better the horse, the more weight it carries to slow it down and make the race more equitable. The difference between the weight of the jockey and the weight assigned to the horse is made up by lead slabs carried in cloth pads under the saddle. Some believe that the heavier the jockey, the better, since the jockey's weight moves with the horse rather than being tied down to the saddle.

Linda Kennedy, biographer of the great handicap horse Kelso, explains the relationship between weight and distance:

• At one mile: two extra pounds = one length

- At one and one-fourth miles: two extra pounds = one and a half lengths

For example, if a horse would normally beat another horse carrying equal weight by five lengths, adding ten pounds to the better horse should result in a close race at one mile. According to Kennedy, the greater the weight on the horse's spine, the greater the strain on the abdomen and the greater the effort to stride. As weight increases, bone, muscle, heart, and lungs must work harder, oxygen debt takes an early toll, and the horse tires faster. The longer the race, the greater the effect. Famed jockey Eddie Arcaro called 130 pounds the "breaking point" for a horse. Three times he tried to win with Citation carrying 130 pounds, and he failed every time. Only Kelso and Forego carried more than 130 pounds consistently and won.

Some have questioned whether handicapping is necessary. Horse racing is the only sport in which a competitor is penalized for being outstanding. "Do they tell Jack Nicklaus he has to give three a side?" trainer Roger Laurin asked. "Would that be fair? Would they make Babe Ruth swing a bat five pounds heavier?"

When racing secretary Lenny Hale assigned weights for the Marlboro, he assigned Affirmed, a four-year-old, 133 pounds; Bid, still only three years old, 124 pounds; and Coastal, 122 pounds. "I don't see how [Affirmed's trainer] Laz Barrera can complain about it, but he will," Hale said.

He was right. Barrera was furious. "I will not comment on it," he said, and then did. "It's the Wolfsons' horse, and they can do with him what they want. But if he were my horse I would not run him." Apparently, the owners agreed, and the next day, Barrera withdrew Affirmed from the Marlboro Cup, citing unfair handicapping weights. He noted that in 1978, Seattle Slew had been given only 128 pounds to Affirmed's 124 pounds—a 4-pound difference—whereas the difference between Affirmed and Bid was 9 pounds. According to Hale, Barrera complained as if it were Hale's fault that fans would be deprived of the "race of the century."

"If my horse raced in the Marlboro, he might win or he might not," Barrera said of Affirmed. "But that's too much weight differential to give him. I'm mighty glad that the racing secretary thinks he's the greatest horse in the country, but I don't want to kill my horse. The Wolfsons understand. They know I'm trying to protect their property." In Barrera's opinion, a fair race would be a weight-for-age contest, in which Affirmed, the older horse, would carry 126 pounds and the three-year-olds would carry 121. Affirmed would therefore skip the Marlboro and aim for the one-and-a-quarter-mile Woodward Stakes at Belmont Park on September 22, which was a weight-for-age event.

General Assembly, also running in the Marlboro, was assigned only 120 pounds. He had just won the Travers Stakes by fifteen lengths, and the up-and-down stock of General Assembly was on the rise again. So instead of a matchup of the two best horses in the country, fans would see a rematch of the Belmont. Russ Harris called it one of the best fields in the seven-year history of the Marlboro Cup. Could Coastal do it again? Could General Assembly finally run like his sire and recapture his earlier glory?

Handicappers also had their eye on Star de Naskra, a four-year-old colt that would be carrying the same weight as Bid. With such a light weight on a more mature horse, they thought that Star de Naskra could fly. The downside was that most of his races had been distances of a mile or less. The Marlboro was one and one-eighth miles.

Instead of focusing on the drama over Affirmed's weight assignment, Andrew Beyer called the weight assignment a slap in the face to Spectacular Bid. "By decreeing that Affirmed would have to spot Bid nine pounds in order to equalize the horses' chances, [Lenny] Hale was saying that Bid was not in the same class as Affirmed," he wrote. With or without Affirmed in the field, Beyer predicted that a fresh Spectacular Bid would win. If Affirmed raced, he would be unable to handle the extra weight and would lose; if he didn't, the race was Bid's almost by default. Beyer thought that Bid was back.

Coastal's trainer, David Whiteley, called Barrera's actions tasteless and unsportsmanlike. "If you have any backbone and consideration for racing, you run the horse," he said. "They've had it pretty easy. The horse is obviously at his best. He went past Forego and Kelso in money winning. If he deserves to be mentioned in the same breath with them, he ought to do a little bit of what they did," which was to carry additional weight in handicaps. Kelso had carried 136 pounds several times, and the giant Forego had once carried 138 pounds. When reminded that Forego had carried 137 pounds in the Marlboro Cup, Barrera replied, "Forego was a gelding." This had nothing to do with weights, but he may have been alluding to Affirmed's approaching syndication at stud. He did not want to do anything that might jeopardize the horse's stud career.

Delp was disappointed that Bid would not be running against the best. "Laz is smart, but it's bad for the sport. . . . This would have been the Race of the Century," he said. "I've never seen a field of this caliber. It's still the Race of the Decade." With Affirmed absent, Delp predicted that Star de Naskra would be his stiffest competition, and he threw a barb at General Assembly. "General Assembly won't win it. That's one horse I know I'm going to beat. I've beaten him five times. He keeps coming back for more."

When Spectacular Bid arrived at Belmont Park on the Friday before the race, he was housed in the barn of Frank Whiteley, father of David and trainer of the great filly Ruffian. To welcome Bid, Whiteley himself had put six bales of straw in the stall—stall number 13. Delp promptly moved Bid to stall 12. So much for not being superstitious.

The morning of the Marlboro broke hot and steamy, with an expected temperature of eighty-four degrees. Wearing a red Marlboro blazer, Delp was sweating and wiping his face with a handkerchief as he heard the catcalls coming from the New Yorkers: "Hey! Watch out for those safety pins!" and "Got all those pins out?" Delp ignored them, focusing instead on his prized Thoroughbred. He believed no accident would befall Bid today, and the outcome would be no accident either.

Bid was his usual antsy, rank self before the race, skipping and hopping his way to the starting gate. But he went in the gate smoothly. The bell clanged, the gates sprang open, and they were off. Bid started well and settled into third place, just behind front-runners Star de Naskra and General Assembly, with Coastal and Text not far behind. The pace was agonizingly slow; at the half-mile mark, Shoemaker had seen enough and let a notch out of Bid's reins. Bid responded and passed the two leaders, but Text made a move as well, and he and General Assembly held on. Text was just a neck behind Bid, and General Assembly was a neck behind Text. Delp, who had no binoculars, asked Harry Meyerhoff what was going on. Harry confirmed that Bid had just taken the lead, and Delp said, "He'll win." When the time for the half mile was posted (a snail-like forty-seven and two-fifths seconds), he boasted, "This race is history."

As the pack rounded the turn for home, Bid extended his lead to a length and a half, and the field was chasing him futilely. "Everybody was whipping and driving and I really hadn't asked my horse to run," Shoemaker said. When he did ask Bid to run, the horse responded, extending his lead down the homestretch with his effortless stride, winning by five lengths over General Assembly in what seemed like an exhibition. The time was 1:46³/₅, just a second behind Secretariat's track record. Coastal was never in contention. He tried to mimic his Belmont finish with a ride along the rail but finished third, one and a half lengths behind General Assembly.

The crowd roared its approval. It was sweet revenge for Bid, who had defeated Coastal by six and a half lengths at the same track where he had lost in the Belmont Stakes. "[Bid] established without a doubt his supremacy over the other members of his generation," wrote Andrew Beyer. "And today's race certainly verified Delp's insistence that the Belmont was not a true performance by his horse."

"The way Bid ran, Barrera may have decided wisely," wrote William Nack in *Sports Illustrated*. Barrera, too, felt justified in his decision. "[Spectacular Bid] showed yesterday that he should have won the Triple Crown," he said on Sunday. "He wins the Marlboro in 1:46³/₅ with Shoemaker hardly using the whip. If Affirmed is in the race and Shoe uses the whip, Spectacular Bid goes in 1:46. Then Affirmed has to run his eyeballs out with 133 pounds to win in 1:45 and change. It is asking too much. He would be knocked out for the rest of the year." Without actually saying it, Barrera implied that Affirmed would have lost to Bid.

Despite Bid's win, Harry Meyerhoff expressed his disappointment at Affirmed's absence. "Our horse ran a great race, and we're sorry we didn't meet [Affirmed]," he said.

Delp now had to decide whether Bid would face Affirmed in the Woodward Stakes on September 22. It was just two weeks away—not a lot of time for a horse to recuperate. Bid had done it before, however, between the Kentucky Derby and the Preakness. But some critics still believed that the rush of races during the Triple Crown had taken something out of Spectacular Bid.

Nature made the decision for Delp. Bid stopped eating on the Tuesday before the Woodward, and when Bettis took his temperature, it was 104 degrees. He summoned a veterinarian, who administered antibiotics. By the next day, Bid was eating five quarts of oats, but the infection had done its damage. Bid would go back to exercising on Thursday, but "it would be too much to ask him to run back in the Woodward," Delp said. He was out of the race. Delp hoped Bid would be ready for the Jockey Club Gold Cup on October 6.

Without Bid in the field at the Woodward, Affirmed cruised to a two-and-a-half-length victory over Coastal. Czaravich, who had been a Belmont possibility before illness struck, finished third. This race was the perfect prep for Affirmed, priming him for the Jockey Club Gold Cup. Bid was recuperating well from his fever, so it looked like the two would finally meet.

Meanwhile, the Meyerhoffs returned to the Keeneland fall sales and bought seven yearlings for $220,000—paying a high of $42,000 for the most expensive yearling. When asked whether he had another Spectacular Bid in the group, Harry Meyerhoff replied, "A couple of champions, no doubt, and some $5,000 claimers, too."

Besides Affirmed and Spectacular Bid, five other horses entered the Jockey Club Gold Cup: Coastal, Czaravich, Bowl Game, Silent Cal, and Gallant Best (the front-runner Bid had chased at the Belmont Stakes). This, not the Marlboro Cup, was shaping up to be the race of the year, with a purse of $381,000—$228,600 going to the winner.

Affirmed was named the 4 to 5 favorite and would be racing from the number-six position; he would carry 126 pounds in the weight-for-age race. Spectacular Bid was even money—the first time since his two-year-old days that he was not the favorite—and would be in the number-three slot; he would carry 121 pounds. Coastal would be beside Affirmed, in the number-seven slot.

Affirmed had changed since his three-year-old Horse of the Year campaign. Described as an elegant and refined three-year-old (compared to the freight train that was Alydar), Affirmed had grown bigger and more powerful as a four-year-old, gaining 200 pounds over the winter of 1978–1979. He was now a more mature horse and a true powerhouse, having won six in a row after losing his first two races of the year.

On September 26 Bid worked a mile and one-eighth in 1:50 and galloped out a mile and a quarter in 2:04. On October 4 he ran half a mile in forty-seven and two-fifths seconds at Pimlico. He arrived at Belmont Park on October 5, just one day before the race. Barrera believed Bid's late arrival gave Affirmed the edge; Affirmed had been stabled at Belmont for a few months now. "The ballgame is being played in [Affirmed's] stadium," he said. "He's been working here when the track has been good and bad and is familiar with it. He's been in his own stall and he knows the surroundings."

On race day, Bid rose at 3:00 a.m., and Mo Hall greeted him with two quarts of oats as a Pinkerton guard stood nearby on twenty-four-hour watch. "Rise and shine, you hoss," Hall said. The temperature was cool; autumn was in full swing. He gave Bid a supply of timothy hay to help fill his belly. About an hour later, Affirmed awoke, crying for his breakfast. His groom did the same for him.

At around 5:50 a.m. Bud Delp arrived in his Cadillac limousine; he was wearing a jacket with the slogan "Spectacular Bid Is Spectacular" on the back. He went into the stall to see how Bid had made it through the night. Several minutes later, he instructed Robert Smith, the exercise rider, to walk Bid a little to limber him up for his morning run. "I'm just gonna give him a little gallop," Delp said. "Nothing more than that. Gotta save something for this afternoon." Bid would then be walked to cool him off, bathed, and given two more quarts of oats.

Barrera showed up at the barn at least an hour later. "I feel very confident," he said. "I'm not nervous. I'm too old in the business for that. I did all my study last night. The race, I take it as it comes now. I did my job. Nothing more I can do. Up to the jockey now. Affirmed, real smart horse, most intelligent horse I ever have. You know what he do all day today? He sleep. He rest. He know what comes later."

When lunchtime came and went and they got no food, the two horses knew it was race day. They fidgeted in their stalls, waiting. "It may not look like it," Smith said, "but Bid knows just what's going on. These horses aren't dumb. . . . I bet Bid'll know Affirmed when they meet, too. It's something the great ones give off to each other."

Bid got a little sleep, while, contrary to Barrera's predictions,

Affirmed got antsy, nibbling at some hay in his stall. Delp downed a beer to calm his nerves. Someone asked Delp how he felt. The cockiness was gone. "I'm uptight now. I feel tense," he said. "I'll go back to my hotel and watch the baseball game. . . . But I guess I'll be thinking about the race all day. How'm I gonna not think about it? I been thinking about it ever since the Preakness. This is the biggie. Anyone got eyes can see that."

Sportswriter William Nack talked to Shoemaker about the race and offered some advice: get Bid out early and challenge Affirmed. "You know, if you let Affirmed get loose on the lead, you've got no chance, especially if you let him get away with a half in forty-nine or fifty," Nack told Shoemaker.

Shoemaker replied, "Yeah, I know, but there's nothing I can do about it."

"Why can't you send your horse up there?" Nack asked.

"That's not his style," the jockey responded. "I'm not going to change his style."

Finally, post time approached. The trainers and grooms put saddles and bridles on the horses. The horses paraded around the manicured paddock, which was freshly planted with an abundance of mums. The bugle called the horses to the post; the jockeys mounted and paraded their horses in front of the 36,187 fans in attendance at Belmont Park. Affirmed was now the 3 to 5 favorite, while Spectacular Bid's odds had fallen to 7 to 5. With workmanlike precision, the assistant starters moved the horses into the starting gate. Only four horses would be racing that day; Silent Cal, Czaravich, and Bowl Game had been scratched.

The starter pressed a button, cutting off the electric current that held the front of the gates together, and as the doors opened, the bell rang, signaling the start of the race. The crowd roared. And away they went. Affirmed broke perfectly and jumped to a one-length lead within the first fifty yards, followed by Gallant Best. As Shoemaker had predicted, Spectacular Bid broke slowly, and he and Coastal battled it out for third, a length and a half behind. Before they had even reached the clubhouse turn, Bid was behind by almost two lengths. For a front-runner like Affirmed, who refused to give up the lead once he had it, that was equivalent to a five-length lead. Even worse, Bid was boxed in by the other three horses—Gallant Best to the inside, Coastal to the outside, and

Affirmed in front—and he had to settle for fourth place. When Coastal dropped back, Bid made a move to the outside and began to stalk Gallant Best and Affirmed.

The race was setting up perfectly for Affirmed. He and Gallant Best ran the first quarter in a pedestrian twenty-five seconds, which meant that Affirmed would have plenty of stamina left for a stretch run. Just as Nack had predicted, the pace was slow, and Affirmed was dictating the speed of the race. Affirmed ran the half mile in forty-nine seconds—again, right where Nack had said he would be.

Gallant Best took the lead from Affirmed by a neck heading into the backstretch but continued the slow pace. The four horses were tightly bunched, with no more than four lengths separating them. Bid strained at the reins, but strangely, Shoemaker made no move to accelerate the pace, electing instead to keep stalking the leaders. No one was seriously challenging Gallant Best or the four-year-old champion.

Affirmed retook the lead just as Bid started to make his move on the outside; he pulled up to within a half length of Affirmed but stayed there, still waiting for something. Seeing that Bid was not going to take the lead, Affirmed's jockey, Laffit Pincay Jr., pulled back and let Affirmed rest some more, slowing the pace yet again. Bid slowed down as well. Going into the far turn, Affirmed gradually turned it up a notch and increased his lead to a length over Bid. Gallant Best was third, Coastal fourth. Bid made another move on Affirmed but was still a half length behind as they rounded the far turn. Affirmed fought back, increasing his lead to a length and a half as Coastal made his move on the inside, coming to within a neck of Affirmed. Bid was now in third place. Was he tiring as he had in the Belmont? Was he incapable of being a mile-and-a-half horse?

Shoemaker asked for more, and Bid reached deep within. As they left the far turn and entered the homestretch, Bid, responding to the whip, slipped in between Coastal and Affirmed and pulled to within a neck. The three horses were now running almost as one, with just half a length separating them. The spectators leaped to their feet, cheering as the horses battled over the last few furlongs. In the homestretch, Affirmed led by a neck over Spectacular Bid, but Bid kept charging. In the past, Bid could have overwhelmed his rivals with one push. But

Affirmed pulls away to defeat Bid in the Jockey Club Gold Cup. (Bob Coglianese)

Affirmed thrived on head-to-head competition, as he had proved in his thrilling stretch runs with his Triple Crown rival Alydar.

In the last seconds, Affirmed pulled away one last time, going under the wire to win by three-quarters of a length. Coastal was third, three lengths behind and unable to keep up with the two champions. Gallant Best finished thirty-one lengths behind Coastal. The crowd roared, knowing they had seen a true battle. Bid had been unable to look Affirmed in the eye and stare him down, as he had done countless other times on the racetrack. Affirmed was the first horse that had taken control of a race and would not let go.

After the race, the Meyerhoffs were more subdued and less emotional than they had been after the Belmont, but they were disappointed in the outcome. Delp praised both horses but said, "You give Spectacular Bid the break that Affirmed had and give Affirmed the break that Bid had, the outcome might have been different." Shoemaker agreed.

"[Affirmed] outbroke my horse about a length leaving the gate. If I had gotten a better start, the pace wouldn't have been that slow." He refused to say that Affirmed was the better horse. Later he told Harry Meyerhoff he had not realized how slow the pace was and admitted he should have gone faster. "I only f—— up once [on Spectacular Bid]," he later told the Meyerhoffs, referring to the Jockey Club Gold Cup. Delp told Ron Franklin that if Shoemaker had ridden Bid in the Belmont, Bid would have won; if Franklin had ridden Bid in the Jockey Club Gold Cup, Bid would have won as well.

William Boniface of the *Baltimore Evening Sun* agreed. "Bill Shoemaker ran a poor race on Spectacular Bid," he wrote. "It was that simple, but most critics are reluctant to say so about the world's leading race-winning jockey. If it had been Ron Franklin . . . they would have overheated their typewriters with the complaints." Boniface said Shoemaker had been outmaneuvered at every turn when he misjudged the early pace set by Pincay and Affirmed, putting himself at their mercy in the final half mile. "He let Pincay slow the pace down to little more than a gallop. . . . He couldn't spot that slow a pace to an ordinary horse and expect to catch him, let alone Affirmed. . . . Shoemaker should have known better."

Barrera disagreed with the media's assessment. "I don't want to insult anybody, but I think Affirmed is the best horse I ever saw. Don't take nothing away from the Bid. He's a hell of a horse. But my horse knows where the wire is, and the party's over once he takes control."

"The pace makes the race," Delp answered. "No horse has ever lived who can give Affirmed the lead in forty-nine [for a half mile] and then get by him. If Bid had the lead and had gone a half in forty-nine, there's no horse living who could have gotten by him either."

Some cited the Woodward as the reason Affirmed had done so well. If the two horses had met in the Marlboro Cup, Bid would have had the advantage of a more competitive race, as Affirmed had been absent from competition for more than two months. Bid's scratching from the Woodward gave Affirmed the perfect tune-up for the Jockey Club Gold Cup. Bid, in contrast, had been ill and had not competed in four weeks, having no opportunity to race before the Gold Cup to tighten him up and condition him.

But according to Steve Cady of the *New York Times,* the older, more mature horse had won. "What yesterday's result seemed to support was the notion that outstanding three-year-olds rarely beat outstanding older horses in the Gold Cup. No three-year-old has won [the Jockey Club Gold Cup] since Arts and Letters succeeded in 1969," he wrote. A maxim in horse racing is that a good four-year-old will beat a good three-year-old most of the time. This was the case with Affirmed; he was simply a more experienced and stronger horse. It would be like an all-American college basketball senior playing a one-on-one game against an all-American high school senior.

Writers were quick to heap praise on Bid for his valiant effort, though. Dan Farley of the *Thoroughbred Record* was impressed with both Bid and Coastal, but especially Bid, who tried repeatedly to catch Affirmed and never gave up. "Bid and Coastal solidified their standing as the best three-year-olds the continent has to offer," he wrote.

Ron Franklin, who was riding occasionally, had finished his last race at Pimlico, hurried back to Delp's home, made himself a bloody Mary, and settled down in front of the television to watch the Gold Cup. "If anybody was going to take my place on Bid, I'm glad it was Shoe," he said. "He knows what he's doing, and he can take the pressure a little better."

After the Gold Cup, Delp was not satisfied. He wanted one more shot at Affirmed, confident that if the two horses broke together and Affirmed did not control the pace, Bid could win. He was considering two races—the Meadowlands Cup and the Turf Classic at Aqueduct Racetrack. According to Barrera, there was a chance that Affirmed might start in the Turf Classic, but he rejected the idea of a match race.

9

The Streak

There's no doubt about it, he's a great horse. He's at least as
good as any horse I've ridden in my career, and maybe better. I
just don't know what it's going to take to beat this horse.

—Bill Shoemaker

DELP ENTERED SPECTACULAR BID in the Meadowlands Cup
that fall. To ensure that Bid would enter, officials at the Meadowlands
had sweetened the pot, raising the purse from $250,000 to $350,000.
Twenty-two other horses were nominated, including Affirmed, but Laz
Barrera decided not to run him. Instead, he sent his latest sensation,
Valdez, to the Meadowlands. Valdez, once considered a Triple Crown
contender, had almost died from a viral infection in the spring but had
recently beaten Kentucky Derby front-runner Shamgo by two and three-
quarters lengths to win the Swaps Stakes in Inglewood, California. It
was his third victory in a row and his fifth in six starts.

Bid drew the rail for the race—not where Delp wanted him to be.
He was still talking about a rematch between Bid and Affirmed. "I think
we deserve another shot," he said. "Whatever it takes to get these two
horses together again, I'd like to see it happen. They could meet next
month." Barrera said, "I'd have to think about it. After tonight, it might
not be necessary," implying that Valdez might spoil the party.

October 18 was a cool night at the Meadowlands—a perfect night
for racing. Going off as the 1 to 9 favorite, Bid got off to his usual slow
start, giving the lead to Text, ridden by Angel Cordero. Text held the
lead for the first quarter mile, with Valdez second. At the half-mile pole,
Text and Valdez switched places, with Bid biding his time in third place.

Shoemaker urged his mount on in the backstretch, and Bid, taking his time, slowly gained ground on the leaders. As they entered the far turn, Bid took off, as if he had been waiting for the right moment. He passed Valdez and Text, and although Valdez fought back, matching Bid stride for stride around the turn, Bid drew away in the homestretch, widening his lead with his precision strides. He finished three lengths ahead of a fast-closing Smarten, who nosed out Valdez for second. He had covered the mile and a quarter in 2:01 1/5, breaking the old track record by two-fifths of a second.

Talk started about a rematch between Bid and Affirmed. "Any time, any place, any distance," Delp said. Tom Meyerhoff even sweetened the pot; when asked about a winner-take-all format for a match race, he offered Affirmed the whole pot, win or lose, if that would get them together. Larry Barrera, Laz's son, said maybe. "There's no need for a match race because Affirmed has proved what he had to prove. But if there is a match race next month, we'd prefer to have it in California." So the race was a possibility. And then it was not. Three days later, Laz Barrera announced that Affirmed was retiring from competition and would stand at stud at Spendthrift Farm in Kentucky. "He does not like the grass," Barrera said, explaining his decision to withdraw Affirmed from the Turf Classic at Aqueduct. Apparently, Affirmed was not running well on grass.

Affirmed retired as the richest Thoroughbred in racing history, amassing $2,393,818. The question was: who was Horse of the Year? Bid had won twelve straight races until his loss in the Belmont, and he had broken two track records. He had exacted revenge on Coastal (who retired after the Jockey Club Gold Cup) and earned $1.2 million, a new record for a single season. Affirmed had seven victories in nine starts, including a win over Bid. But Bid's fans reminded everyone that Affirmed had been voted Horse of the Year in 1978, despite being beaten badly by 1977 Triple Crown winner Seattle Slew—twice.

"It looks like they are scared of me," Delp said. "Affirmed is going into hiding. The whole world is waiting for a match race, and they're pulling out. I thought they were better sports than that. I guess they're ready to concede Horse of the Year honors to Bid." He claimed that Bid had done more during the fall than Affirmed had done all year. "He's beaten older horses twice and did it decisively while conceding them a lot of weight. . . . He won more money while setting a world's record for purse earnings and he won more stakes and was beaten only twice, the same as Affirmed in 1979."

Andrew Beyer thought the Eclipse Award belonged to Spectacular Bid. "It's going to be the same old story: The world will be wrong and I'll be right," he wrote. Beyer predicted that because Affirmed had beaten Spectacular Bid most recently in the Jockey Club Gold Cup, voters would forget about Bid's previous performances—his twelve-race winning streak and his Derby and Preakness wins—and vote based on the results of that race. "I thought Spectacular Bid's three-fourths length loss under those disadvantageous circumstances [Bid's four-week layoff, the lack of other front-runners in the Gold Cup] was a heroic performance. Under more neutral conditions, he would have whipped Affirmed."

Pimlico general manager Chick Lang thought Bud Delp should be named Trainer of the Year. "It is nothing short of remarkable how Delp has brought this horse back to peak condition. After the Belmont, I don't know how many horsemen came up to me and said that if they had the horse, they would have stopped him and pulled his shoes. . . . But Bud tried to keep him in light exercise and heal his feet at the same time."

When all the votes were tallied, it was not even close: Affirmed won Horse of the Year. Spectacular Bid was voted Champion Three-Year-Old Male, a small consolation prize. Laz Barrera was named Trainer of the Year. For the Spectacular Bid team, the results were a slap in the face. To Delp, the awards were a joke and a disgrace. He called Bid's year the greatest by any horse ever—only Citation and Man o' War had won as many as twelve straight stakes. He blamed the racing establishment, which had shunned them from the beginning. "Politics were again involved," he said, leaving the Eclipse Awards with a bitter taste in his mouth. Eclipse Award voters were like fans voting for baseball All-Stars, he said, looking at career statistics rather than those of the current season. The Affirmed camp had run from a match race with Bid, he claimed, because they did not want to risk losing the Horse of the Year title. It was a "chicken decision," he said. "I wanted a match race and so did the world. It would have been a great show. I can assure you that if this horse stays healthy, there's no one we'll duck. We'll run against anyone anywhere."

❦

Winter came, and the Meyerhoffs decided to continue to race Spectacular Bid instead of putting him out to stud. So Bid was flown west to
Santa Anita during the first week of December to prepare for next year's
racing season, accompanied by Franklin and Delp. And once again, the
writers were ready for Delp. "Is The Bid as good as blabbermouth trainer
Bud Delp keeps shouting?" asked John Hall of the *Los Angeles Times*.
"How does a guy get so obnoxious? . . . Wouldn't it have been better for
the world if that safety pin in the Belmont barn had wound up in Delp's
mouth instead of his horse's foot?" California fans did not care; at Bid's
first workout at Santa Anita, 5,000 people showed up before dawn to
watch him breeze.

Basking in the warm climate of Southern California, Bid bided his
time and rested until the racing season began in January. The Meyerhoffs
rented a house not too far away in Acapulco and spent the winter there.
Their plans for Bid were similar to Affirmed's in 1979: keep him in California and race him at Santa Anita and a few other tracks in the area
before heading back east later in the year. Their goals were to break the
all-time earnings mark set by Affirmed and to capture the elusive Horse
of the Year honors. If they could not beat Affirmed on the racetrack
again, they would eclipse all his records. Such a decision was risky. Bid
would likely command $10 million in syndication fees to go to stud; by
racing him, they risked injuring the colt and jeopardizing his stud career.

If looks were any indication, Spectacular Bid could not have been
healthier. He had filled out over the winter and was even more muscular. He had also grown, measuring over sixteen hands. "He can get very
strong at times," said exercise rider Robert Smith. "As a horse gets older,
naturally he'll strain at the bit more. I have to restrain him from running
quicker." Bid was also more rambunctious and irritable, a sign that he
was reaching the age of a stallion. Charlie Bettis said, "He's always trying to bite and kick. He doesn't try to do serious damage, but he wants
everyone to know he's irritated. Aside from little temper tantrums, he's
the most relaxed horse I've ever been around. He walks like an old man,
very slow and never in a hurry."

Delp planned to run Bid in the Malibu Stakes on January 5, the San
Fernando Stakes on January 19, the Strub Stakes on February 3, and
the Santa Anita Handicap on March 2. Bid was likely to run into an old

rival, Flying Paster, who had gone back to California to recuperate after the Preakness Stakes. His hiatus had put him in sound condition. But Harry Meyerhoff, with Bid's two losses behind him, had never lost his confidence. "We're gonna win 'em all," he said—something Affirmed had not done when he wintered in California. Affirmed had finished third in the Malibu Stakes and second in the San Fernando Stakes before running the table in the rest of his races.

When the Santa Anita season was over, Bid would move to Hollywood Park and run in the Californian Stakes and perhaps a few other races. Harry Meyerhoff planned to take Bid east in the fall. "It's hard to look too far ahead, and I haven't discussed this in detail with Bud Delp, but I'd like to run him at the Meadowlands again," he said. He also planned to run him in the Marlboro Cup, Woodward Stakes, and Jockey Club Gold Cup again. Last year, Bid had won only one of the three. This year, Meyerhoff hoped Bid would be the first horse to sweep all three races.

Franklin had accompanied Delp to Santa Anita to ride horses, but that did not pan out for him. During the season at Santa Anita, he failed to win on forty-four mounts. And criticism over his riding fueled his fury. People were saying that he could not ride a decent race; that he was a dopehead, an idiot, as Delp had said back at the Florida Derby. Franklin got in a fight with Darrel McHargue over the latter's riding tactics but later blamed it on himself, admitting that his temper was causing trainers to second-guess using him as a rider. "My temper gets the best of me," he said. "I can't control it. I go too far. I keep on going and then I'm always sorry afterwards that I did it. . . . It's a part of me. Something just snaps inside when things don't go the way I want them to."

Franklin had no agent, and Delp was not letting him ride horses anymore, preferring to use him as a hot walker and paying him $65 a week. "A nineteen-year-old isn't supposed to have ulcers," Delp said. "The best thing, the right thing, was to bring him back to earth some. He's still capable of being any kind of rider, but right now we're trying to take it a step at a time. Right now I'd describe him as a hell of a student." It was a giant step backward for a jockey who, just eight months earlier, had ridden a Kentucky Derby and Preakness winner.

❧

In his first race of 1980, the Malibu Stakes on January 5, Bid faced only four other horses in the short, seven-furlong race. Race day was warm and sunny—typical of Southern California in winter. Bid was assigned 126 pounds, the heaviest in the field, and seemed ready to resume his racing career, pawing at the ground in the paddock before the race. Flying Paster, eager to get another shot at Bid, was carrying 123 pounds. Bettors sent Bid off as the 3 to 10 favorite.

Spectacular Bid broke from the gate in his usual lumbering style. He let How Rewarding pass him and was last entering the clubhouse turn, but not too far off the leader, Rosie's Seville. Flying Paster broke well and was in third place before giving it up to How Rewarding, who, after a slow start, was making a mad dash to the front and battling Rosie's Seville for the lead. Bid was still in last place. Shoemaker inched Bid up between horses and into fourth place, just behind Flying Paster. When the Paster made his move on the inside around the far turn, Bid saw his rival and went with him. Throughout the turn, it was a four-horse race, with Rosie's Seville still hanging on and Known Presence making a move. Once they entered the homestretch, though, Spectacular Bid took over, even though he had gone around the turn four horses wide, just as he had done in the past with Franklin. He bolted into the lead as if his feet were not even leaving the ground, almost like a trotter. Bid extended his lead to three lengths, then four, as Shoemaker hand-rode him almost the whole way, using the whip only once. In fact, Shoemaker had to slow Bid down to conserve the horse's energy.

The winning margin was five lengths over poor Flying Paster, who was being whipped all the way down the stretch but could not catch Bid. Once considered Bid's equal or even his superior, the Paster had been beaten badly yet again—this time on his home track, and with no excuses.

Bid knew he had won. He was led to the winner's circle, got his chocolate doughnut, and heard soothing sounds of encouragement from Bettis and Delp, which calmed him down after the race.

In winning the Malibu, Bid broke another track record; the winning time was three-fifths of a second faster than the old track record, set back in 1954, and just one-fifth of a second off the world record, set in 1972. By comparison, Affirmed had finished third in the Malibu in 1979. If Shoemaker had let Bid loose all the way to the finish line, he could have set a world record for the distance. "He had his running shoes on," Shoe-maker said. "When we straightened out in the stretch, I hit him once, and he took off and left the others." Dr. Alex Harthill examined Bid after the race and told Delp and Bettis that Bid's heartbeat was so slow, "it was like he'd been in his stall all day."

Writers gushed at Bid's easy win. Barry Irwin of the *Thorough-bred Record* had to remind everyone how good Flying Paster had been before he ran up against Spectacular Bid. "Flying Paster is no slouch. This writer went on record . . . as saying that he was the best California-trained three-year-old seen since Sham a half-dozen years earlier.[1] . . . It is through knowing how good Flying Paster is that we can fully appreci-ate the ability and quality of Spectacular Bid."

Only three horses dared to compete against Bid in the San Fernando Stakes on Saturday, January 19. It had rained all week, and Delp had considered scratching Bid if the rain continued, but the track was in good condition at race time. Once again, Flying Paster was his main competition, and this time, Bid went off as an incredible 1 to 98 favor-ite—the shortest odds on a horse since Man o' War commanded 1 to 100 in 1920. The pari-mutuel department at Santa Anita officially listed him at 1 to 9, but based on the amount of money bet on him, he was 1 to 98. The tote board could not accommodate more than two figures.

Bid broke slowly again, with pacesetters Relaunch and Timbo tak-ing control of the race and running up a six-length lead over Flying Pas-ter heading into the clubhouse turn. Bid was another length back. In the backstretch, the two horses expanded their lead to ten lengths over the favorites as Bid passed Flying Paster, taking over third by two lengths. Was ten lengths too much of a deficit to make up? Bid answered the ques-tion before the end of the backstretch. "And there goes the Bid, quickly moving up third on the outside, right to the leaders!" the announcer exclaimed as the gray colt bolted forward and challenged Relaunch and Timbo. Bid saw the amount of ground he had to make up and went after the leaders. The move was so sudden, so quick, that writers in the press box wondered whether Shoemaker had gone to the front too soon and was chasing a fast pacesetter, as Franklin had done in the Belmont.

Bid passed Timbo with ease and raced neck and neck with Relaunch around the far turn, getting a breather after his lightning move. Then, as he had done in so many races, he found another gear and turned it up a notch, taking the lead by a neck, then a length, then two lengths.

But here came the Paster once again. As if he had been shot out of a gun, Flying Paster flew past a tiring Relaunch and took aim at Bid, trailing him by a head and running with momentum. The crowd roared as it finally got to see the true rivalry that had only been hinted at for the past eighteen months. Did Bid have anything left in him? Were they about to witness a major upset?

When Shoemaker saw the Paster out of the corner of his eye, he panicked and started whipping Bid furiously, and Bid responded. He still had something in reserve. As Bid tried to pull away, a stubborn Flying Paster stuck to him, but by the final sixteenth, the race was no longer in doubt. Shoemaker had to hold Bid up again by the time he reached the finish line. This time, the winning margin was a length and a half, but it had seemed closer. Relaunch finished in third, fifteen lengths behind the Paster.

"I thought I had you, I really did," Don Pierce, the Paster's jockey, told Shoemaker after the race.

"I did too," Shoemaker said.

"Today I might have if my horse had had another race. I thought I was going to go right by him. I might get him sometime, but not today," Pierce said. He paused. "Maybe never."

Delp had only good things to say about Flying Paster's effort. "Flying Paster is a helluva horse. He probably could beat any horse in America today—except Spectacular Bid. And the Bid can run with any horse that ever lived."

California journalists were confounded, wondering how Affirmed had beaten Spectacular Bid. The horse was a year older now, had put on some weight, and had grown into an impressive-looking colt. His strides were effortless, as if he were out on a leisurely gallop. But no one could catch him. "Only by seeing the power and strength of Flying Paster's challenge could anybody appreciate precisely how incredible Spectacular Bid's race really was," wrote Barry Irwin of the *Thoroughbred Record*. "If Flying Paster never runs any better than he ran in the meeting's first hundred-grander, he will have accomplished enough to convince horsemen he is a first-class colt; Spectacular Bid, on the other hand, is in a class by himself."

After the San Fernando, Delp caused some controversy when he said the race had been a "weight control" exercise, meaning that because Bid would be running in the Santa Anita Handicap in six weeks, he had not wanted the horse to turn in a blazing performance that would result in excessive weight being assigned to him. It sounded as if he were making excuses for the close margin of victory. Delp was a shrewd man and was always thinking in advance. But whatever had happened in the San Fernando to appease handicappers went out the window in the Strub Stakes.

Bold Bidder, Spectacular Bid's sire, had set a new track record of 1:59³/₅ for one and a quarter miles in winning the Charles H. Strub Stakes fourteen years earlier. That record still stood. Now Spectacular Bid was going to take a crack at it.

Who would be his challengers? There would not be many. Laz Barrera, maybe still hoping for another win against Affirmed's previous rival, entered Valdez in the Strub. Valdez had won his last race, the one-and-one-sixteenth-mile San Pasqual Handicap, on January 27. Flying Paster and Relaunch were the only other challengers as Bid tried to become the fourth horse to sweep the Strub Series, which consisted of the Malibu Stakes, the San Fernando Stakes, and the Strub Stakes. Bid carried a high weight of 126 pounds; Valdez, 122 pounds; Flying Paster, 121 pounds; and Relaunch, 116 pounds—hardly anything.

At the start, Relaunch took a huge lead as he passed the grandstand for the first time—about six lengths. Valdez was in second; Flying Paster was close behind in third, followed by Spectacular Bid in last place. The first quarter was clocked at a mercurial twenty-two seconds; Relaunch was flying, but there was no way he could sustain that pace. As they entered the backstretch, Relaunch stretched his lead to seven lengths, and then Bid began to move up. He passed Flying Paster and Valdez to take second place, then set his sights on the light-gray Relaunch, who was now ten lengths in front. Throughout the backstretch, Valdez kept up with Bid. The half-mile time was forty-four and three-fifths seconds. The pace was blistering.

On the backstretch, Bid and Valdez ran neck and neck, closing the gap on an exhausted Relaunch. The two caught Relaunch on the far turn, and then Bid inched his way ahead of Valdez. The stubborn Relaunch somehow managed to hold on to the lead, but entering the homestretch, Bid found that second wind and pulled away. Then, once again, the Paster came from behind. At one time seven lengths in back of Bid and Valdez, Flying Paster moved up around the far turn. Taking advantage of the tiring Valdez, who drifted wide on the turn, he went inside and took over second place at the top of the stretch. Don Pierce asked him for his best, and Flying Paster gave him everything he had. But Bid was in top gear. He led by two and a half lengths and then pulled away even more, winning by three and a quarter lengths as he passed under the wire.

The time was 1:57⁴/₅—a world record on dirt. The winning time shattered Bold Bidder's track record by almost two seconds and beat the American record of 1:58¹/₅ set by the great Noor in 1950 and equaled by Quack in 1972. The only faster mile and a quarter had occurred on hillside turf courses, which ran downhill in parts. The pace was so fast that even Flying Paster's second-place finish broke the track record. Valdez finished a well-beaten third, nine lengths back.

Delp was beside himself after the race, and the usually talkative trainer was almost speechless. "I said before he turned three that he was one of the greatest horses of all time, so I can't say anything new," he told reporters.

Shoemaker echoed what he had said the first time he rode Bid: "There's no doubt about it, he's a great horse. He's at least as good as any horse I've ridden in my career, and maybe better. I just don't know what it's going to take to beat this horse—maybe a lot of weight is the only way they'll do it." Delp probably blanched when he read that quote.

Don Pierce was impressed. "Flying Paster ran his best race. It just wasn't good enough. Maybe we just can't beat him. He really gave his all; we have no excuses."

Writers lauded Bid's achievement. Barry Irwin of the *Thoroughbred Record* wrote, "Affirmed had as his hallmark an iron will that refused to be beaten. Yet Spectacular Bid has an incredible brilliance that, at maturity, seems capable of breaking the iron lock of Affirmed. Still to be proven to this observer is that he has the overpowering strokes of Secretariat. But nothing we have seen since Secretariat has been so awe inspiring as Bid."

Bid had now won four races in a row. He had won twenty of twenty-four races in his career. And he had just become only the fourth horse to win the Strub Series; the other three were Round Table,[2] Hillsdale, and Ancient Title.

Bid was now entering the handicap season, and racing secretaries were taking notice. When Bid entered the $350,000 Santa Anita Handicap, the racing secretary assigned him a career-high 130 pounds for the mile and a quarter race—according to Eddie Arcaro, that weight was the breaking point for a horse. Using Linda Kennedy's formula, 2 pounds equaled one and a half lengths; Bid had never carried more than 126 pounds, so a 4-pound addition meant a three-length disadvantage. The weight was a great equalizer.

On race day, rain came in the morning off the San Gabriel Mountains. It started as a gentle drizzle and then blossomed into a torrential downpour, making conditions miserable for the 49,285 racing fans who had showed up and turning the racetrack into a mud pit. Four of the five trainers had their farriers put mud calks on their horses, special horseshoes with a projection on the heel (similar to a cleat) to prevent the horse from slipping in the mud. Delp conferred with Shoemaker throughout the day and even called farrier Jack Reynolds, who assured him that Bid had an excellent shoe for the mud, so they decided not to change shoes.

In this race, to keep the mud out of his mount's face, Shoemaker sent Spectacular Bid close to the lead, pacing him so he would not run out of steam. Beau's Eagle started quickly but then slowed the pace, establishing a two-length lead as they passed the stands the first time. Bid was second, and Flying Paster was third. The first quarter was a slow twenty-four and two-fifths seconds, but Beau's Eagle continued to add to his lead; it was as if the other horses were running in slow motion. When he stretched his lead on the backstretch to four lengths with a half mile to go, fans wondered whether Bid's good fortune had run out.

Shoemaker asked Bid for an extra gear, and he moved on Beau's Eagle. The pesky Flying Paster made a move, too, and as they passed the five-sixteenths pole, the three were locked in a battle for first. The Paster, on the outside, lost some ground, and Bid stuck a neck out in front of the tiring Beau's Eagle. When they reached the top of the stretch, Bid's margin had extended to a full length. Shoemaker tapped him twice with the whip, and Bid continued to lengthen his lead. He accelerated in his leisurely manner and coasted to an easy win, covering the sloppy mile and a quarter in an impressive 2:00³/₅. He ran the final quarter mile in twenty-three and four-fifths seconds—too fast for any horse at the end of a race—and won by five lengths over Flying Paster, who carried 123 pounds, 7 pounds less than his rival. It was the fourth time in a row the Paster had finished second to Bid and his sixth straight loss to him. Not even a weight advantage could get Flying Paster any closer to Bid.

"We tried to hook him a little earlier, but it didn't seem to make much difference," Don Pierce said. "I don't think there's any way we're going to beat that dude. I guess the only way anyone will beat him is to tie an anchor on him." Owner B. J. Ridder said he had had enough of Bid and would not let Flying Paster face him again.

"The only thing that may beat him is weight," Delp said. "I don't know what they'll put on us now. Sure, we'll have to carry some, but then it's up to us if we want to run." Like Barrera before him, Delp was setting the stage to refuse to run if the weight was too high.

With the win, Bid moved past the $2 million mark in career earnings—the second horse in history to reach that milestone. The colt bought for only $37,000 had now earned $2,089,417, and Affirmed's earnings record was locked in his sights. He also became only the sixth horse to win the Santa Anita Handicap under so much weight; only Seabiscuit, Thumbs Up, Mark-Ye-Well, Round Table, and Ack Ack had carried as much weight as Bid. Three of those horses were in the National Museum of Racing and Hall of Fame.

Flying Paster had proved that chasing after Bid was lucrative. His four runner-up finishes to Bid had earned him $150,000, raising his earnings to $877,060 and making him the fourth-richest California-bred winner of all time. The next time out, his owners went for grass. He entered the San Luis Rey Stakes on March 15, but the result was not much better. Racing against turf specialist John Henry, the Paster lost badly to him, fading to sixth. Bid's old rival Golden Act took seventh place.

Spectacular Bid came out of the taxing Strub in remarkable shape. When assistant trainer Charlie Bettis rode him on a workout, his hands and arms hurt from having to restrain the horse. Bid was squealing and playing the entire time, and when he got back to his stable, he ate all his feed.

On March 11, 1980, the Meyerhoff family stunned the racing world by announcing that Spectacular Bid had been syndicated for a world-record $22 million. Seth Hancock, owner of Claiborne Farm in Lexington, Kentucky, was instrumental in closing the deal; it was a real coup for him. "There was a lot of competition for [Bid] since we announced last summer that he was coming to Claiborne," he said. "It was easy, real easy, to put [the deal] together. I just got up a list of sixty of our best people and then picked twenty of the best ones that had mares to suit him. All twenty said they wanted in." Those twenty people—including breeders and owners from Europe, New York, and Kentucky—jumped at the chance to put up $550,000 each for a share of the breeding rights and an opportunity to offer a mare to breed with Bid.

Bid's syndication was quite a contrast from Secretariat's, which Hancock had also organized back in 1973—before the colt had even won the Triple Crown. That deal had been difficult to put together, requiring a lot of backroom deals and cajoling, since few people had been willing to take a chance on a three-year-old so early in the season. But Bid already had a fantastic three-year-old season under his belt and was on his way to a remarkable four-year-old campaign. He had been tested, and people were confident in Bid's ability. When asked about the timing of the syndication deal, Harry Meyerhoff said, "[Bid] did what we said he would do under every possible condition out west. He set a world record, a track record, and won on fast tracks, a good track, and a muddy track. We felt his value would not increase that much more no matter what he does the rest of the year, so we started moving on it yesterday."

The deal shattered the previous richest syndication—$16.5 million for Troy, a British horse that had won the Epsom and Irish Derbies. Affirmed stood at stud under a syndication deal worth $14.4 million. Once he retired, Bid would be joining Secretariat, Damascus, Honest Pleasure, Round Table, and Nijinsky II as Claiborne Farm's premier stud horses. Since Hancock's announcement in July 1979 that Bid would retire there, the horse's value had passed the $20 million that experts estimated he would be worth if he had won the Triple Crown. Hancock had waited for Bid to prove himself, and his patience had paid off. The horse purchased for a paltry $37,000 was now worth almost 600 times that.

The Meyerhoffs collected $11 million from the deal. They also kept half the shares, which meant that they could breed mares to Bid at no

charge. Since they owned no mares themselves, they were going to broker deals with broodmare owners. The Meyerhoffs would get a mare to
breed to Spectacular Bid, and they would give one foal from that breeding to the broodmare's owners. When the two horses were bred again,
the Meyerhoffs would keep that foal.

Meyerhoff said that Spectacular Bid would continue to race for
Hawksworth Farm, and the family would continue to make decisions
regarding the colt. "The syndication will not alter the schedule we had
planned," he said, "and we hope to race him seven or eight more times
before he is retired to stud."

On April 4 the Meyerhoffs gave Bud Delp a package worth $1.5
million, with payments to be spread over fifteen years for tax purposes.
Such a payment is customary to reward the trainer when a top horse
goes to stud. "I could have had a share of Spectacular Bid, and that
probably would have been more lucrative," Delp said. "But I'm just a
working man, and I'd rather have the money up front. Dealing in breeding seasons is a rich man's game." Harry Meyerhoff also promised extra
compensation to the rest of Bid's team, which included Charlie Bettis,
Robert Smith, and Mo Hall.

Meanwhile, Madelyn Jason and Grace Gilmore, who had sold Spectacular Bid for a song, got their due. Spectacular's success as a mare
caught the attention of Englishman Robert Sangster, who bought a half
interest in her for a reported $1 million.

Delp managed to sneak in another race for Bid—the Mervyn LeRoy
Handicap at Hollywood Park on May 18. He was a last-minute entry
on the Friday before the race, which was on Sunday. Delp had predicted
that the racing secretaries would be on to Bid by now, and he was right.
Bid was assigned 132 pounds, as much as Affirmed had ever received and
the highest weight of Bid's career. "It's a lot of weight, but we've got an
awful lot of horse," Delp said.

He would be facing the regulars: Flying Paster, who was giving it
another go—especially when Gordon Campbell heard that the Paster
would be carrying ten pounds less than Bid—and Beau's Eagle, whose
handlers hoped the eleven-pound weight advantage would benefit him
this time. Other horses challenging Bid that day included Peregrina-

tor, Life's Hope, and Replant. The Friday Delp entered Bid in the race, he gave the horse a sharpening workout; Bid covered three furlongs in thirty-four and four-fifths seconds.

When B. J. Ridder was asked what it would take for Flying Paster to beat Bid, he revealed that Laz Barrera had told him a secret: keep Bid on the inside because, apparently, he did not like to run between other horses and the rail. In the race, Don Pierce gave the strategy a chance. Staying true to form, Bid was off the pace as Replant led into the clubhouse turn. Flying Paster stayed with Bid toward the back of the field and moved to the outside. Pierce was right where he wanted to be, and Bid was boxed in on the rail. Shoemaker first tried to find room outside Peregrinator, who was hugging the rail in front of Bid, but the colt moved off the rail and blocked any chance of Bid getting through. Shoemaker waited, and when an opening developed between Peregrinator and Flying Paster, he went for it. Eight lengths behind after the first quarter mile, Shoemaker urged Bid on, and the horse slipped between horses with a twenty-two-second quarter mile down the backstretch. He then had to squeeze between Beau's Eagle and Replant. Replant relented, but Beau's Eagle hung on. The two battled neck and neck around the far turn—Bid on the inside of Beau's Eagle—but in the homestretch, Bid turned it up a few notches and extended his lead to win by seven lengths over Peregrinator, who closed for second place in the field of six. So much for Barrera's strategy.

The final time was 1:40²/₅, almost a full second faster than the winning time of Affirmed, who had carried only 130 pounds on the same track. Flying Paster finished fourth; Bid had now beaten him seven times. Bid earned $120,400 for the victory, bringing his earnings to $2.2 million—about $185,000 short of Affirmed's record. It was Shoemaker's 7,841st victory, his 796th stakes win, and his 115th win in a race worth $100,000 or more.

Delp's big concern had always been Bid's health, especially out on the racetrack (even though Bid's one injury had occurred in his stall). Delp was especially careful of other horses around Bid—anything that might spook him, startle him, or cause him to rear up and wrench a knee.

On May 12 he escaped a near disaster. Bid was galloping under exercise rider Robert Smith when the horse became clumsy and bobbled slightly, pulling out of the workout. The sudden jolt unseated Smith, who fell to the ground and left Bid riderless for about a furlong. An alert outrider waited until Bid had drifted off the rail and then came up on his left and brought him to a slow stop before he could cause himself any injury. This time, there was no one to blame. Both Bid and Smith emerged unscathed, but the incident reminded Delp what a valuable commodity he had in Bid, and how important luck is in racing.

On another occasion, a backstretch worker was walking a horse behind Bid and got too close to him. "Don't you know what stop means?" Delp yelled at the boy, stepping in front of his horse and blocking his way until Bid had moved a good distance in front of the horse. He was worried that the horse might clip Bid's heels and injure him.

Delp was overprotective and spared no expense. One racetrack provided three security guards twenty-four hours a day to watch over Bid. Delp himself employed a night watchman who looked after the horse from 7:00 p.m. to 5:00 a.m.—the hours when Delp or Bettis could not be there. The horse always had empty stalls on either side of him to make it quieter, and Delp made sure there was not a filly in the stall behind Bid so the horse would not try to climb over the wall. Whenever Bid left his stall, Delp walked in front of him like the servant of a king, removing any pebbles and rocks in his path so he would not bruise a hoof.

Bid's staff walked him every day for fifty-five minutes, regardless of his workouts. They placed poultices on his front legs to keep his ankles cool; once they removed the poultices and cleaned the legs, he stood in a rubber tub filled with warm water and Epsom salts. Then Hall massaged his lower front legs. Bid was bathed every day, and Bettis would dip a plastic glass into ice water and pour it into a loose blue bandage around the horse's left front ankle.

Delp kept Bid at Hollywood Park, where six horses would challenge him in the Californian Stakes on June 8. As expected, Bid was assigned the highest weight of 130 pounds—not as much as he had carried in the Mervyn LeRoy Handicap, but enough weight to throttle Citation.

Maybe that would be enough, the other trainers and owners thought, to make it a real horse race. Bid's winning streak, now at six races, would have to end sometime, would it not?

At about 7:30 a.m. on race day, Delp sent Bid to the track for his morning jog. Toward the end of the jog, Bid's hind foot nicked the right front hoof, knocking the shoe off. When Delp touched the area around the hoof, Bid didn't seem to be in a lot of pain. "After what happened the morning of the Belmont with the safety pin in his stall, it did go through my mind that maybe we are jinxed. However, I knew it wasn't as serious as the safety pin injury." Delp cut away some of the torn skin and cleaned the area with peroxide and methylate, an antiseptic. This was not an injury to the bottom of the hoof, which takes most of the pounding on the dirt, and since the hoof was not tender, Bid could still race.

The lost horseshoe was a problem, though. Delp called his farrier, Jack Reynolds, who lived in Detroit, and Reynolds agreed to catch the next plane to Los Angeles. A few minutes later, Delp's phone rang; it was Reynolds. The last plane of the day to Los Angeles had just left Detroit. "At that point, I popped another beer and called the Meyerhoffs, who were staying at a hotel in Beverly Hills," Delp said. Tom Meyerhoff chartered a Learjet in Chicago, which picked up the farrier in Detroit and began the flight to Los Angeles. There was one problem. High winds forced them to land in Denver, and the airport was preventing all planes from taking off. Once the jet had been cleared for takeoff, Delp arranged for the Inglewood chief of police to meet Reynolds at the airport and escort him to the track.

But time was running out and Delp had to find another farrier. He walked Bid over to the saddling enclosure; Bid's foot was wrapped in cotton so he would not step on anything. Delp, as usual, flicked stones and pebbles out of his way. When they got to the saddling enclosure, the farrier there took a nail, hammer, and shoe and prepared to put the shoe on Bid. According to Delp, the farrier was "shakin' like a leaf." Delp turned around and walked out, unable to watch. The nervous farrier put on the shoe.

On the way to the post, Delp felt a hand on his shoulder; it was Jack Reynolds. Tom Meyerhoff called the incident the $10,000 horseshoe, based on the cost of the Learjet.

In the race, Bid got off to a good start, for a change. He stalked the leaders, Bolger and Replant, down the backstretch. Then, entering the far turn, he turned on the gas and easily passed the leaders; by the home-stretch, he was six lengths ahead of Paint King. Shoemaker just sat on Bid, not asking for any speed, and Bid's final margin of victory was four and a quarter lengths over Paint King. Caro Bambino finished third, another three and a quarter lengths back.

In winning his seventh straight race, Bid had covered the mile and an eighth in 1:45⁴/₅, well below the track record that had been set in 1964 and just two-fifths of a second slower than the world record set by Secretariat. If Shoemaker had urged Bid during the homestretch at any point, it could have been another world record for Bid. The $184,450 purse gave him almost $2.4 million in career earnings, passing Affirmed on the all-time earnings list. He was now the richest Thoroughbred in history.

And what about the last-minute shoe? Delp said it slipped a little during the race but did no damage. "There was no question in my mind that he was going to break a track record," Delp said. "This horse loves to run through the stretch. We're not looking for world records, we're look-ing for wins every time out and a healthy horse."

Shoemaker finally stopped equivocating and proclaimed Bid "the best horse I've ever ridden."

Hollywood Park executives wanted Bid to run in the Hollywood Gold Cup Handicap on June 22, but Delp refused, citing the hard track at Hollywood Park. "Your track is showin' wear and tear on my horse," he said. "I've got to get him out of here." So Bid went to Chicago to race in the Washington Park Stakes (formerly known as the Washington Park Handicap) at Arlington Park on July 19. Arlington Park officials wanted Bid so badly that they were willing to do anything to get him there. Knowing that a handicap might scare off Delp and company, offi-cials dropped the handicap provision for only the second time in fifty-two runnings of the race. They also added a provision that if the winner of a Triple Crown race ran in the stakes, the purse would double from $125,000 to $250,000. That was enough to convince the Meyerhoffs to come.

Bid left California after going undefeated at two racetracks. Columnist John Hall, who had criticized Delp when Bid first arrived in California for the winter, had been converted to a Bid—and Bud—fan. He proclaimed Delp a great trainer for keeping Bid at a sustained peak through the winter and spring. Bid, he wrote, "has won at all sorts of distances on all types of tracks. He set Santa Anita's track record for seven furlongs, set a world record for a mile and one quarter in the Strub Stakes, and splashed through the slop to win the Big Cap in a monsoon. . . .The Bid goes right to the top of my all-time list. I put three in a super class above all else—Citation, Spectacular Bid, and Affirmed. The rest can eat cake." That was quite a turnaround from the cynic Hall had been at the beginning of the Santa Anita season. Hall even framed a letter Delp had written to him in response to one of his stories. Delp had signed it, "Bud and Bid."

When Bid arrived in Chicago, he was treated to bundles of rye straw, bottled drinking water, empty stalls on either side, and twenty-four-hour security. Delp was given a camper next to Bid's barn, complete with a cook and a bartender, and a room at the hotel next to the track. Bid would be carrying 130 pounds again, but the crowd did not care and sent him off at odds of 1 to 20. Most of the other trainers admitted they were competing for second- and third-prize money. Bid prepped for the race on Thursday, running a half mile in forty-six seconds.

The weather was uncooperative again. The heat was unbearable in Chicago, and the forecast called for rain on the day of the race. Delp planned to scratch Bid if the track was sloppy. "I'm not going to do anything to jeopardize this horse," he said. "This horse will not be abused; I'll promise you that. If he's ever not at his dead-level best, he'll be retired immediately. He's gonna leave me just like he came to me—kicking and playing." When race day came, however, there was only a sprinkle of rain—just enough to cool things down to a bearable eighty-four degrees. Delp looked over the track and said, "Damascus,[3] kiss your track record goodbye."

Five horses raced against Bid. Hold Your Tricks, sharing the second-highest weight at a modest 119 pounds, held a two-length lead down the backstretch, with Bid settling for fourth place. Shoemaker swung Bid to the outside—just as Franklin would have done—and as the pack approached the far turn, Bid felt the need to make his move, without any prodding from Shoemaker. He drew even with Hold Your Tricks, then sped away with Shoemaker hand-riding him. He won by a remarkable ten lengths.

Damascus's record, shared with Jatski, had been replaced by a new track record, Bid's seventh. His time was 1:46¹/₅ over one and one-eighth miles. According to Shoemaker, Delp wanted him to let Bid run. "And he did. He likes to run. You don't want to cramp his style. At the end, he was tired. It was hot today, and he hadn't raced in several weeks." It was his eighth win in a row.

Dan Farley of the *Thoroughbred Record* said the performance "further confirmed Spectacular Bid's status as one of the best American-breds ever and certainly the best—by many lengths—we have to offer this season."

Racecourses wanted Bid to run at their tracks to attract big crowds. Belmont Park announced that Bid was among seventeen horses invited to compete in the $300,000 Marlboro Cup on September 6. Monmouth Park printed posters announcing that Bid would race in the $250,000 Haskell Handicap on August 16. It was as if the circus were coming to town.

The Haskell was a handicap, and Delp pressured the racing secretary to keep Bid's weight down or else his horse would not run. This put officials in a quandary: they longed to have Bid run at their track, but they also wanted to follow the handicapping rules and equalize the race so there would be some competition. Delp won. Bid was assigned 132 pounds, equal to his career high. Andrew Beyer said that after his last romp under that weight, it should have been 135 or even 140 pounds. "If Bid had won under 135 in New Jersey, [New York Racing Association] secretary Lenny Hale would have been obliged to make him carry 137 or 138 [in the Marlboro Cup]."

It was a shrewd move; Delp and the Meyerhoffs were thinking ahead. But Bid's weight of 132 pounds (as much as Affirmed had ever carried) encouraged six other horses to enter the Haskell, and Bid was conceding 15 to 22 pounds to them. Facing Bid for the first time was the impressive filly Glorious Song, who had won six of nine starts and earned more than $400,000 that year. The Haskell was held at Monmouth Park, the site of Bid's first loss—his romp in the mud at the Tyro Stakes as a two-year-old.

Starting as the 1 to 9 favorite in the Haskell Handicap on August 16, Bid came out of the gate slowly again. He was seventh after a quarter mile and had moved up to just sixth after a half mile. Steelwood and Boyne Valley battled for the lead, with The Cool Virginian third and Glorious Song fifth. Fans grew nervous when Bid did not make his typical move on the backstretch. But Shoemaker, remaining patient, had his eye on the filly, and when she made her move heading into the turn, Spectacular Bid went with her, needing no encouragement from his jockey. Bid knew she was the one to beat. Around the turn, Steelwood, Boyne Valley, and Tunerup were leading, with Glorious Song coming up between horses and Bid following her on the outside. Glorious Song emerged from the turn as the leader, with Bid on her heels, four horses wide. When he tried to pass her, she held him off, battling with him down the stretch. But Bid was not to be denied; it took several whips from Shoemaker to get him to pull away at the finish to win by one and three-quarters lengths. It had been a hard-fought race, given Bid's recent victories, but he had once again found that extra gear and defeated a challenger.

Or had it been a hard-fought race? Conspiracy theorists thought Delp was doing the same thing he had done in the San Fernando Stakes: making it seem that the race was closer than it actually was, in the hope that the racing secretaries for the Marlboro would think the weight was affecting the horse and take it easy on Bid. If he had blown the competition away, 132 pounds would not be enough. But if he struggled. . . .

In the winner's circle, Delp pointed a finger at Monmouth racing secretary Kenny Lenox and said, "I told you. I told you that weight spread would make him go all out today." He added, "That filly made him run. She's a hell of a horse to be giving fifteen pounds to—the best filly in the country, if you ask me." And with that, the performance was over; the media had gotten the sound bite he wanted them to have.

The war of words continued. Delp noted that the great Swaps had never carried more than 130 pounds, and Secretariat had carried 119 pounds in the Whitney Handicap as a three-year-old, when he was upset by a horse named Onion. "The spread in these handicaps is what worries

me so much. But I'd carry 140 in the Marlboro if the others tote 137."
He was sounding more like Laz Barrera every day.

New York Racing Association (NYRA) racing secretary Lenny Hale ignored Delp, assigning Bid 136 pounds for the Marlboro Cup—one more than he had given Affirmed the previous year, twelve more than Secretariat, and eight more than Seattle Slew. The next highest weight was given to a horse called Winter's Tale, the recent winner of the Suburban Handicap, at 123 pounds. Bid was carrying 4 pounds more than he had ever carried and 13 pounds more than the next closest horse. Dr. Patches, one of the nation's top sprinters, was assigned 114 pounds—a difference of 22 pounds.

While Andrew Beyer admitted that it was a lot to carry, it was a weight worthy of a champion. "Hale is paying Spectacular Bid a supreme compliment, but it is the sort of compliment that trainers and owners rarely appreciate," he wrote. Beyer urged Delp and Meyerhoff to accept the weight assignment. "If either of the men possesses an iota of sportsmanship, Spectacular Bid will run at Belmont on Saturday. The colt has sailed through this season without a serious challenge; there is not a Thoroughbred in America remotely in his class. The only thing left to challenge him is weight, and if Bid can successfully carry 136 pounds, he will join a very select circle of horses."

On Wednesday, Delp said he was training Bid and intended to enter him in the race. But Russ Harris of the *New York Daily News* did not believe it. "Think about it. Why should Spectacular Bid pack 136 pounds in the Marlboro and give eighteen pounds to the three-year-old Jaklin Klugman? Delp can wait for the $200,000 Woodward Stakes on September 20 when Bid will carry only 126 pounds, the same impost as the older horses, against 120 for the three-year-olds." Harris pointed out that Kelso and Forego were geldings, meaning that they had no stud careers to jeopardize, and they had raced as older horses and could handle the tougher weight assignments. Radiographic studies of the acquisition of bone mineral in horses from age one day to twenty-seven years have shown that they do not achieve maximum bone mineral content until they are six years old. And that is what trainers worry about: the effect of weight on those fragile leg bones.

On Thursday, Delp proved Harris right. He did not show up at

Thursday's press breakfast, when post positions were drawn for the Marlboro Cup. He withdrew Bid from the race, saying the weight was too punitive. He also berated racing secretary Lenny Hale, calling him incompetent. "Lenny Hale either has too much pressure on him or he doesn't know how to handicap a race properly," Delp said. "Hell, weight stops freight trains. Two weeks later, it's equal weights [in the Woodward Stakes, a weight-for-age race]. What am I, stupid?" Several years later, Hale responded to Delp's accusations. "Mr. Delp said Bid was the greatest horse to ever look through a bridle," he said. "I asked him to prove it, and he came up short."

The action stunned and angered the New York racing establishment. At the press breakfast, Hale was treated to a hero's welcome by the New York media and trainers, who could not resist taking shots at Delp. Trainer P. G. Johnson suggested that Delp would not run Bid at 136 pounds because he wanted to start him in a handicap at the Meadowlands, and the New Jersey secretaries might find it hard to justify giving Bid 119 or 120 pounds. It was a slap at Monmouth racing secretary Bob Kulina, who had given Bid 132 pounds for the Haskell—more than Secretariat, Citation, or Affirmed had ever carried. Some thought that if Bid had been given 134 pounds at the Haskell, Hale's jump to 136 would not have seemed so punitive.

Doug Worswick, trainer of 10 to 1 shot Tanthem, claimed that after Hale issued his weights on Monday morning, Worswick knew that Bid would not run in the Marlboro. Bill Shoemaker's agent had confirmed at 3:00 p.m. that same day that Shoemaker would ride Tanthem in the Marlboro because Bid was out of the race. "Yet for the next three days, Delp publicly was vacillating, just so he could have the satisfaction of pulling the rug from under the Marlboro Cup at the last possible moment," wrote Andrew Beyer. Beyer then took a slap at Delp's Maryland claiming background. "Despite the two years he has spent with Spectacular Bid in the upper echelon of the sport, Delp has not advanced too far from his bush league racing origins."

The editors of *Blood-Horse* commented that Bid had nothing to lose and everything to gain by racing in the Marlboro. "For almost two years now, trainer Buddy Delp has been saying Spectacular Bid was the greatest horse that ever looked through a bridle, and then he denied it, impliedly conceding the four-year-old might not be up to carrying 136 pounds nine furlongs, bypassing the race." They cited many great horses that had carried equal or more weight, including Forego three times and Kelso, Discovery, and Bold Ruler twice. Man o' War, Forego, Discovery, Exterminator (another gelding), and Whisk Broom II carried 138 pounds or more, and Discovery even carried 143 pounds for one and three-sixteenths miles.

Delp took another slap at Lenny Hale, saying that he was under too much pressure. Instead of Hale assigning the weights, Delp suggested having four racing secretaries assign weights and then taking the average of the four to come up with a fair weight. It did not happen.

Without Bid in the race, Winter's Tale took the Marlboro Cup by four and a half lengths over Glorious Song. Winter's Tale's trainer, Mack Miller, said he thought the weights were fair. Had Bid run and won, he would have been the first multiple winner of the Marlboro Cup.

Next it was on to the Woodward Stakes, the race Bid had missed the previous year because of a virus. The challengers were dwindling, since they were simply racing for second- and third-place money. Talk started of a walkover, a one-horse race in which there were no challengers. "[A walkover] would symbolize in the most tangible form they know of that Spectacular Bid is truly the greatest horse of modern times," wrote Barry Irwin of the *Thoroughbred Record*. Since it was not a handicap, Bid would be carrying only 126 pounds. That scared away a lot of the competition. Even Winter's Tale was scratched after X-rays revealed a chip in the bone above the knee. Only two other horses were entered—Temperance Hill, winner of the 1980 Belmont Stakes and Travers Stakes, and sprinter Dr. Patches. Owners of both horses said they would run their horses if the NYRA wanted them to, but curiously, they were not asked to run. After meeting with NYRA officials, the owners of Dr. Patches and Temperance Hill scratched their horses.

This meant that Bid would run the Woodward by himself. It would be the first walkover since 1949, when Coaltown had gone to the starting gate alone at the Havre de Grace Racetrack. According to Brian Landman of the *Tampa Bay Times,* it was racing's greatest gesture of respect.

Most of the time, some other horse would run in the race just to collect the 20 percent of the purse awarded to the second-place finisher. But not this time.

Bid had come close to a walkover before. In February, he had been the only horse entered in the San Antonio Stakes at Santa Anita—all other horses had withdrawn. So Delp and the Meyerhoffs withdrew Spectacular Bid as well. Delp then told Laz Barrera, trainer of Valdez, "You don't have to hide your horse now. You can go ahead and run him." That just gave Barrera one more reason to dislike Delp.

In hearing about the Woodward walkover, the Meyerhoffs also got a surprise announcement: Since there were no other horses in the race, officials had the option of giving the winner only half the guaranteed purse, plus the nomination fees, but not the entry money. Spectacular Bid would get $73,000 for winning the race, but that was all. He also had to make a real effort; he couldn't just canter around the racetrack for a mile and a quarter. The Meyerhoffs were furious with the decision and talked of racing under protest or not racing him at all. Delp was livid. He accused NYRA officials of chasing Dr. Patches and Temperence Hill away from the race to repay him for withdrawing from the Marlboro Cup. Curiously, Hale would not say whether that was true. "We felt like the New Yorkers got together and they decided that they were going to do this to us," Tom Meyerhoff said. There was still some bad blood between the two camps, dating from the feud between Franklin and Cordero, the safety pin incident at the Belmont, and the weight assignments for the Marlboro Cup.

In the end, Bid showed up and walked onto the track alone, a post parade of one, with boos and catcalls still lingering over Delp's decision to withdraw from the Marlboro. "Everybody else was at the Marlboro, where were you?" one person asked. Bid was not used to the boos; he had not heard any since the Belmont Stakes. It was unfair, but New York fans have little sympathy for anyone, much less a horse.

Bid was loaded into the starting gate—alone—and when the bell clanged, he took off by himself. He needed no challengers to run a good race; all he needed was his love of running, and he ran like an animal uncaged. Shoemaker had to hold him back to prevent him from wasting too much energy. He galloped the one and a quarter miles under

Spectacular Bid, with Bill Shoemaker aboard, racing by himself in the Woodward Stakes walkover. (Bob Coglianese)

strong restraint in an impressive 2:02²/₅—the same time in which he had finished the Kentucky Derby. It was a good exercise and tune-up for his next start, the Jockey Club Gold Cup on October 4. Bid earned his $73,000—half of what he would have earned if just one other horse had run. His winning streak was at ten. He remained unbeaten during 1980.

Despite the bitter feelings associated with the race, Delp had always dreamed of seeing Bid in a walkover, and it finally came true. He announced that Bid might race two more times after the Jockey Club Gold Cup: the Meadowlands Cup on October 16, and the Washington, DC International Stakes, a grass race at Laurel Park on November 8.

Seven other challengers entered the Jockey Club Gold Cup, including turf great John Henry, Temperence Hill, and Bid's old foe Instrument Landing. "My only instructions to Shoemaker will be to win the race.

We're not looking to set any track records," Delp said. Bid appeared ready to take the Gold Cup denied him the previous year by his rival Affirmed. If he did that, the surpassing of Affirmed would be complete.

However, on the morning of the Gold Cup, bad luck reared its head. Delp and veterinarian Alex Harthill discovered something troubling. Spectacular Bid was hurt.

For two years, Delp had been keeping a secret from horse racing fans: Bid had a bad foot. Throughout his two-year-old campaign, he had suffered from a swollen left ankle. They had watched the ankle closely after every race, checking for any heat that would signify something more serious. But it was always cool to the touch, and Bid never came up lame during his three-year-old campaign. However, the morning after Bid had won the Malibu Stakes at Santa Anita on January 5, 1980, Delp noticed that the horse's left ankle was swollen again. Delp had the ankle X-rayed with a portable X-ray machine, and the images came back negative. With a little rest and treatment, the swelling subsided, and he won the San Fernando Stakes two weeks later. "It is conceivable that the injury . . . could have been there after the Malibu," Delp said. "We had him X-rayed periodically throughout the season and had no cause to be concerned."

Delp treated Bid with Butazolidin, an anti-inflammatory drug, and they encountered no more problems with the ankle. In August, however, Dr. Harthill took X-rays with a more sophisticated machine at the Delaware Veterinary Clinic and found a sliver of bone separated from the bottom of the inside sesamoid in the left foreleg. While not serious, it was something they needed to monitor, and Delp occasionally touched the leg and flexed the muscles in that area to see whether Bid experienced any pain.

The day before the Jockey Club Gold Cup, Delp gave Bid a tough workout, and the ankle swelled again. Since this had happened before, Delp was not overly concerned, but he still checked for heat and tenderness. There was none. Dr. Harthill took new X-rays and found a new chip in the sesamoid region. Although Bid could still race, the situation was becoming more complicated. There was a greater risk of further injury with this second chip.

Then the whole situation became messy. Rumors were flying around the barns that Harthill was with Delp, which always meant that something interesting was happening. The morning of the Gold Cup, Delp had Bid gallop a little. He then put Bid's legs in ice to tighten the tendons and reduce any swelling. At 9:00 that morning, Dr. Manuel Gilman, the NYRA veterinarian, came by to examine Bid as part of the prerace routine. A NYRA vet needed to examine each horse and declare it physically sound to race. The vet would check the legs, feeling for any heat; take the horse's temperature and pulse; and occasionally ask that the horse be jogged. Bid's legs were in a tub of ice, and Delp refused to take them out, so there would be no examination. Gilman left but promised to return in an hour to complete the exam. "I'll come back when these people have their act together," he said in front of a barn full of reporters. Once Gilman left, Delp instructed Mo Hall and Charlie Bettis that if he was not there when the vet returned, the only thing they should allow Gilman to examine was the identification tattoo inside Bid's lower lip.

When Gilman came back, Bid was no longer in the tub. His left leg was not bandaged, but the right one was. Gilman asked Hall to remove the bandage so he could examine the leg; Hall and Bettis refused. Gilman demanded to speak to Delp, who told Gilman via phone that they would remove the bandages, but he was not to touch the horse, flex the muscles, or take Bid from the stall. Gilman left again, angry. "I'll go to the stewards and tell them that I tried to do my job twice and was refused. After that, I don't know what will happen," he said.

The stewards confirmed that Bid needed a proper examination before he could run in the Gold Cup. Later that day, when Gilman examined the latest X-rays of Bid's ankle, he saw the bone chips. That made a jog almost mandatory, and when Gilman asked to see the horse jog, he was denied because, he was told, Bid had just eaten, and jogging after eating can cause colic.

A steward warned Delp that Bid risked being scratched for failure to cooperate with the NYRA veterinarian's examination. Delp promised a jog for Gilman when he returned to the barn at 4:00 that afternoon, only two hours before post time. When Delp arrived shortly before four, he conducted his regular exam of the left foreleg and flexed it. Bid winced. That was all Delp needed to see.

He took the Meyerhoffs into the tack room and recommended that Bid be scratched—and retired. The Meyerhoffs agreed. "He was ninety-eight percent perfect, but you don't take chances with a $22 million horse," Delp said. "I'm not going to send him out on the racetrack when he's not one hundred percent. It's as simple as that."

"There was a very fine line," said Dr. Harthill. "He probably could have run and won easily, but there was no point taking a chance."

At 4:00, when the NYRA chairman and president showed up at Delp's barn to talk about his refusal to let Gilman conduct his examination, they were told that Spectacular Bid had been scratched and was retired. "So the era ended when a band of Marylanders refused to back down to New York racing," wrote Dale Austin of the *Baltimore Sun*. "Both sides are probably glad it has come to an end."

Marshall Cassidy, the track announcer, told the crowd of 24,035 that Bid had been scratched, and the spectators, unaware of the drama that had been unfolding for hours, responded with boos. In Bid's absence, 1980 Belmont Stakes winner Temperence Hill cemented his chances of capturing Three-Year-Old Male Championship honors, winning the race by five and a half lengths over the legendary turf horse John Henry. "I do know one thing," said Joe Cantey, Temperence Hill's trainer. "I'm glad Bid wasn't in there."

The next day, several news sources reported Harthill's assertion that X-rays showed bone chips in Bid's ankle. Delp, however, called the report a lie. His explanation to reporters was that the colt had been scratched because he was not "one hundred percent fit." The *Daily Racing Form*'s columnist Herb Goldstein hammered Delp and Meyerhoff, asking: If Spectacular Bid had been in such poor condition, why wasn't he scratched earlier in the day? Why did it take three visits from a vet and a call to racing stewards to get the horse examined? "Spectacular Bid has been class personified in the Thoroughbred. Would that the same could be said about his owners and trainer," Goldstein wrote.

The real story was not about deception or trickery, although Delp's denials earlier in the day could have been replaced by a more honest assessment, such as, "His ankle is bothering him a bit. We'll see how it goes." Russ Harris wrote that some NYRA officials felt that Delp and Meyerhoff were still angry at them for reasons dating to the Belmont and chose the day of the Jockey Club Gold Cup to "give them the shaft." Delp denied it, and NYRA chairman Ogden Mills Phipps said he did not believe it either. Tom Meyerhoff believed that it was part of the ongo-

ing feud between Delp and NYRA officials. "I know that he was not getting along with Dr. Gilman or Lenny Hale, and it had gotten personal,"
he said. "I do know that Bud said he'd scratch him before he'd let [Gil-
man] look at him. And we did scratch. . . . I do know that there was some
ill will between them."

Dan Farley of the *Thoroughbred Record* praised Delp's team for their
cautious approach to Bid's health. He wrote that the horse racing community had "no real reason to ponder the motives of those who played
major parts in Bid's last day at the racetrack . . . if Bid were not one hundred percent, he should not have been asked to do what he never before
had done."

With that in mind, Delp's outrage at Bid being asked to carry 136
pounds on a chronically injured leg in the Marlboro Cup did not seem so
unsportsmanlike. His routine of icing the horse's legs, applying liniment
and bandages, and massaging the legs did not seem like overdoing it. His
refusal to race Bid on Hollywood Park's hard surface did not seem rude.
He seemed like a trainer who was watching out for his horse—a horse
whose leg was not 100 percent and could have sustained further damage. Delp had devoted himself to Spectacular Bid for three years, turning over much of the supervision of the rest of his stable to his brother.
He had watched the colt's every move.

On Thursday, October 16, 1980, Spectacular Bid and the great harness
racer Niatross took one last trip around the track at the Meadowlands—
the site of two of Bid's wins. The crowd of 21,000 applauded the two
champions, the New Yorkers apparently forgetting that they had booed
Bid in his walkover several weeks earlier. The two horses were announced
as the first inductees into the Meadowlands Hall of Fame.

Spectacular Bid's record at retirement stood at twenty-six wins in
thirty races, with one second and one third. At 87 percent, it was the
highest winning percentage among the twenty-five richest colts in Thoroughbred history, better than even Secretariat and Affirmed. In 1982 he
was inducted into the National Museum of Racing and Hall of Fame.
Bid raced at fifteen different racetracks in nine different states, winning
at all of them. He won thirteen Grade 1 stakes; he broke seven track
records and equaled another. He still holds the world record for a mile

and a quarter. His walkover in the Woodward Stakes was the last one in an American race to date.

Spectacular Bid was named champion at ages two, three, and four; he carried 130 pounds or more five times and won every time; he had winning streaks of twelve stakes races in a row and ten races in a row, including a perfect nine-for-nine record as a four-year-old (while he was having trouble with his left ankle). He won setting the pace, and he won coming from off the pace. Only two horses—Coastal and Golden Act—passed him in the homestretch and stayed there, and that was when he was hurt. Now *that* is spectacular.

Epilogue

"RACING REALLY NEEDS a superstar, like any other sport," Bud Delp told a reporter in 1980. "The exposure that it's getting this year with Bid, and last year with Bid, I think is the greatest thing that ever happened to horse racing. . . . It's a sport. We need new people. We need new faces and we need exposure and the only way you're going to get exposure is to have a superstar. It's unfortunate that we don't have one every year."

At the 1980 Eclipse Awards, Spectacular Bid won Horse of the Year, and Bud Delp won Trainer of the Year. Owner of the Year, however, went to Mr. and Mrs. Bertram Firestone, owners of the filly Genuine Risk, who had won the 1980 Kentucky Derby.[1] (They were also the owners of General Assembly.) In his typical rebellious fashion, Delp boycotted the awards dinner because he believed the Meyerhoffs had been "slighted, snubbed, even maligned." "How in the world is it possible for me to be Trainer of the Year if Spectacular Bid didn't run?" he asked. "And why did he run? The Meyerhoffs decided to race him as a four-year-old." Delp called the decision one of the greatest sporting gestures ever made in horse racing. "They didn't do it for the money; they did it for the glory of seeing the horse run," he said.

The Meyerhoffs could have retired Bid at the end of his three-year-old campaign and made a handsome profit from syndication. But they took a chance, knowing that Bid could get injured, and continued to run him for another year. Insurance premiums for the year totaled $1.7 million—almost $600,000 more than the horse made in 1980, and that did not take in account the cost of travel, training, and security. "To some horsemen, this was a needless, dangerous risk," wrote Billy Reed of the *Louisville Courier-Journal.* "Nevertheless, the Meyerhoffs are sports people who wanted to give something back to the game."

Delp said the Meyerhoffs' lack of connections had cost them the award. Although the Firestones were from Virginia, they were part of the racing establishment, having owned several racetracks in Florida. The voters took that into consideration, especially the writers. Three groups of people voted for the Eclipse Awards: staffers of the *Daily Racing Form,* members of the National Turf Writers Association, and racing secretaries from tracks associated with the Thoroughbred Racing Association. The writers sided with the Firestones, the racing secretaries with the Meyerhoffs.

Delp blamed the article by New York–based *Daily Racing Form* writer Herb Goldstein for swaying voters. Goldstein had objected to team Bid scratching the horse on the day of the Jockey Club Gold Cup. He claimed racing had suffered when Delp and the Meyerhoffs misled NYRA officials about Bid's true condition. "There can be little doubt that Spectacular Bid's connections sought to delude the people here who are specifically charged with guarding the integrity of the sport," he wrote. "There are those connected with racing who only take from the sport and believe they have no obligation to it." It was damning in its tone and in its allegations against the Meyerhoffs.

Delp continued to lash out at Goldstein. "The Meyerhoffs went through hell up there [New York] and I can't believe it would have happened if they were from the New York establishment," Delp said. "What difference does it make if they're from Maryland? New York is not the only place where there's racing and thank God for that." Bob Maisel of the *Baltimore Sun* agreed with Delp, blaming the "New York backlash" for the Meyerhoffs' failure to win. "I don't think a lot of people forgave the Meyerhoffs for taking the edge off the New York fall series," he wrote. "There is nothing like a New Yorker scorned. It probably cost the Meyerhoffs in the voting."

Dale Austin, also of the *Sun,* had written back in October, "So when the rumor spread Friday that Bid was injured and would scratch out of the Jockey Club Gold Cup, you could see the glee in the chauvinistic New Yorkers. Few of those who commented on it expressed remorse over the upstart Marylanders who were taking all the races and the money."

✍

In November 1980 Spectacular Bid settled into his new home at Claiborne Farm. He was examined by a veterinarian, had his shoes removed, and was given a tranquilizer to calm him down. He was then released into a two-acre paddock with some thirty-five people watching him to make sure he did not hurt himself. But there was no need for that. He paraded around the paddock like a show horse, with his tail up in the air; he ran up to the fence and greeted Secretariat, who was curious about this newcomer. He was put in Round Table's old stall, right across the shed row from Secretariat.

Bid passed his fertility tests with flying colors and successfully bred his first mare, a brown- and white-spotted half-bred nurse mare, on December 1. He was bred to forty mares his first season, starting in mid-February.

The Meyerhoffs threw a black-tie party for Spectacular Bid in November. They invited 100 guests and served filet mignon, caviar, escargot, and baby lamb chops. During the festivities, Bill Shoemaker grabbed the microphone and, in uncharacteristic fashion, railed against the establishment. He called Delp the best trainer in the country and said he had never ridden for a "classier guy" than Meyerhoff. "Some of the New York sportswriters don't like Harry Meyerhoff," he said. "Screw 'em."

Bid was also remembered at Gulfstream Park in January 1981 with "A Salute to Bid." Park officials enshrined Bid in its Garden of Champions and unveiled a bronze plaque in his honor. The Meyerhoffs, Bud Delp, and Ron Franklin spoke about the horse to the thousands in attendance, which included Kentucky establishment types such as Leslie Combs, New Yorker Pat Debary, and Harold Snowden, a board member at Hialeah Park, where the Meyerhoffs had been snubbed at the Flamingo Ball. "At Gulfstream, they still claim that the 1979 Florida Derby was the most outstanding individual effort in the career of history's all-time leading equine money winner," wrote Paul Moran of the *Fort Lauderdale News*. "It was, admittedly, a great effort forged out of necessity by the colt. . . . Spectacular Bid won that Florida Derby by more than four lengths, converted many of the skeptics and went on to fashion a career that is now etched in history."

Unfortunately, Bid's record as a sire did not compare with his racing career. He started well, siring twenty-eight stakes winners from his first four crops of foals—an outstanding 16 percent of winners. One of his colts from that first crop, Spectacular Love, won the 1984 Futurity Stakes over Chief's Crown, who placed in every Triple Crown race the next year. But Spectacular Love did little else, finishing eighth that year in the Breeders' Cup Juvenile to Chief's Crown. He finished with four wins, one place, and one show in nine starts, earning only $179,500. In 1984 Bid had another stakes winner, and that was enough for the syndicate to raise his stud fee from $150,000 to $225,000. But in 1985 only three of his offspring won graded or group stakes, with Spectacular Joke winning the Prix Maurice de Gheest and the Prix du Palais Royal in France.

Looking at the yearling sales, Bid's first crop of foals sold for an average of $708,182. By 1986, they were averaging only $141,000. As a result, his stud fee plunged to $80,000 for 1986. Most of his sons and daughters needed time to develop—something that breeders and buyers had little patience for.

By 1991, Bid's fee had fallen to $15,000, and the average price for his yearlings fell to $21,875. Sensing that competition from the other stallions at Claiborne was dropping his fee, Harry Meyerhoff suggested moving Bid to Milfer Farm in Unadilla, New York. Meyerhoff had been discussing the idea with Milfer's owner, Jonathan H. F. Davis, who was looking for a horse to boost the New York breeding scene. The previous year, Tom Meyerhoff had toured the facility, and he agreed that it was the right place for Bid. Seth Hancock did not oppose the idea, and when the shareholders were polled, 87 percent approved of the move—more than the 75 percent needed.

The move did not help Bid's progeny or his stud fee. Only two of his forty-four stakes winners were bred at Milfer; he closed out his career standing for a paltry $3,500. He did have several successful colts and fillies, but they were not the kind of horses people read about in the news. Lotus Pool, born in 1987, raced forty-three times, mainly in Europe, winning only eleven races but earning $694,543. Lay Down, born in 1984, earned $593,423, even though he won only eleven of twenty-nine starts. In total, Bid produced 253 winners and 47 stakes winners.

"Bid was a freak," Delp said. "But he had a twin in his bottom line, and it caught up to him. All we got from him was a bunch of soft-boned horses who would pop a splint[2] on you if you sent them out for a gallop." But a review of Bid's progeny shows that twenty-six of his offspring raced more than forty-five times, including Illustrious Bidder, who raced ninety-nine times but won only fourteen races. It seems like many were hardy but not fast.

Looking back, Seth Hancock of Claiborne Farm said he would not have syndicated the colt today. "I've learned that pedigree really does matter; it's a rare horse who can overcome a weak pedigree," he admitted. Bid overcame his pedigree and became one great horse in a line of average horses both before and after him.

"People go out and spend millions of dollars on breeding, and many times they don't come up with much," said Walter Kelley, trainer at Elmendorf Farm, where Spectacular Bid's second dam, Stop on Red, was born. "Never in a million years would I have thought Stop on Red would be the second dam of a horse like Spectacular Bid. Here's a filly that if I could have given her away, I would have. It goes to show you, that if you get lucky enough to put the right genes together, anything can happen. With Spectacular Bid, there must have been some genes somewhere that just clicked."

The Meyerhoffs continued to race, but no horse ever came close to achieving the fame and success of Bid. Harry and Teresa divorced in 1992, leaving the horse business to Harry and Tom. They had a few successes after Bid. They bought Silent King as a yearling for $22,000 and put the now fifty-two-year-old Shoemaker on him in 1984. He rallied from twenty-one lengths behind to finish second in the Blue Grass Stakes; however, he managed only a ninth-place finish in the Kentucky Derby and a seventh-place finish in the Belmont Stakes. Silent King won $255,376 for the Meyerhoffs. Calipha, a gray filly from the Bold Ruler line, won the $200,000 Black-Eyed Susan Stakes for them in 1994 and earned $378,739 over her career.

Besides Spectacular Bid, the best horse Delp trained for the Meyerhoffs was Dispersal, who was considered a 1989 Kentucky Derby favorite after winning the Louisiana Derby. He was leading in the Blue Grass Stakes until he injured his shins and badly bumped the eventual winner, Western Playboy. He was withdrawn from the Triple Crown races, which led to the unforgettable stretch runs between Sunday Silence and Easy Goer. Dispersal came back, though, finishing second in the 1989 American Derby and third in the Breeders' Cup Sprint. In 1990 Dispersal ran even better, winning six of eight races that year, and he was considered the favorite for the Breeders' Cup Classic. However, the front-running horse drew the outside position, requiring him to run an extra distance to get to the rail and take the lead, and he finished a disappointing twelfth. Dispersal's career record was twelve wins, three seconds, and two thirds in twenty-two starts; his earnings topped $1.1 million.

Overall, thirty-five years of shopping had given Harry Meyerhoff 220 yearlings. With Delp's help, twenty won stakes races, and three became millionaires. Only seven never started.

In 2016, at age eighty-six, Harry Meyerhoff died of a stroke. Four days later, one of his horses, Marengo Road, won the $75,000 Miracle Wood Stakes at Laurel. "Racing really lost a hero," said Michael Trombetta, Marengo Road's trainer. "He was a wonderful man."

"It was a once-in-a-lifetime feeling," said Tom Meyerhoff of Spectacular Bid's whirlwind campaign. "I had only been involved [in horse racing] for four years then, my dad had been involved for fifteen years, but I don't think he had ever won more than a $50,000 stakes before. This was huge, and we've had nothing like it ever since." Tom continues to buy and race horses.

❧

After his success with Spectacular Bid, Delp went back to claiming horses, spending summers in Chicago and winters in Louisiana before moving back to Maryland in the early 1990s. "Delp started with horses like that because he had to, but he's never left them because he doesn't want to," wrote Maryjean Wall of the *Lexington Herald-Leader*.

In 2000 Robert Meyerhoff, Harry's brother, asked Delp to take over his stable. One colt named Include won four straight starts as a three-year-old. The next year, Include was almost unbeatable; he finished in the money in eight of nine races, won the New Orleans Handicap, and took the $750,000 Pimlico Special in a thrilling stretch run against Albert the Great, the nation's third-ranked horse at the time. The race was decided in the final strides. "I don't know about that tight finish," Delp said. "Spectacular Bid never did that to me." Include finished his four-year-old season as Maryland's Champion Older Male and Horse of the Year; he retired at age five with ten victories in twenty starts and winnings of more than $1.6 million.

For all his contributions to the sport and his excellent handling of Spectacular Bid through the 1978–1980 seasons, Delp was elected into the National Museum of Racing's Hall of Fame in 2002. He had trained 68 stakes winners and saddled 3,674 winners for nearly $41 million in earnings. Delp estimated that two-thirds of those wins had been from claimers, befitting a trainer who had constantly been reminded that he was not part of the establishment. "My dad wasn't a very emotional person, but when he found out he was inducted into the Hall of Fame, I remember the first thing he did was tear up," said Cleve Delp, his youngest son. "He said, 'This was something they can't take away from me.'" The Hall of Fame plaque hung in his office for years. It represented the recognition he so deeply needed, a validation of a job well done after years of hard work in the shadows of more well-known trainers—except for those three years when he had basked in the spotlight.

Delp died of liver cancer in 2006 at age seventy-four. "What he did in this business was amazing," Cleve said. "He went from claiming cheap horses and doing a lot of the work himself, working for his stepfather and pretty much hustling, to reaching the pinnacle of his profession."

"I loved Bud Delp," Andrew Beyer said. "He was honest, straightforward and funny. And he was a self-made man who disdained trainers who had the advantage of family connections. Long before Bid came along, he revolutionized the claiming game in Maryland with his aggressive wheeler-dealer approach, shaking up a game in which trainers rarely claimed from one another. He was regarded strictly as a shrewd wheeler-dealer until Bid came along and let him demonstrate what a superior horseman he was."

After Ron Franklin's disappointing season at Santa Anita in 1980, he enjoyed several successful years at Pimlico Race Course and Delaware Park. He was edged out (by one win) for top rider at Delaware Park in 1981, where he ranked first in winning percentage (27 percent). It looked like things were finally turning around for the young jockey. "I made my one mistake," he said, referring to his involvement with drugs in 1980. "It will never happen again. I have too much at stake."

In 1981 he moved out of Delp's house and into a town house about a mile away. According to Delp, the decision was mutual. "I felt it was time for Ronnie to learn some responsibilities, things like buying his own groceries and cleaning his room." It sounded as if Delp were still talking about the sixteen-year-old Franklin.

Franklin's temper problems continued. In November 1980 he was fined for fighting with fellow jockey Rudy Turcotte. Franklin admitted starting the fight. "I was egging him on about something and I just kept it up. I should have left him alone, but I didn't." In May 1981 he was fined again for slapping jockey Kenny Black in the jockeys' lounge; Black had cut him off in an earlier race. Curiously, Delp condoned the action. "Ronnie's tough on things like that," he said. "It's no big deal. It happens all the time in this business."

On April 13, 1982, just before the fifth race at Keeneland, detectives from the Lexington Police Department arrived at the jockeys' room and arrested Franklin, charging him with the transfer of cocaine. He and some friends were expecting a delivery of cocaine via Federal Express; however, they were nervous about the parcel's arrival and had called FedEx fourteen times, asking if their package had arrived, attorneys said. A suspicious FedEx employee contacted the police. Arrested along with him was Gerald Delp, one of Bud Delp's sons and Franklin's agent.

A judge sentenced Franklin to sixty days in jail. He was also fined $500, put on four months' probation, and ordered to enter a drug treatment program while in jail. Gerald Delp received the same sentence. The charges had been reduced to a misdemeanor; otherwise, Franklin and Delp could have faced up to ten years in prison and a $10,000 fine.

The sixty days in jail were the worst two months of Franklin's life; he hated confinement and longed for the open spaces he had frequented as a child. During the day, he sold soap, shampoo, and candy in the commissary to other inmates. He kept some of the candy for himself, and his weight ballooned to 130 pounds. At night, he could not fall asleep and stared at the cinderblocks in his cell, wide awake and short of breath. He was released just six days before Spectacular Bid was inducted into the Hall of Fame in Saratoga, New York, but he thought it would have been inappropriate to go to the ceremony.

"He has two big strikes against him," Delp said, "but he seems like a remarkably changed person. If he's got any real fortitude and smarts, he's on his way to a beautiful life in racing. The potential's there, it's up to him."

Billy Reed of the *Louisville Courier-Journal* said Franklin was the kind of kid people pulled for, and each slip was a disappointment to everyone. "You wanted this kid to make it, somehow. You hoped that he would overcome it all—the scuffling boyhood, the lack of education, the fame that came too big and too soon, the drug thing. You wanted this simple child bent and shaped by pressures that he never comprehended to find happiness in the end."

By 1983, Franklin seemed to be back on track. He had 824 career wins under his belt, and in 1982 he had finished third among jockeys at the Fair Grounds Race Course in Louisiana with 70 winners. He was also battling it out for first place among jockeys at Louisiana Downs. He got married in December and became a born-again Christian. "I have a little more muscle now and maybe more brains," he said. "I realize there is no future in drugs. There is a future [in horse racing] if I work hard enough." But his temper was still out of control. Stewards fined him $100 for hitting another jockey with his whip at the end of a race.

Franklin parted ways with Delp in 1984 after an argument over Franklin's marriage. Delp believed that the marriage, which came with two children, was not in Franklin's best interests. Later that year, the jockey received his license to ride in Maryland, but the Maryland Racing Commission warned him that "any future involvement with drugs will be cause for immediate suspension." He returned to his home state and said he intended to ride there permanently. He stayed less than two weeks, claiming that his wife hated it there. A year later, they split up. There was a nasty divorce, and Franklin's wife burned his clothes and papers in the front yard of their home.

In 1985 he came back to Maryland to be with his father, who was battling cancer. He rode for Bud Delp's brother, Richard, and Dick Dutrow, one of the "Big Four" trainers in Maryland. "Ronnie is a good, strong rider," Richard Delp said. "He hasn't caught on here yet, but he will." Later that year, he slipped again. His father had died, and just before Christmas, Franklin checked himself into Taylor Manor Hospital in Ellicott City, Maryland, an inpatient facility that specializes in drug and alcohol addiction. It did not help. Acting on information from an outside source, Maryland stewards asked Franklin to take a drug test on April 24, and he tested positive for marijuana. He was suspended by the Maryland Racing Commission with the recommendation that his license be revoked.

Franklin kept struggling; while he was suspended, he nailed sheet metal for $200 a week from 7:00 a.m. to 3:30 p.m., five days a week, to pay for all the attorneys he had retained for both his divorce and his appeal. To keep in shape, he cared for horses at Woodbine Farm in Virginia. He had hoped to get a license in another state, but reciprocity rules prevented that. "Franklin couldn't get a license in Hong Kong," one Maryland official quipped.

In April 1987 he was granted a license as an exercise rider. "I'm all the way back," Franklin said. "I think I've got it beaten." Shortly thereafter, he was reinstated as a jockey, and the *Daily Racing Form* noted, "Franklin has looked better and better with every ride. . . . It's way too early to make a definite judgment, but it looks like Franklin might have finally, at the age of twenty-seven, added some much-needed mental maturity to the physical tools which have enabled him to do so well in seasons past."

In 1987 he rode Angelina County to a win in the $55,350 Snow Goose Handicap. He was seeing a drug counselor every week and submitting a urine sample twice a week. "I do that mainly to keep a safety on myself," he said. "I don't have to do it, but it helps me keep a focus on things. It serves as a support system." He even got his high school diploma from a nearby community college.

By 1988, he had been clean for two years and was battling Kent Desormeaux for the top spot in the Laurel Park jockey standings. He also got married again. "This is my last comeback," he said. "I know that I either have to quit for good or not ride horses anymore."

Then his last comeback fell apart. In May 1991 Franklin was suspended by the Delaware Racing Commission after testing positive for drugs. He completed a ten-day relapse program. In September 1992 he failed another drug test and was suspended indefinitely by the Maryland stewards; it would be the last time he raced. The Maryland stewards would not reinstate his license, and he was barred from racetracks. "It is a sad situation," said steward Bill Passmore. "Ronnie has had so many problems in the past that you'd hope that he'd be able to put that behind him, but for him, drugs seem to be a curse."

Franklin continued to follow his dream of riding horses. He was granted an exercise rider's license in the fall of 1995 on the condition that he complete a rehabilitation program, continue drug counseling, and be subjected to random drug testing. When that random testing revealed cocaine in 1996, his license was revoked. By 1999, his exercise rider's license had been reinstated, and he was exercising horses at Laurel Park in the mornings for $8 a ride while working for a cabinetmaker in Brooklyn, Maryland.

Eventually, Delp changed his tune about the Belmont and laid all the blame at the feet of Franklin. In an interview with *Pressbox*, Delp said, "Ronnie rode a terrible, terrible race. He just should've relaxed behind those horses, let that 80–1 shot [Gallant Best] go where he wants to go—don't worry about him—and then we win the race without a doubt." Then, in the next breath, he proclaimed, "Coastal didn't belong in the same barn with him. But Bid was hurt. When he was coming down the stretch, I almost cried, because I felt so bad for the horse, because I could see him laboring. And I said to myself, 'I've screwed up; I should have scratched him.'" So which was it—a terribly run race or a hurt Bid? Delp seemed to vacillate, based on his mood.

In 2000 Franklin's exercise rider's license was revoked again when he failed to participate in drug rehabilitation efforts, as required by the Maryland Racing Commission. In 2004 he was making ends meet by hauling cement at construction sites. "I miss horses," he said. "That's the thing that hurts the most. Racing is a natural thing for me." Several times he tried to get the racing commission to reinstate him as a jockey, even as late as 2007, when he was forty-seven years old. He was denied each time, although the commission reinstated his exercise rider's license in 2005.

Franklin's battle with drugs is common among jockeys; many great riders such as Pat Day, Jerry Bailey, Pat Valenzuela, and Kent Desormeaux have battled addiction. Some recovered, but others were not so lucky. Chris Antley, who won the Kentucky Derby twice, died from an overdose in 2000 at age thirty-four. Cocaine is prevalent among jockeys because it gives them a feeling of invincibility. It also helps them keep their weight down and gives them the energy required to control a 1,000-pound animal going forty miles an hour. Dominick Bologna, director of the New York Racing and Wagering Board's substance abuse program, said, "If you had to invent a drug just for jockeys, cocaine would be it."

Franklin's meteoric rise to the top of the horse racing world was followed by a precipitous fall due to drugs, and he never recovered. The story of Ron Franklin is one of inexperience coupled with talent and promise, of success coupled with setbacks. Drugs robbed him of his lifelong dream.

In 2016 Franklin was diagnosed with lung cancer. He died two years later on March 8, 2018. Despite the suspensions, he amassed 1,403 wins and more than $14 million in earnings. But after Spectacular Bid, he never rode in another Triple Crown race. He exercised horses for different farms, doing whatever he could to stay connected to the animals. He had a deep faith in Christianity and resisted the notion that his early success caused him to get into drugs. "I'm an addict," he said. "That's what I am. I recover, though. And I'm recovered now. And recovery is a lifelong thing. . . . I look at it as just today. It makes it a lot easier." Two years before he died, he was asked if he wished things had gone differently for him. He paused for a long time and then said, "No, not really. No. I'm not second-guessing nothing."

Shoemaker continued to ride after Spectacular Bid, but the mounts were fewer as trainers preferred younger, more motivated jockeys. He rode the great turf horse John Henry to victory several times. Then in 1986, in one of the best rides of his career, he was racing in the pack aboard longshot Ferdinand at Churchill Downs and saw a small opening on the rail. He took the opening and raced to the front, winning his fourth Kentucky Derby at age fifty-four—the oldest jockey ever to win the Derby. He retired in 1990 after forty-one years of racing and 8,833 victories (a record at the time). He had been the country's leading jockey in money ten times and the leading jockey in races won five times. After his retirement from racing, he trained horses for a living.

In April 1991, after having a few beers with Don Pierce, Shoemaker was driving his 1990 Ford Bronco when he reached for his cell phone, lost control of the vehicle, and rolled over an embankment. His spinal cord was severed, leaving him a quadriplegic. Ironically, after surviving so many accidents on horses, he suffered his worst injury in a vehicle. Despite having a blood alcohol level of 0.13 (exceeding the California limit of 0.08), authorities did not press charges, since it was a one-vehicle accident. Shoemaker continued to train horses, his mounts earning nearly $3.7 million. He retired for good in November 1997. On October 12, 2003, Shoemaker died in his sleep at age seventy-two. National Thoroughbred Racing Association president Tim Smith said, "Bill Shoemaker, pound for pound, was one of the best athletes of the twentieth century, with a rare combination of poise, grace, and courage. He was an ambassador for our game, and the entire sport will miss him."

Controversy continued to follow Angel Cordero. Riding Codex in the 1980 Preakness Stakes, he was in the lead heading into the homestretch when the Kentucky Derby winner, a filly named Genuine Risk, made her move on the colt. Cordero looked behind him, saw Genuine Risk, and drifted wide, carrying Genuine Risk with him. He brushed up against the filly, and her jockey, Jacinto Vasquez, claimed that Cordero hit the filly's head with his whip. Genuine Risk immediately backed off, and Codex went on to win the Preakness by four and three-quarters lengths. Vasquez and most of those in attendance who did not have money on Codex cried foul. But in a baffling move, the stewards decided that although there had been intimidation on Cordero's part, it was not enough to warrant disqualification. Fans inundated Pimlico with calls of protest and disgust at the stewards' decision. Cordero received hate mail for months, including several death threats.

Once again, Cordero had to deny charges in 1981 that he was involved in race fixing. Former jockey Jose Amy testified at a fellow jockey's racketeering trial that Cordero and six other jockeys had discussed with him how they had fixed races in New York.

In the 1983 Belmont Stakes, Cordero, riding Slew o' Gold, was in the lead when Caveat made a move along the rail. Cordero forced Au Point, who was running between them, toward the rail, slamming Caveat into it. Caveat recovered and won the race, but he injured a ligament and was retired after the Belmont. Woody Stephens, Caveat's trainer, confronted Cordero after the race and chastised him, "Angel, I was a raggedy boy, and I came out of Kentucky the same way you were a raggedy boy who came out of Puerto Rico. The horses did everything for me, and they did everything for you, and I never hurt a horse. But you steered my horse into a fence and ruined him."

In 1986 Cordero was riding in the fourth race at Aqueduct Racetrack aboard a horse named Highfalutin when the horse fell. Cordero was tossed off, and another horse trampled him, lacerating his liver and breaking his leg just below the knee. He underwent four hours of surgery and was in the hospital for several weeks. Then forty-three, he was determined to come back from this serious injury. "When I leave this game, I want to leave on my own," he said. "I don't want to leave because I got hurt, or because my business wasn't any good." Sure enough, he came back that same year to win his eleventh title at Saratoga.

In 1990 Cordero was suspended for seven days for impeding the progress of Rubigo, ridden by jockey Chris Antley. Rubigo fell, and Antley lacerated his elbow, causing him to miss a week's worth of races.

Aqueduct would prove to be a hard-luck place for Cordero, and another accident there sidelined him for good. Running in the second race on January 12, 1992, he was thrown from his mount during a four-horse accident and hit the inner rail. He required emergency surgery to remove his spleen; he also had a bruised kidney, several broken ribs, and a fractured elbow. "For forty-eight hours after the accident, we didn't think Angel would [survive]," said Dr. Gary Wadler. "Any further injury to his abdominal area and I fear he might not be as lucky as he was this time."

Four months later, choking back the words, Cordero announced his retirement from racing. His record: 7,076 victories and more than $164 million in purses. In addition, he was the leading jockey at Saratoga for thirteen out of fourteen years. He won the Eclipse Award for Outstanding Jockey in 1982 and 1983 and rode three Kentucky Derby winners. In 1988 he was inducted into the National Museum of Racing and Hall of Fame. He also collected more than 200 suspensions and fines during his career.

Flying Paster, the horse that was supposed to beat Spectacular Bid in the Kentucky Derby in 1979, turned into an outstanding sire in California. He produced thirty stakes winners, including millionaire Flying Continental. Flying Paster died in 1992 at Cardiff Stud Farm in Paso

Robles, California, at the young age of sixteen. In twenty-seven races for the Ridders and Gordon Campbell, Flying Paster finished with thirteen victories, seven seconds—most of those to Spectacular Bid—and two thirds, earning $1,127,460. Had it not been for Bid, Flying Paster might have been one of the great horses of the 1970s.

Coastal, Bid's nemesis who denied him the Triple Crown, retired in 1979 with eight wins in fourteen starts and earnings totaling $493,929 in two years of racing. He died at twenty-nine at Summerhill Stud in South Africa.

As Bid grew older, his iron-gray coat turned even more dappled and then white, like his mother, Spectacular. And despite the polarizing personality of his trainer, he remained loved and popular. Fans still wrote letters to him over the years, requesting locks of hair, a horseshoe, or a halter.[3] "He liked to ham it up," said Jonathan H. F. Davis, owner of Milfer Farm. "If you brought a camera, he seemed to know he was on stage. He'd stand still and wait for you to snap his picture."

On June 9, 2003, Bid had a heart attack and died—twenty-four years to the day after his Belmont Stakes defeat, and two days after Funny Cide failed in his bid to win the Triple Crown at Belmont. He was buried at Milfer Farm.

Steve Haskin of *Blood-Horse* wrote, "Over the course of an entire career, at ages two, three, and four, Spectacular Bid was the greatest horse I have ever seen. There have been better-looking horses than the Bid. There have been better-moving horses, and better-bred horses. But he had one quality that separated him from the others—he could do everything. He was as close to the perfect racing machine as any horse in my time."

After Bid's death, Delp recalled, "I saw him last summer and he was running and romping around." He said, "Bid had a good life both at Claiborne and at Milfer. They loved him up there. I guarantee you he liked his twenty-three years in retirement better than the three years I had him."

That is debatable. Bid loved to run, and he loved to win. When *Blood-Horse* ranked the top 100 American Thoroughbreds of the twentieth century, it put Spectacular Bid at number ten, ahead of such champions as Affirmed, War Admiral, and even Seabiscuit. The Associated Press ranked him at number nine in its Horse of the Century poll, and

Spectacular Bid in retirement, galloping in his paddock. (Barbara Livingston)

in their book *A Century of Champions,* Tony Morris and John Randall placed him ninth in the world during the 1900s and third behind Secretariat and Citation among American horses—ahead of Man o' War.

In a fantasy race devised by the *Louisville Courier-Journal* featuring most of the Triple Crown winners and Spectacular Bid, Alysheba, Sunday Silence, Exterminator, and Swaps, Spectacular Bid beat Citation by a nose in a track record. Secretariat was third by a head.

"I think Spectacular Bid could reasonably be rated as a close number two on the all-time list, after Secretariat, and he deserves extra credit for his great consistency (in comparison to Secretariat, who lost three times in his 1973 season)," said Andrew Beyer. Brian Zipse, senior writer with *Horse Racing Nation,* said, "A true runner in every sense of the word, Spectacular Bid could do whatever he wanted against his competition. Speed enough to wire any race, he could also wait, before uncorking a ferocious late run. The way he won that Florida Derby, after the trouble he was ridden into, was a moment in racing I will never forget. No list of the greatest horses in American racing history is complete without the inclusion of Spectacular Bid."

Horse racing attendance peaked in 1976, when 79.3 million people attended the races, according to the US Statistical Abstract. By 1979, when Spectacular Bid was chasing his Triple Crown, that number had shrunk 8 percent to 72.7 million people. By this time, the trial of Tony Ciulla had resulted in several investigations and the conviction of former jockey Con Errico for fixing races, as well as the revocation of four other jockeys' licenses. Jacinto Vasquez got a one-year suspension; Cordero, though implicated, was not charged with any wrongdoing.

Congress and state legislatures threatened to get involved amid allegations that trainers were doping horses. State racing associations moved quickly to assure the betting public that the sport was clean. But it was too late; the sport was suffering from what Andrew Beyer called a crisis of integrity.

After three Triple Crown winners in the 1970s, the 1980s had none. In 1981 Pleasant Colony won the Kentucky Derby by three-quarters of a length and followed that up with an even more impressive victory in the Preakness. Trained by a man who, like Delp, boasted that the Belmont would be a piece of cake, the horse finished a disappointing third to Summing.

In 1982 even the owners seemed disinterested in the Triple Crown. The odds-on favorite to win the Kentucky Derby, Linkage, passed up the Derby to focus on the Preakness. The eventual winner of the Derby, Gato del Sol, did not run in the Preakness. For the second time in three years, three different horses won the three races of the Triple Crown.

To bolster interest in the sport, breeders held a series of championship races in the fall to help determine Horse of the Year. Called the Breeders' Cup, these races drew impressive crowds at the numerous parks where they were held, but that was just one day (eventually, two days) of the year. Overall attendance continued to decline.

By 1990, attendance was down to 63.8 million. Five years later, it fell by almost 40 percent to 38.9 million. Racetracks stopped reporting attendance figures after 1995. Many blamed the casinos that were popping up all over the nation. In 1987 only Nevada and New Jersey allowed casino gambling; by 1997, the number of states allowing it had increased to thirty-one. To combat the decline in attendance (and revenue), racetracks installed casinos of their own. By 1997, seven struggling tracks had installed video gambling and slot machines to attract more people into the parks.

Another troubling statistic was that the audience was aging; the cigar-chomping, fedora-wearing handicapper was getting older. More than half the spectators at racetracks were over fifty; only 12 percent were under the age of thirty. The majority were also male; only 30 percent of racegoers were female.

Meanwhile, the Triple Crown continued to be elusive. In 1989 Sunday Silence and Easy Goer replayed the exciting 1978 Triple Crown rivalry between Affirmed and Alydar. Sunday Silence won the Derby and the Preakness by two and a half lengths and a nose, respectively. But Easy Goer spoiled the Triple Crown sweep with a commanding eight-length win over Sunday Silence in the Belmont.

From 1997 to 2014, horse racing fans were teased with nine horses that won the first two legs of the Triple Crown, only to falter in the Belmont. In 1997 Silver Charm lost to Touch Gold by three-quarters of a length; in 1998 Real Quiet was beaten by Victory Gallop by a nose in a photo finish. Charismatic broke a leg in the stretch at Belmont in 1999 and never raced again. War Emblem stumbled out of the gate in the 2002 Belmont, almost falling to his knees, and managed only an eighth-place finish. In 2003 and 2004, Funny Cide and Smarty Jones captured Americans' hearts with their no-frills, common upbringing, but they both faded in the stretch at Belmont and lost. Big Brown went into the Belmont undefeated in 2008 but was mysteriously pulled up in the stretch and did not finish.

In 2011 the Jockey Club commissioned a study from McKinsey & Company that found Thoroughbred racing was in a state of crisis. Without new growth strategies, wagering on Thoroughbred racing would decline by 25 percent in the next decade, and the number of tracks would decline by 27 percent, according to the report. Why? Horse racing experts already knew the main reason: competition from casinos. But the report addressed several other issues:

- Public perception. Only twenty-two percent of the public had a positive impression of horse racing.
- Animal welfare. A National Thoroughbred Racing Association survey in 2008 found that the top three concerns among fans were health and safety of the horses, performance-enhancing drugs, and therapeutic overages.
- Dilution of the best racing. Horses were running less often; lifetime starts for the top three Kentucky Derby finishers plummeted from twenty-five in 1990 to eight in 2008. Average field size had dropped eight percent from 1990 to 2010.

McKinsey & Company recommended decreasing the number of races, which would create larger fields and higher revenue from wagering. It also suggested changes to the wagering system and improved television coverage.

The hunt for a Triple Crown winner went on. I'll Have Another in 2012 and California Chrome in 2014 failed to capture the Belmont. Chrome's defeat marked thirty-five years since Spectacular Bid's failed attempt to win the Triple Crown. Why was it taking so long for another Triple Crown winner to emerge?

One new theory was that horses were being bred for speed, not stamina; as a result, they could not handle the long distance of the Belmont. The Humane Society argued that breeding for speed had made horses' legs more fragile. High-profile breakdowns such as Charismatic, 2006 Kentucky Derby winner Barbaro, and 2008 Derby runner-up Eight Belles seemed to lend credence to this theory.

Enter American Pharoah and Justify. In 2015 American Pharoah broke the thirty-seven-year drought started by Spectacular Bid. In just four years, horse racing was treated to two superhorses that captured the Triple Crown. Triple Crowns seem to come in clusters, and no one can explain this phenomenon. Horse racing enthusiasts don't try to explain it; they just enjoy it, knowing that another thirty-seven years may pass before they see another.

Spectacular Bid was just one safety pin away from the Triple Crown. If Mo Hall had remembered to put pepper on the bandages, if the pin had fallen differently, if Bid had stepped just a few inches to the right or left, the collapse at Belmont could have been averted. Delp put it best: only an act of God kept Spectacular Bid from winning the Triple Crown. Most will remember Bid for his loss of the Triple Crown, and that is a shame, for he did so much more: rebounding from injury, going undefeated during his four-year-old season, winning three Eclipse championships, and running in a walkover. Perhaps Delp was right. Spectacular Bid was the best horse ever to look through a bridle.

Acknowledgments

MY FIRST BOOK took me ten years to write; this one took me about two. I researched and wrote like a man possessed, taking four trips to Kentucky and one to Baltimore. Although I had been a fan of horse racing for forty years, there was a lot to learn, and I lived six hours from the nearest racetrack.

I would like to thank Jennifer Kelly for recommending the University Press of Kentucky for my book. It turned out to be a perfect fit. Anne Dean Dotson, Natalie O'Neal, David Cobb, and the entire editorial and marketing teams were all willing to help at any time. It was an honor to work with them.

Cathy Schenck and Roda Ferraro at the Keeneland Library were invaluable resources, letting me have the run of the library during my trips to Kentucky. I researched back copies of the *Daily Racing Form, Thoroughbred Record,* and *Blood-Horse* and fourteen volumes of the Meyerhoffs' scrapbooks, giving me enough reading material for months. Chris Goodlett of the Kentucky Derby Museum also gathered materials for me, including valuable papers from the Jim Bolus collection.

Interviews were a huge part of the information-gathering process. Asking people about a horse that raced thirty-eight years ago was tough going, but the interviewees gave it their all. Doug Arnold at Buck Pond Farm gave me a tour of the place, allowing me to reconstruct Bid's birth and picture what the farm looked like back in 1976. Ed Caswell, the farm manager in 1976, and Helmut Jackson, nephew of the Proskauers, told me about Buck Pond Farm and Bid's birth and upbringing and provided vital information on the horse's early years.

Bud Delp and Harry Meyerhoff had passed away by the time I began this project, so I relied on their relatives for insights into these two great personalities. Bud's brother, Richard, took me back to that fateful day when Bid stepped on a safety pin the morning of the Belmont, and Bud's son Gerald Delp told me about his father. Teresa Meyerhoff Pete and Tom Meyerhoff recounted the excitement and thrills of owning a superhorse and provided great stories of their interactions with Bid, Delp, and Ron Franklin.

Lyn Jason Cobb, daughter of Madelyn Jason, was gracious and helpful; she put me in contact with Janet Linfoot, who had done research on twin horses and gave me some valuable information on Spectacular Bid's granddam. Cobb also provided pictures of Spectacular, which are used in this book with her permission.

I thank my good friend Fred Wyman for putting me in touch with many great jockeys, including Sandy Hawley, Don Pierce, and Ron Franklin. Franklin was forthcoming about not only his brief stint with fame but also his fall from stardom. I was fortunate to be able to talk with him several times before his death in 2018. He was a first-rate person who deserved better in life.

Seth Hancock of Claiborne Farms talked to me about the syndication of Spectacular Bid, providing great insight into the process as well as some perspective on Bid's career at stud. King Leatherbury told me stories about the "Big Four" of Maryland racing and how Bud Delp was a big part of that. Billy Christmas gave me a tour of Pimlico and filled me with stories of Bid, Delp, and the Meyerhoffs. Robin Richards taught me about leads and what might have happened to Bid's hoof during the Belmont Stakes.

Journalists were helpful in their recountings of Spectacular Bid. Andrew Beyer gave me his thoughts on Bid, as did the late William Nack, who told me about his conversation with Bill Shoemaker before the Jockey Club Gold Cup. Brian Zipse of Horse Racing Nation, a big fan of Bid, gave me his evaluation of the horse's career, which helped me understand Bid's place in history. Barry Irwin, a former writer for the *Thoroughbred Record* and the breeder and owner of 2011 Kentucky Derby winner Animal Kingdom, was gracious enough to read the manuscript, point out some errors, and give me a quote I could use. Nick Costa of pastthewire.com and Vince Misiewicz also volunteered to read the manuscript for accuracy.

Photos taken thirty-eight years ago are scarce and costly, but I got my hands on some. Jim McCue, Mary Cooke, Becky Ryder, Adam Coglianese, Helena Hau with *Blood-Horse,* Cathy Schenck, Roda Ferraro, Lyn Jason Cobb, Barbara Livingston, and the Associated Press all helped me track down photos of Bid and his entourage. I thank them for their help.

Where would writers be without editors? My father, Leon Lee Sr., was an English professor and performed the first pass on the manuscript, and my brother, Leon Lee Jr., took another pass. Dan Crissman helped with developmental editing, encouraging me to bring out parts I had merely glossed over, and Christina Roth did a fantastic job of not only catching style mistakes but also fact-checking. Her contribution lent a great deal of polish to the product. Linda Lotz provided the final edits, making the final manuscript even better. She also taught this former journalist some things about *The Chicago Manual of Style* and the use of the past-perfect tense. Writers are always learning.

My friends, family, and launch team did everything they could to get the word out about this book, and I thank them for their time and efforts. A special thank you goes to my wife, Apirada, for being my motivator and source of encouragement throughout this journey, as well as serving as my "assistant." She offered ideas and support and knew the right thing to say when I needed it most. Starbucks deserves a shout-out, even though I paid a lot of money for the coffee I drank there. It was like my second home office, where I spent hours writing, researching, and editing.

And finally, I want to thank the members of Teenage Fanclub. On a long journey home from Kentucky, the music from the Scottish group lifted me up and kept me going all the way through Kentucky, Tennessee, and Georgia. It became the soundtrack of this book; I listened to the group as I researched, wrote, and edited. Their music will remind me of this book, and this book will remind me of them.

Appendix A
Spectacular Bid's Pedigree

		NASRULLAH (GB), brown 1940
	BOLD RULER (USA), dark brown/brown, 1954	
		MISS DISCO (USA), brown 1944
BOLD BIDDER (USA), brown, 1962		
		TO MARKET (USA), chestnut, 1940*
	HIGH BID (USA), brown,1956	
		STEPPING STONE (USA), brown, 1950
		PALESTINIAN (USA), chestnut, 1946
	PROMISED LAND (USA), gray, 1954	
		MAHMOUDESS (USA), gray, 1942
SPECTACULAR (USA), gray, 1970		
		TO MARKET (USA), chestnut, 1948*
	STOP ON RED (USA), chestnut, 1959	
		DANGER AHEAD (USA), chestnut, 1946

NEARCO (ITY), brown, 1935	PHAROS (GB)
	NOGARA (ITY)
MUMTAZ BEGUM (FR), brown, 1932	BLENHEIM (GB)*
	MUMTAZ MAHAL (GB)
DISCOVERY (USA), chestnut, 1931	DISPLAY (USA)
	ARIADNE (USA)
OUTDONE (USA), brown, 1936	POMPEY (USA)
	SWEEP OUT (USA)
MARKET WISE (USA), brown, 1938*	BROKERS TIP (USA)*
	ON HAND (USA)
PRETTY DOES (USA), brown, 1944*	JOHNSTOWN (USA)
	CREESE (USA)
PRINCEQUILLO (IRE), brown, 1940	PRINCE ROSE (GB)
	COSQUILLA (GB)
STEP ACROSS (USA), brown, 1941	BALLADIER (USA)
	DRAWBRIDGE (USA)
SUN AGAIN (USA), chestnut, 1939	SUN TEDDY (USA)
	HUG AGAIN (USA)
DOLLY WHISK (USA) brown, 1930	WHISAWAY (USA)
	DOLLY SETH (USA)
MAHMOUD (FR), gray, 1933	BLENHEIM (GB)*
	MAH MAHAL (GB)
FOREVER YOURS (USA) gray, 1933	TORO (USA)
	WINSOME WAY (IRE)
MARKET WISE (USA), brown, 1938*	BROKERS TIP (USA)*
	ON HAND (USA)
PRETTY DOES (USA), brown, 1944*	JOHNSTOWN (USA)*
	CREESE (USA)*
HEAD PLAY (USA), chestnut, 1930	MY PLAY (USA)
	RED HEAD (USA)
LADY BEWARE (USA), dark brown/brown, 1937	BULL DOG (FR)
	RUNAWAY LASS (USA)

Source: Used with permission from Pedigree Online, http://www.pedigreequery.com/spectacular+bid.

* Horse is listed twice in the pedigree.

Appendix B
Spectacular Bid's Record

Date	Length of Race	Name of Race/ Stakes	First	Second	Third	Winning Time
6/30/78	5 ½ furlongs	Maiden	Spectacular Bid	Strike Your Colors	Instant Love	1:04³/₅
7/22/78	5 ½ furlongs	Allowance	Spectacular Bid	Silent Native	Double Proud	1:04¹/₅
8/2/78	5 ½ furlongs	Tyro Stakes	Groton High	Great Boone	Our Gary	1:04⁴/₅
8/20/78	6 furlongs	Dover Stakes	Strike Your Colors	Spectacular Bid	Spy Charger	1:10⁴/₅
9/23/78	7 furlongs	World's Playground (G3)	Spectacular Bid	Crest of the Wave	Groton High	1:20⁴/₅
10/8/78	1 mile	Champagne Stakes (G1)	Spectacular Bid	General Assembly	Crest of the Wave	1:34⁴/₅
10/19/78	1 ¹/₁₆ miles	Young America (G1)	Spectacular Bid	Strike Your Colors	Instrument Landing	1:43¹/₅
10/28/78	1 ¹/₁₆ miles	Laurel Futurity (G1)	Spectacular Bid	General Assembly	Clever Trick	1:41³/₅
11/11/78	1 ¹/₁₆ miles	Heritage Stakes (G2)	Spectacular Bid	Sun Watcher	Terrific Son	1:42
2/7/79	7 furlongs	Hutcheon Stakes	Spectacular Bid	Lot o' Gold	Northern Prospect	1:21²/₅
2/19/79	1 ¹/₁₆ miles	Fountain of Youth (G3)	Spectacular Bid	Lot o' Gold	Bishop's Choice	1:41¹/₅
3/6/79	1 ⅛ miles	Florida Derby (G1)	Spectacular Bid	Lot o' Gold	Fantasy 'n Reality	1:48⁴/₅
3/24/79	1 ⅛ miles	Flamingo Stakes	Spectacular Bid	Strike the Main	Sir Ivor Again	1:48²/₅
4/26/79	1 ⅛ miles	Blue Grass Stakes	Spectacular Bid	Lot o' Gold	Bishop's Choice	1:50
5/5/79	1 ¼ miles	Kentucky Derby (G1)	Spectacular Bid	General Assembly	Golden Act	2:02²/₅
5/19/79	1 ³/₁₆ miles	Preakness Stakes (G1)	Spectacular Bid	Golden Act	Screen King	1:54¹/₅
6/9/79	1 ½ miles	Belmont Stakes (G1)	Coastal	Golden Act	Spectacular Bid	2:28³/₅

Date	Length of Race	Name of Race/ Stakes	First	Second	Third	Winning Time
8/26/79	1 ¹/₁₆ miles	Allowance	Spectacular Bid	Armada Strike	Not So Proud	1:41³/₅
9/8/79	1 ⅛ miles	Marlboro Cup Invitational Handicap (G1)	Spectacular Bid	General Assembly	Coastal	1:46³/₅
10/6/79	1 ½ miles	Jockey Club Gold Cup	Affirmed	Spectacular Bid	Coastal	2:27²/₅
10/18/79	1 ¼ miles	Meadow-lands Cup (G2)	Spectacular Bid	Smarten	Valdez	2:01¹/₅
1/5/80	7 furlongs	Malibu Stakes (G2)	Spectacular Bid	Flying Paster	Rosie's Seville	1:20
1/19/80	1 ⅛ miles	San Fernando Stakes (G2)	Spectacular Bid	Flying Paster	Relaunch	1:48
2/3/80	1 ¼ miles	Strub Stakes (G1)	Spectacular Bid	Flying Paster	Valdez	1:57⁴/₅
3/2/80	1 ¼ miles	Santa Anita Handicap (G1)	Spectacular Bid	Flying Paster	Beau's Eagle	2:00³/₅
5/18/80	1 ¹/₁₆ miles	Mervyn Leroy (G2)	Spectacular Bid	Peregrinator	Beau's Eagle	1:40⁴/₅
6/8/80	1 ⅛ miles	Californian Stakes (G1)	Spectacular Bid	Paint King	Caro Bambino	1:45⁴/₅
7/19/80	1 ⅛ miles	Washington Park Handicap (G3)	Spectacular Bid	Hold Your Tricks	Architect	1:46¹/₅
8/16/80	1 ⅛ miles	Haskell Handicap (G1)	Spectacular Bid	Glorious Song	The Cool Virginian	1:48
9/20/80	1 ¼ miles	Woodward Stakes (G1)	Spectacular Bid			2:02/₅

Glossary

allowance race: Race in which the racing secretary determines how much weight each horse will carry, based on its age, sex, money earned, or past performance.

apprentice jockey: Rider who has not ridden a certain number of winners within a specified time. Also known as a "bug."

backstretchers: People who work with the horses in the stables and barns, which are typically located near the backstretch of the track.

bit: Piece of metal or other material placed in the horse's mouth that helps the jockey communicate with the horse.

blinker: Cup-shaped device intended to limit a horse's vision and prevent it from swerving away from objects or other horses on either side.

blowout: Short, fast workout shortly before a race that sharpens a horse's speed.

bowed tendon: Tear or swelling of the tendon, causing it to appear bowed.

breeze: To exercise a horse at a moderate speed.

broodmare: Female horse used for breeding.

bug: Apprentice jockey.

claiming race: Race in which each horse that runs is for sale. If a horse is "claimed," or bought, the title to the horse is handed over to the buyer after the race begins, regardless of the horse's condition after the race. If the horse wins, the original owner collects the winnings. Claiming races are at the bottom of the racing hierarchy, below stakes, handicaps, and allowance races, but they account for most races run on US tracks.

colic: Condition that causes abdominal pain and is especially dangerous for horses. It is a symptom of possible obstruction in the intestines, which may require surgery. Many horses have died from colic.

colt: Male horse, usually under the age of five.

corn: Rupture of blood vessels in a horse's hoof.

coupling: Distance between a horse's last rib and the point of the hip. A short-coupled horse has a short distance between the rib and hip.

cuppy: Track condition in which the surface is dry and loose and collapses under a horse's hooves.

dam: Horse's mother.

Eclipse Awards: The premier awards in American Thoroughbred horse racing. They are named for the eighteenth-century British horse Eclipse, who was unbeaten.

farrier: Person who trims and shoes horses' hooves for a living.

filly: Female horse, usually under the age of five.

frog: Underside of the hoof. It acts as a shock absorber for the horse's foot and encompasses about 25 percent of the bottom of the hoof.

furlong: One-eighth of a mile.

gelding: Horse that has been castrated.

groom: Person who takes care of a horse when it is not on the track.

group stakes: Term for graded stakes in other countries.

halter: Rope or strap with a noose placed around the head of a horse, used to lead it.

hand: Measurement that equals the width of the palm, including the thumb—about four inches. Horses are measured in hands.

hand ride: Race in which the winning jockey does not have to use the whip.

handicapping: Assigning different weights to horses based on their ability, intended to equalize the field. High-performing horses are assigned more weight than those that are not as good or have not proved themselves.

hardboot: Horseman from Kentucky.

hot walker: Person who walks a horse after a race or a workout to allow the muscles to cool down. Lack of a proper cooldown can result in poor blood circulation and can cause the body to go into shock.

in the money: Finishing first, second, or third (win, place, or show) in a race. Bettors bet on a horse to finish in one of these places. Technically, it can include horses that finish fourth and fifth, especially in exotic wagers.

length: Measurement of the distance by which a horse wins a race. The length of a horse from nose to tail is about eight feet.

maiden: Horse that has never won a race. When a horse wins his maiden, he wins his first race.

mare: Female horse over the age of four.

outrider: Person who escorts horses to the starting gate and makes sure they are calm and ready to race.

paddock: Small field or enclosure where horses are kept.

photo finish: Race that is so close that a camera has to be used to determine the winner.

pole: Marker next to the rail that signifies how much distance is left in the race. Poles are placed throughout the racecourse.

race rider: Jockey who outmaneuvers another jockey.

scratch: Withdraw a horse from a competition.

second dam: Grandmother of a horse.

sire: Father of a horse.

sprint: Race of a mile or less.

stakes race: Race in which the owner has to pay a fee to run a horse; the track then adds more money to make up the total purse.

stallion: Any male horse over the age of four, especially those that are breeding.

stewards: Officials who oversee the rules of horse racing. They investigate possible infractions, conduct hearings, and take disciplinary action if they find any wrongdoing.

stud: Stallion.

supplementary addition: Entry of a horse into a stakes race after the deadline for nominations has passed. The owner usually has to pay a supplementary fee.

syndication: The process of selling shares in a racehorse or its breeding rights.

tack room: Place where saddles, bridles, and other equipment are kept.

weaning: Process of separating a foal from its mother to begin its own feeding and training regimen.

yearling: Horse that is one year old. All horses become yearlings on January 1, regardless of when they were born.

Notes

Introduction

Sources by Page Number

1 ". . . but not to witness." Steve Snider, "Chateaugay Given Good Chance to Beat 'Triple Crown' Jinx," *Nevada State Journal,* May 14, 1963.
1 ". . . see another Triple Crown champion." Chauncey Durden, "That Testing Last Quarter," *Richmond Times-Dispatch,* June 2, 1968.
1 . . . skyrocketed to 24,954. Bill Bracher, "Time Study," *Cincinnati Enquirer,* May 15, 1977.
2 . . . even three Triple Crowns in six years. Steve Cady, "How Can You Explain Increase of Triple Crown Winners?" *New York Times,* June 4, 1979.
2 ". . . making the all-pro backfield." Ibid.

1. Beginnings

1. Since Halma and Alan-a-Dale, eleven other father-son combinations have won the Derby, including two grandfather-father-son combinations. Gallant Fox and Omaha, a father-son combination, both won the Triple Crown.

2. A short-coupled horse has a short distance between the last rib and the point of the hip.

3. Since 1979, grays have had more luck in the Derby, with Gato del Sol, Winning Colors, Silver Charm, Monarchos, and Giacomo winning the prestigious race.

Sources by Page Number

4 . . . soldiers had been killed or wounded. "Thomas Marshall (U.S. politician)," Wikipedia, https://en.wikipedia.org/wiki/Thomas_Marshall_ (U.S._politician).
6 . . . owners could do nothing to save the track. Joseph P. Pons Jr., "The Breeders," *Blood-Horse,* May 14, 1979.

6 ". . . she's going to have twins again." Bill Christine, "Thoroughbred Racing: A Winning Twin Is Equine Rarity," *Los Angeles Times,* October 25, 1991.

6 ". . . for both twins to survive." Ibid.

6 ". . . Twins never make good racehorses." Associated Press, "Spectacular Bid Set for Saturday's Stakes," *Indianapolis Star,* July 16, 1980.

7 ". . . She was born to be a mother." Janet Linfoot, interview by the author, March 2, 2016.

7 ". . . a lot of stamina to have made it." Glenye Cain, "Bid's Breeder Remembers the Ride," *Daily Racing Form,* June 14, 2003.

7 ". . . she'd just kind of gallop along." Ibid.

7 ". . . she had speed, so I kept her." Joseph P. Pons Jr., "Spectacular Bid's Breeder," *Blood-Horse,* October 23, 1978.

9 ". . . short-coupled, and Bold Bidder was that, too." Ibid.

9 "'. . . you've overmatched your mare a bit?'" Pons, "The Breeders."

10 ". . . strong colt. Shows quality." Dave Anderson, ed., *The Red Smith Reader* (New York: Skyhorse Publishing, 2014), 69.

10 . . . would make him even stronger. Cain, "Bid's Breeder Remembers the Ride."

10 ". . . that run-in shed if he wanted to." Anderson, *Red Smith Reader,* 71.

10 ". . . nippy in the field but not a bully." Logan Bailey, "Meyerhoffs Bought a Champ for Only $37,000," *Daily Racing Form,* April 26, 1979.

11 . . . asked whether the mare had had triplets. Ibid.

11 . . . dark bay or brown, and gray/roan. "About Thoroughbreds," Keeneland Racing and Sales, https://www.keeneland.com/racing/about-Thoroughbreds.

11 . . . only twenty-eight gray broodmares were recorded in England. Margo Weise, "The Continuous Grey of the Alcock's Arabian," White Horse Productions, http://www.whitehorseproductions.com/images/HorseRacing/Mumtaz%20and%20Tetrarch/Writings/The%20Continuous%20Grey%20°f%20the%20Alcock.doc.

11 ". . . they apparently don't go for speed." Gene Kessler, "Do You Know?" *Lincoln (NE) Star,* January 16, 1930.

11 ". . . little more than yaks." Bob Considine, "On the Line: Backhand Praise for White Sox," *Rockford (IL) Register-Republic,* June 29, 1953.

2. Sold

1. Keeneland abolished the July sale in 2003 and now accepts all Thoroughbreds at its September sale.

2. The Jockey Club rejects names for a variety of reasons. One cannot name a horse after another horse that has won a stakes race within the last twenty-five years. Names cannot be more than eighteen letters and cannot consist entirely

of initials. One cannot reuse the name of a famous horse. For example, one cannot name a horse Man o' War or Secretariat; those names are retired forever. The Jockey Club estimates that it rejects 90 percent of names for some reason.

   3. Delp later had a third son, Cleve.

Sources by Page Number

14 ". . . there was a horse I wanted to bid on." Dave Anderson, ed., *The Red Smith Reader* (New York: Skyhorse Publishing, 2014), 71.

15 ". . . know what a bowed tendon was." "Biographical Sketch Prepared by Jim Bolus for 1989 Breeders' Cup Biography Book," Jim Bolus Collection, Kentucky Derby Museum.

16 ". . . finish at home and get my diploma." Judy Mann, "A Very, Very Long Way to the Winner's Circle," *Washington Post,* March 28, 1979.

16 ". . . before it was too late." Ibid.

16 ". . . [Harry] came in and that was it." Judy Mann, "Being Wealthy Isn't All There Is to Life; Wealth Not All There Is to Good Life," *Washington Post,* March 30, 1979.

16 ". . . didn't marry him for his money." Nellie Blagden, "Okay, Harry & Teresa Meyerhoff Aren't Household Names: What About Their Three-Year-Old?" *People,* June 11, 1979.

16 "'. . . a humble family and now you're wealthy.'" Mann, "Being Wealthy Isn't All There Is to Life."

17 ". . . I knew something about racing." Tom Meyerhoff, interview by the author, July 8, 2017.

17 ". . . I've been behind many bars." Ross Newhan, "Meyerhoffs Love to Horse Around," *Los Angeles Times,* May 27, 1979.

17 ". . . more equal than the two of us are." Ibid.

17 ". . . is who sleeps with Teresa." John Schulian, "Teresa Meyerhoff Changes Cinderella Story," *Tallahassee Democrat,* June 10, 1979.

17 ". . . millionaire to own a Thoroughbred . . . in years." Mann, "A Very, Very Long Way to the Winner's Circle."

17 ". . . the type to own a classic race horse." Newhan, "Meyerhoffs Love to Horse Around."

18 ". . . doesn't impress me that much." William Nack, "Some More Yelps from Bud Delp," *Sports Illustrated,* June 11, 1979, 67.

19 ". . . any darling of the establishment." Frank Phelps, "With Racing over, Only Boos Remain," *Lexington Leader,* October 7, 1980.

19 ". . . better horses because of the better purses." King Leatherbury, interview by the author, May 11, 2017.

19 . . . treat horses like individuals, not animals. Kent Baker, "Delp Is Successful, Outspoken—and Respected," *Baltimore Sun,* May 20, 1979.

19 . . . who did things a little differently. Skip Bayless, "Bid's Bud: His Act Is the Real Thing," *Dallas Morning News,* May 3, 1979.

19 ". . . or dictator's sense of inflated self-worth." Bill Lyon, "Delp Finally Escapes Used Horse Business," *Boca Raton News,* May 4, 1979.

20 ". . . to be too broke to buy a hamburger." Billy Reed, "Man of the Week: Bid's Trainer, Bud Delp," *Louisville Courier-Journal,* April 29, 1979.

20 ". . . that's when you get in trouble." Baker, "Delp Is Successful, Outspoken—and Respected."

20 ". . . most of the time, he was right on." Gerald Delp, interview by the author, April 10, 2016.

20 . . . parted ways soon after that. Reed, "Man of the Week."

21 ". . . survive was in the claiming business." Neil Milbert, "Spectacular Trainer: Bud Delp," *Illinois Racing News,* August 1990, 24.

21 ". . . rivalries boiled and tempers flared." Marty McGee, "Remembering Maryland's Fab Four," *Daily Racing Form,* date unknown.

21 . . . so Dutrow would not claim him in a race. Leatherbury interview.

21 ". . . called him the 'King of Claimers.'" Delp interview.

21 ". . . must wonder how they stand at times." Dan Mearns, "Coming Home," *Thoroughbred Record,* May 30, 1979, 1697.

21 ". . . whenever he has something to talk about." Billy Reed, "Delp's Pride and Joy Bids to Be Known as the Greatest Ever," *Louisville Courier-Journal,* July 16, 1980.

21 . . . so completely gutted in such a short time. "32 Dead Horses Left in Laurel Fire's Wake," *Cumberland (MD) Evening Times,* November 4, 1964.

22 ". . . or the Black-Eyed Susan Stakes." Steve Haskin, "Delp's Daughter Stirs up Memories of the Bid," February 18, 2017, http://cs.bloodhorse.com/blogs/horse-racing-steve-haskin/archive/2017/02/18/delp-s-daughter-stirs-up-memories-of-the-bid.aspx.

22 ". . . just as well with a class horse, if I had one." "Biographical Sketch Prepared by Jim Bolus for 1989 Breeders' Cup Biography Book."

22 ". . . along in those days after the fire." Evan Hammonds, "Still Budding," *Blood-Horse,* August 5, 2002, http://www.bloodhorse.com/horse-racing/articles/10808/still-budding.

23 ". . . as much about horses as Bud Delp." Shelby Strother, "Riding a Horse's Coattails Can Be Best Ride of All," *Wilmington (DE) Morning News,* March 15, 1979.

23 ". . . that's not our job." Marla Ridenour, "Bid's Three Owners Take Their Spectacular Success in Stride," *Lexington Herald,* April 26, 1979.

24 ". . . we would have to go for any given sire." Meyerhoff interview.

24 ". . . Looks like a runner." Clive Gammon, "Big Horse Comin'," *Sports Illustrated,* April 23, 1979, 107.

24 ". . . might have affected his price a little." Timothy T. Capps, *Spectacular Bid: Racing's Horse of Steel* (Lexington, KY: Eclipse Press, 2001), 31.

24 ". . . and what prices we were thinking." Meyerhoff interview.

24 . . . thought the horse looked like a tweed coat. Buddy Martin, "Triple Crown's Heir Apparent," *New York Daily News,* June 3, 1979.

24 . . . raved about the horse's "perfect ass." "Spectacular Bid—Racing's Superhorse," *Florida Today,* March 11, 1979.

24 ". . . Here's your next champion." "Biographical Sketch Prepared by Jim Bolus for 1989 Breeders' Cup Biography Book."

25 "'. . . certainly was a nice-looking yearling.'" Joseph P. Pons Jr., "Spectacular Bid's Breeder," *Blood-Horse,* October 23, 1978.

25 ". . . we were averaging in the $80,000 area." Jack Murray, "Spectacular Bid Can Afford to Laugh," *Cincinnati Enquirer,* April 28, 1979.

25 . . . and the lowest was $10,000. Cathy Schenck (librarian, Keeneland Library), interview by the author, February 24, 2016.

26 ". . . horses walking in the opposite direction." "About the Middleburg Training Center," Dog Branch Farm website, January 15, 2016, http://www.dogbranchfarm.com/breakingtraining.htm.

26 ". . . and she's been a horsewoman for some time." William C. Phillips, "Adjectives Galore Now Thrown 'Bid's Way Continuously," *Daily Racing Form,* May 21, 1979.

26 ". . . knew what he was supposed to do." Ibid.

26 ". . . fun of him or laughing at him." Dave Koerner, "He's Still 'Plain Old Ronald,' but He's No Longer a Quitter," *Louisville Courier-Journal,* April 15, 1979.

26 . . . the doctor said nothing was wrong. Richard H. P. Sia, "Franklin: From Neighborhood Wise Guy to Derby Winner," *Baltimore Sun,* May 8, 1979.

27 ". . . who didn't like people bullying." Ron Franklin, interview by the author, March 7, 2016.

27 ". . . behind no windows," he was fond of saying. Nellie Blagden, "A Drug Bust, a Paternity Suit—Troubles Come in Battalions for Jockey Ronnie Franklin," *People,* July 9, 1979.

27 . . . school officials still promoted him. Skip Myslenski, "Derby Favorite Spectacular Luck for Jockey," *Chicago Tribune,* May 4, 1979.

27 ". . . he was never afraid of anything." Sia, "Franklin: From Neighborhood Wise Guy to Derby Winner."

27 ". . . best thing for him to do was to quit." Koerner, "He's Still 'Plain Old Ronald.'"

28 ". . . looking for a hot walker's job." Ibid.

28 . . . with double negatives and dropped *g*'s. Eric Siegel, "Ronnie Franklin: The Repentant Jockey Rides Again," *Baltimore Sun,* May 11, 1980.

28 ". . . Don't worry, we'll teach you." Ron Franklin, interview by the author, March 7, 2016.

28 . . . he got ready for work. Myslenski, "Derby Favorite Spectacular Luck for Jockey."

28 ". . . remember wanting to be somebody." Koerner, "He's Still 'Plain Old Ronald.'"

29 ". . . that's what I'm trying to do." Ron Franklin, interview by Katherine Veitschegger, April 28, 2010.

29 . . . the top 10 percent of all athletes. Tom Biracree and Wendy Insinger, *The Complete Book of Thoroughbred Horse Racing* (New York: Dolphin Books, 1982), 241.

29 . . . maximum performance from an animal. Ibid., 243.

29 ". . . Horses run fast for him." Alan Goldstein, "Ron Franklin, School Dropout, Earns Top Grades Quickly as a Jockey," *Baltimore Sun*, May 20, 1979.

3. Potential

1. Seethreepeo ran for Hawksworth Farm, collecting thirteen wins in forty-five starts. I Know Why was claimed by King Leatherbury and finished first in twelve of his fifty-six starts.

2. Since a furlong is one-eighth of a mile, this race was eleven-sixteenths of a mile.

3. Bettors would get their $2 back as well.

4. The five-sixteenths pole, located next to the rail, signifies that five-sixteenths of a mile is left in the race. Markers are placed throughout the racecourse to tell jockeys how much farther they have to go.

Sources by Page Number

30 ". . . How the hell would you know?" Jack Mann, "How Bud Almost Did . . . with Bid," *Turf and Sport Digest*, June 1980.

30 ". . . What do you know about horses?" Kent Hollingsworth, "Spectacular Bid," *Blood-Horse*, April 14, 1984, 2745.

31 ". . . 'He needs to be with me [at Pimlico].'" David Schmitz, "Greatest Horse Ever to Look through a Bridle," *Blood-Horse*, June 21, 2003, 3390.

31 ". . . could see that Bid was best." Ibid.

31 ". . . you can overdo it, right from the get-go." Ibid.

31 ". . . There isn't a bit of heat anywhere." Bob Maisel, "Spectacular Bid Eludes Price Tag," Meyerhoff Collection, Book 3, Keeneland Library.

31 ". . . thought he was going to run and didn't." Ibid.

31 ". . . would've been 1 to 5 if they had seen him." Ron Franklin, interview by the author, June 3, 2017.

32 ". . . but Franklin might be an exception." Dale Austin, "Silver Ice Captures Va. Belle Stakes," *Baltimore Sun,* February 5, 1978.

33 ". . . than anybody I've ever known." Ross Peddicord, "Franklin Leads Scramble to Replace Chris McCarron as Riding Champion," *Baltimore Evening Sun,* February 10, 1978.

33 "'. . . he is going to run very well.'" Maria Ridenour, "Bid's Three Owners Take Their Spectacular Success in Stride," *Lexington Herald,* April 26, 1979.

34 ". . . beat on until they're black and blue." Steve Cady, "A Black and Blue Rainbow," *New York Times,* January 25, 1979.

34 ". . . He did look great, didn't he?" William C. Phillips, "Adjectives Galore Now Thrown 'Bid's Way Continuously," *Daily Racing Form,* May 21, 1979.

35 ". . . prospects in the race he paid $14.60." William Phillips, "Spectacular, to Say the Least," *Daily Racing Form,* July 3, 1978.

35 ". . . this is a special kind of horse." Teresa Meyerhoff Pete, interview by the author, January 5, 2017.

36 "'. . . don't move on him the whole race.'" Mann, "How Bud Almost Did . . . with Bid," 17.

38 ". . . he'd [have] won by ten." Karl Feldner, "Agent Goof Gives Jockey Bid," *Pensacola News Journal,* May 3, 1979.

39 ". . . coming at him and falling back." Mann, "How Bud Almost Did . . . with Bid," 17.

39 ". . . two-year-olds just don't do that." Brian Zipse, interview by the author, September 21, 2016.

39 "Lenny. . . Cauthen. . . Idiot. . . Please call." Jack Mann, "Bid's Handlers Wonder What If?" *Annapolis Capital,* September 13, 1998.

40 ". . . He wants the best for the horse." Dale Austin, "Spectacular Bid Captures Champagne Stakes by 2¾," *Baltimore Sun,* October 9, 1978.

41 ". . . He was one of those horses." William Nack, interview by the author, July 9, 2017.

41 ". . . and hope he gets [to the Triple Crown races]." Ed Schuyler Jr., "Spectacular Bid Grabs Champagne after Showing Heels to 'Assembly,'" *Louisville Courier-Journal,* October 9, 1978.

41 ". . . Maybe next year." Austin, "Spectacular Bid Captures Champagne Stakes."

41 ". . . who's the champ from the quarter pole home." Hollingsworth, "Spectacular Bid."

42 ". . . but they'll never forgive him." John Crittenden, "Bid Races Clock and Bankbook," *Miami News,* February 15, 1980.

43 ". . . That made it a hard race." Mann, "How Bud Almost Did . . . with Bid," 17.

43 ". . . didn't know Bid was a great horse." Ibid.

43 . . . a full blinker on the right side. Ibid.

43 ". . . didn't sit well with the Meyerhoffs." Jack Mann, "The Word on Buddy Delp's Walk," *1989 Kentucky Derby Magazine,* 136.

43 ". . . get a Shoemaker, you just do." Don Zamarelli, "A New Definition of the Word Spectacular," *Blood-Horse,* November 6, 1978, 5248.

43 . . . break away under a horse's hooves. "Bobble," in Industry Glossary, Equibase Company, http://www.equibase.com/newfan/glossary-full.cfm.

43 ". . . It's as simple as that." Zamarelli, "New Definition of the Word Spectacular," 5248.

44 ". . . an outsider to step on their territory." Bob Maisel, "Delp's Quotes Sounded Different in Print," *Baltimore Sun,* April 29, 1979.

45 ". . . to see how much horse he really is." William C. Phillips, "Delp's Beside Himself," *Daily Racing Form,* October 30, 1978.

45 ". . . Man, [Franklin's] horse was running." Billy Reed, "'Bid,' Franklin Kid Show 'em with a Record Run in Futurity," *Louisville Courier-Journal,* October 29, 1978.

45 . . . won the World's Playground. Mark Simon, "Learning without Mistakes," *Thoroughbred Record,* November 22, 1978, 1938.

45 ". . . like a lot of them are prone to do." Zamarelli, "New Definition of the Word Spectacular," 5248.

45 ". . . could have been that cool." Phillips, "Delp's Beside Himself."

46 ". . . a Triple Crown winner." Andrew Beyer, "Spectacular Bid Only Tick behind Recent Greats; Trainer Delp in His Element," *Washington Post,* October 31, 1978.

46 . . . between $8 million and $9 million. Meyerhoff Collection, Book 1, Keeneland Library.

47 ". . . left him at the stall in Maryland." Gordon Forbes, "It's Yet Another Spectacular Bid," *Philadelphia Inquirer,* November 12, 1978.

47 ". . . winning the Triple Crown next year." Dave Feldman, "Spectacular Bid: Delp Predicts Triple Crown for Colt," *Wilmington (DE) News Journal,* December 27, 1978.

48 ". . . good condition, and he does his job." Bob Maisel, "The Morning After," *Baltimore Sun,* November 16, 1978.

48 ". . . Come up to the stable gate and say that." Ross Peddicord, "Silent Cal Upsets Star De Naskra at Laurel," *Baltimore Sun,* November 19, 1978.

48 ". . . broken vertebra, this would all be secondary." Ibid.

49 ". . . eats thirteen quarts of oats a day." Feldman, "Spectacular Bid: Delp Predicts Triple Crown for Colt."

49 ". . . he'll win the Triple Crown with ease." Ibid.

49 ". . . any Thoroughbred for that matter." Telegram, Meyerhoff Collection, Book 2, Keeneland Library.

4. The Field Shapes Up

1. Dr. Harthill, veterinarian to twenty-six Kentucky Derby winners, was no stranger to controversy. He was arrested in the 1950s in Louisiana for trying to bribe an employee of a testing laboratory. In 1968 he gave Dancer's Image, a colt who had chronic sore ankles, a dose of phenylbutazone ("bute") to reduce inflammation on the Sunday before the Kentucky Derby. Dancer's Image won the Derby, but a postrace urinalysis revealed the drug's presence, and the horse was disqualified. Since bute usually takes only two days to clear out of a horse's system, most people believe that either the test was wrong or someone gave Dancer's Image another dose of bute just days before the Derby.

Sources by Page Number

51 ". . . when you're preparing for the big ones." Teddy Cox, "Gulfstream," *Daily Racing Form,* February 5, 1979.

51 ". . . I am really pleased." Ibid.

51 ". . . just knocked your eye out." Art Grace, "A Tap on the Shoulder," *Blood-Horse,* February 19, 1979, 898.

51 ". . . ensure his safety and well-being." Bob Adair, "Spectacular Bid Starts Quest to Emulate Slew, Affirmed," *Louisville Courier-Journal,* February 7, 1979.

51 ". . . takes a Kentucky Derby for granted." Cox, "Gulfstream."

53 ". . . thinking that mud is terrific." Randy Schultz, "Bid Spectacular, Even in the Rain," *Palm Beach Post,* February 8, 1979.

53 ". . . the easiest races he's ever had." Associated Press, "Spectacular Bid Beats Speed with Speed," *Louisville Courier-Journal,* February 8, 1979.

53 ". . . go past the finish line driving." Phil Pepe, "Who's First? 'Bid' or Rider," *Lexington Leader,* February 21, 1979.

53 ". . . can't afford another twenty days." Jack Mann, "Happy Party in Florida for Super Horse," *Washington Evening Star,* February 8, 1979.

54 ". . . after he wins the Triple Crown." Associated Press, "Insurance on 'Bid' Upped to $10 Million," *Lexington Herald,* February 28, 1979.

54 ". . . Spectacular Bid is not for sale." Joe Hirsch, "Spectacular Bid Hasn't Been Sold and Is Not for Sale, Meyerhoff Says," *Daily Racing Form,* February 27, 1979.

54 ". . . we've got the best horse of the century." David Condon, "Spectacular Bid—1979's Wonder Colt," *Chicago Tribune,* February 13, 1979.

54 ". . . to scare off some challengers." Ibid.

54 ". . . my lifetime. Including Secretariat." Andrew Beyer, "Spectacular Bid: List of Doubters Is Thinning Out: Bid Looks Like the Real Thing," *Washington Post,* March 5, 1979.

55 ". . . but I say he can be beat." Grace, "Tap on the Shoulder," 898.

55 ". . . he got clear, I knew it was over." Andrew Beyer, "Spectacular Bid Devastates Field at Gulfstream," *Washington Post,* February 19, 1979.

55 ". . . and I'm his regular rider." Steve Cady, "Spectacular Bid Trounces Field in Florida Stop on Derby Route," *New York Times,* February 19, 1979.

55 ". . . I felt like he was taking *me* for a ride." Mike Klingaman, "A Spectacular Hero," *Baltimore Sun,* May 9, 1999.

55 ". . . even better for the Florida Derby." Beyer, "Spectacular Bid Devastates Field at Gulfstream."

57 ". . . My heart is clean." Gerald Eskenazi, "Trainer Accuses Jockeys," *New York Times,* May 2, 1975.

57 . . . trainer's allegations "irresponsible." Stephen Crist, "Angel Cordero: The Jockey Fans Love to Hate," *New York Times,* December 12, 1982.

57 ". . . I'm not a bad person, really." Ken Rosenberg, "Angel Cordero: I'm Not a Bad Person," *Tampa Tribune,* June 7, 1980.

57 ". . . and a few that they do not." Crist, "Angel Cordero: The Jockey Fans Love to Hate."

58 ". . . I'm going to make him run." Associated Press, "Six to Oppose 'Bid' Tuesday in Fla. Derby," *Louisville Courier-Journal,* March 4, 1979.

58 ". . . will get beat by thirteen lengths." Ibid.

58 ". . . He wants to run now." Shelby Strother, "Spectacular Bid—Racing's Superhorse," *Florida Today,* March 11, 1979.

58 ". . . could have got the horse killed!" Bob Whitley, "Golden Act May Be Derby Sleeper," *Pittsburgh Post Gazette,* May 4, 1979.

58 . . . shame as tears welled in his eyes. William Leggett, "It Wasn't Much of a Joy Ride," *Sports Illustrated,* March 19, 1979.

58 ". . . kick you right into next year. . . . I hope he does." Billy Reed, "Shoemaker May Get Call from Delp to Ride Bid," *Louisville Courier-Journal,* March 9, 1979.

58 ". . . You go *outside* with this S.O.B." Billy Reed, "Big Day for 'Bid' No Picnic for Young Rider," *Louisville Courier-Journal,* March 7, 1979 (emphasis added).

58 ". . . is that he knows how dumb he is." Maryjean Wall, "Rice Will Have to Revive Franklin's Fading Star," *Lexington Herald,* March 20, 1979.

58 ". . . Ronnie really screwed it up." Andrew Beyer, "Spectacular Bid Prevails Despite Poor Derby Ride," *Washington Post,* March 6, 1979.

60 . . . Franklin showed "bad judgment" and "panic." Ibid.

60 ". . . a tribute to Spectacular Bid's ability." Reed, "Big Day for 'Bid' No Picnic for Young Rider."

60 ". . . the image of Maryland." Editorial, "Humiliated: Scolding of Spectacular Bid's Jockey by Trainer Inexcusable," Meyerhoff Collection, Book 3, Keeneland Library.

60 ". . . understand what they're saying—Spics!" Reed, "Big Day for 'Bid' No Picnic for Young Rider."

60 ". . . to ride the best horse in the country." Ibid.

60 ". . . decision to make. But I love him." MaryjeanWall, "Trainer, Jockey Discontent in Spectacular Bid Camp," *Lexington Herald,* March 8, 1979.

60 ". . . have to watch it and see what happens." Ibid.

61 ". . . he'll find out what intimidation is." Ibid.

61 . . . stages of speed during the race. Dave Goldman, "The Look of Class," *Thoroughbred Record,* March 14, 1979.

61 ". . . he wanted to see me hurt." Ross Peddicord, "Franklin's Family Happier Now," *Baltimore Sun,* Meyerhoff Collection, Book 4, Keeneland Library.

61 ". . . submarined by a champion." Steve Cady, "Rider Still Uncertain for Spectacular Bid," *New York Times,* March 8, 1979.

61 . . . Franklin as the long shot at 20 to 1. Jack Mann, "Franklin Unlikely to Ride in Derby," *Washington Star,* March 8, 1979.

61 ". . . all of Spectacular Bid's races." Steve Cady, "Franklin Still Spectacular Bid's Rider," *New York Times,* March 13, 1979.

61 . . . Franklin was "overwhelmingly happy" and cried. Ibid.

61 ". . . and a dedicated one. He listens good." Ibid.

62 ". . . I don't give a damn." Teddy Cox, "A Tearful Delp: Franklin to Ride Spectacular Bid," *Daily Racing Form,* March 13, 1979.

62 ". . . in the upper echelons of racing." Andrew Beyer, "Franklin Keeps Spectacular Bid; Keeping Franklin Is a Big Gamble," *New York Times,* March 12, 1979.

62 ". . . experience means virtually everything." Reed, "Shoemaker May Get Call from Delp to Ride Bid."

62 ". . . for the sake of that horse." Barbara H. Bailey, "Bid's Irons Belong to Franklin," Meyerhoff Collection, Book 4, Keeneland Library.

62 . . . said it was "like a beach." Billy Reed, "Heat at Hallandale: Trainer Grover 'Bud' Delp Gets His Dander up, but He and Spectacular Bid Cool Out Together," *Louisville Courier-Journal,* March 6, 1979.

62 ". . . that could have been prevented." Ibid.

63 ". . . So how good is he?" Ibid.

63 ". . . the first sign of nervousness." Edwin Pope, "Delp Sounds Pretty Spectacular over 'Bid,'" *Lexington Herald,* February 17, 1979.

63 ". . . that somebody else gets a higher one." Douglas S. Looney, "He's Got the Right Horse Here," *Sports Illustrated,* November 23, 1978.

63 ". . . who's ever looked through a bridle." Beyer, "Spectacular Bid: List of Doubters Is Thinning Out."

63 ". . . in all the turf clubs in the world." Shelby Strother, "Riding a Horse's Coattails Can Be Best Ride of All," *Wilmington (DE) Morning News,* March 15, 1979.

64 ". . . could have won even with the weight." Associated Press, "Flying Paster Upset by Pole Position," *San Bernardino County Sun,* March 18, 1979.

64 ". . . I ran against him, and I know." Associated Press, "Golden Act Wins Louisiana Derby after Velasquez' Foul Claim Denied," *Louisville Courier-Journal,* March 19, 1979.

65 ". . . important thing in racing is luck." Dave Koerner, "Can Bid's Luck Hold?" *Louisville Courier-Journal,* March 24, 1979.

65 ". . . I'd knock his teeth out." Ibid.

65 ". . . ignorant thing that ends a horse like this." Ibid.

65 ". . . I am a little curious why." Judy Mann, "Being Wealthy Isn't All There Is to Life; Wealth Not All There Is to Good Life," *Washington Post,* March 30, 1979.

65 ". . . and some not so great." Nellie Blagden, "Okay, Harry & Teresa Meyerhoff Aren't Household Names: What About Their Three-Year-Old?" *People,* June 11, 1979.

65 ". . . dinner with friends in Palm Beach." Edwin Pope, "There's No Mystery to Belmont Finish, Spectacular Bid Just Had a Bad Day," *Lexington Herald,* June 12, 1979.

65 ". . . sure I know what establishment is." Ibid.

65 ". . . didn't know the horse's were that good." Ibid.

66 ". . . the persons to whom they will speak." Betty Cuniberti, "Bidding Adieu to a Barmaid's Life," *Washington Star,* May 20, 1979.

66 ". . . considered ourselves regular people." Teresa Meyerhoff Pete, interview by the author, January 5, 2017.

66 ". . . It's tough getting used to it." Linell Smith, "Teresa Meyerhoff Has a Spectacular View of the Winner's Circle," Meyerhoff Collection, Book 5, Keeneland Library.

66 ". . . They soon should be." Schultz, "Bid Spectacular, Even in the Rain."

66 ". . . it would be one like this one, though." Ibid.

66 ". . . I'll ride my own race and try to win." Dave Koerner, "Feuding Franklin, Velasquez Will Be in Outside Positions," *Louisville Courier-Journal,* March 23, 1979.

66 ". . . be the worst rider in the world." Ibid.

67 ". . . to find a way to get him beaten." Andrew Beyer, "'Bid' Rout Expected; Spectacular Bid Expected to Breeze to Wire; Spotlight on Franklin in Flamingo," *Washington Post,* March 24, 1979.

67 ". . . manage to sit on him, Ronnie?" Randy Schultz, "Spectacular Bid Runs Away with Flamingo," *Palm Beach Post,* March 25, 1979.

67 ". . . What would I have done then?" Ibid.

67 ". . . It's worse than Muhammad Ali's." Dave Koerner, "Flamingo Runaway Has Spectacular Bid on Rose-Strewn Path," *Louisville Courier-Journal,* March 25, 1979.

67 ". . . opened up four or five lengths. Effortless." Ibid.

68 ". . . I've always had faith in you." Schultz, "Spectacular Bid Runs Away with Flamingo."

68 ". . . to keep his mind on business." Koerner, "Flamingo Runaway Has Spectacular Bid on Rose-Strewn Path."

68 ". . . The answer is emphatically yes." Andrew Beyer, "Spectacular (?) Bid; 'Superhorse' Is Decidedly Slowing Down; Trainer Delp May Soon Find His 'Lemon' Is out of Juice," *Washington Post,* March 27, 1979.

68 ". . . take any chances—even with a ten-length lead." Ibid.

68 ". . . right now for one such bad trip." Ibid.

69 ". . . He's a superhorse." Ibid.

69 ". . . confident about my colt's chances." Leon Rasmussen, "A Class by Himself," *Thoroughbred Record,* April 9, 1979.

69 ". . . Spectacular Bid has been beating in Florida." Ibid.

69 ". . . made some ridiculous statements." Paul Oberjuerge, "Flying Paster, West's Best, Bids for Spectacular Upset," *San Bernardino County Sun,* April 8, 1979.

69 ". . . probably never lose another race." Steve Cady, "Spectacular Bid Has Trainer Smelling Roses," *New York Times,* March 5, 1979.

70 ". . . my horse is in good shape." Dave Koerner, "Delp Confident Spectacular Bid Will Demolish Blue Grass Rivals," *Louisville Courier-Journal,* April 26, 1979.

70 ". . . and just thinks there's no hereafter." Jim Bolus, "Adams Says Spectacular Bid Will Lose," *Louisville Courier-Journal,* April 7, 1979.

70 . . . he should gallop with a cane. Maryjean Wall, "Delp Should Have Stuck to Original Story without Pinning Blame," *Lexington Herald-Leader,* June 14, 1979.

71 ". . . cut your throat if he gets a chance." Neil Milbert, "Spectacular Bid's Trainer Sees Red before Blue Grass," *Chicago Tribune,* April 26, 1979.

71 ". . . thwart any future offer we might make." Ibid.

71 ". . . candidate at Keeneland in many years." Joe Hirsch, "Spectacular Bid's Work in 1:22³/₅ Delights Delp," *Daily Racing Form,* April 18, 1979.

71 ". . . sets him up for the Kentucky Derby." Dave Koerner, "'Perfect'; Delp Praises Spectacular Bid after Derby Colt's Public Drill," *Louisville Courier-Journal,* April 18, 1979.

72 ". . . I think he can break the track record." Andrew Beyer, "Bid's Slow Win

Prompts Debate; Jockey Says Bid 'Playing,'" *Washington Post,* April 27, 1979.

72 "... and we beat him all the time." Jack Mann, "How Bud Almost Did . . . with Bid," *Turf and Sport Digest,* June 1980, 18.

73 "... playing with them the rest of the way." Ibid.

73 "... an open-and-shut Kentucky Derby." Beyer, "Bid's Slow Win Prompts Debate."

73 "... a mile and an eighth better than [one minute] fifty." Dave Koerner, "Bid Wins Again, but Adams Isn't Convinced," *Louisville Courier-Journal,* April 27, 1979.

73 "... two or three lengths difference between either horse." Ibid.

74 "... the tall roan colt thrives on it." Associated Press, "Delp Works 'Bid' Hard for Derby," *Baltimore Sun,* April 12, 1979.

74 ... keep him from going to Churchill Downs. Teddy Cox, "Rumors Fly after Spectacular Bid Is Visited by Vet," *Daily Racing Form,* April 9, 1979.

74 "... after all of those ridiculous reports." Ibid.

74 "... didn't even have to put the stick to him." Dave Koerner, "Flying Paster's Best Race Ever Wins Hollywood Derby," *Louisville Courier-Journal,* April 15, 1979.

74 "... Spectacular Bid beat everybody on the East." Ibid.

75 "... the equal, at the very least, of Affirmed." Barry Irwin, "Flying to Kentucky," *Thoroughbred Record,* April 25, 1979.

75 "... the best I've ever had." Oberjuerge, "Flying Paster, West's Best, Bids for Spectacular Upset."

75 ... were "not rooting for us." Billy Reed, "Delp Blasts Establishment, Praises Harthill, Bid's Vet," *Louisville Courier-Journal,* April 26, 1979.

75 "... get lucky and stumble into a great horse." Ibid.

75 "... and I'm not going to now." Ibid.

75 ... jealousy of him riding Spectacular Bid. Dave Koerner, "He's Still 'Plain Old Ronald,' but He's No Longer a Quitter," *Louisville Courier-Journal,* April 15, 1979.

5. Derby Fever

1. Meaning that it was a hand ride, in which the jockey did not have to use the whip.

2. Forego, a gelding, finished fourth in the Derby but went on to race until he was eight years old, collecting thirty-four wins in fifty-seven starts and earning almost $2 million.

Sources by Page Number

77 ". . . the Kentucky Derby could be a war." Steve Cady, "East vs. West: Spectacular Bid Meets Flying Paster at Last," *New York Times,* April 30, 1979.

78 . . . the other called it a toss-up. Ibid.

78 ". . . He should be dynamite." "Trainers Give Edge to Paster in Derby," *New York Times,* April 30, 1979.

78 ". . . and won the Wood Memorial." Ibid.

78 ". . . Pierce is hard to beat." Ibid.

78 ". . . got the best horse, you'll win your share." Ibid.

78 ". . . They're dead-even, in my opinion." Ibid.

79 ". . . run the race of his life Saturday." Andrew Beyer, "'Bid' Still the Best in Field; 'Greatest Handicapper' Sees No Bet," *Washington Post,* May 4, 1979.

79 ". . . anyway, and he shouldn't have run." Don Pierce, interview by the author, June 3, 2017.

79 ". . . had to go to the bathroom." Maryjean Wall, "Campbell Figures Flying Paster Will Earn Respect," *Lexington Herald,* May 1, 1979.

80 ". . . That's the way I am." Edward L. Bowen, "Derby Prelude," *Blood-Horse,* May 7, 1979, 2247.

80 ". . . That's where the pressure is." Dave Koerner, "Spectacular Bud? Delp Bloats Listeners with Quotes Concerning His 'S.O.B.' of a Horse," *Louisville Courier-Journal,* May 1, 1979.

80 ". . . every fraction of his talent every second." Mike Sullivan, "Spectacular Boasts Made Delp's Victory that Much Sweeter," *Louisville Courier-Journal,* May 6, 1979.

80 ". . . That's all people think about." Wall, "Campbell Figures Flying Paster Will Earn Respect."

80 ". . . disseminated for public debate." Randy Harvey, "Ronnie Franklin: A Kid on the Spot," *St. Louis Post-Dispatch,* May 6, 1979.

81 ". . . biggest gamble in Kentucky Derby history." Billy Reed, "Franklin Remains Confident in Hot Seat, Despite Skeptics," *Louisville Courier-Journal,* April 27, 1979.

81 ". . . the seventh game of the World Series." Randy Harvey, "Franklin's Ridden out Hard Times," *Atlanta Journal-Constitution*, May 5, 1979.

81 ". . . knows how to take care of himself." Ibid.

81 . . . called the workout "perfecto." Dave Koerner, "Luis Keeps the Barrera Family in Limelight with Screen King," *Louisville Courier-Journal,* May 2, 1979

81 ". . . the Churchill Downs track to a plowed field." Ibid.

81 ". . . Is he always like this?" Andrew Beyer, "Tale of 2 Trainers and Defense of 1 City—Louisville," *Washington Post,* May 2, 1979.

81 ". . . look in a mirror and say, 'Delp, you're a dumb S.O.B.'" Ibid.

82 ". . . basket case before he gets to the Derby." Clive Gammon, "Big Horse Comin'," *Sports Illustrated,* April 23, 1979, 102.

82 ". . . What else can I say?" Joel Bierig, "Meyerhoffs 'Sit in' for Delp, Take the Heat at Dinner," *Louisville Courier-Journal,* May 3, 1979.

82 ". . . like Foolish Pleasure (Jolley's 1975 Derby winner)." Ibid.

82 ". . . he don't belong in the race." Koerner, "Luis Keeps the Barrera Family in Limelight with Screen King."

83 . . . "nor will General Assembly or Flying Paster." Steve Cady, "Maiden Is Surprise Kentucky Derby Entry," *New York Times,* May 4, 1979.

83 ". . . Spectacular Bid can't go over a mile." Jack Mann, "Bid Gets His Chance to Convince the Last Doubter Today," *Washington Star,* May 5, 1979.

83 ". . . I have a conviction and I have to follow it." Ibid.

83 ". . . It's his money, though." Cady, "Maiden Is Surprise Kentucky Derby Entry."

84 . . . and three chose General Assembly. Associated Press, United Press International, "Writers Coast-to-Coast Select for 105th Derby," *Lexington Herald,* May 5, 1979.

84 ". . . previous victories proved his brilliance." Beyer, "'Bid' Still the Best in Field."

84 . . . Tom only laughed. Jack Murphy, "Fascinating People Go with Fast Horses," *San Diego Union,* May 8, 1979.

84 ". . . worried about it. I think we'll win." Teresa Meyerhoff Pete, interview by the author, January 5, 2017.

84 ". . . in the night thinking of him." Sandy Banisky, "If Spectacular Bid Bombs, Life's Still a Run for the Roses," *Baltimore Sun,* May 4, 1979.

84 . . . the next race on the schedule. Associated Press, "Infield Throng at Derby Happy, Hardy," *Newport News (VA) Daily Press,* May 6, 1979.

85 ". . . of thrill and tension and worry." Exhibit, Kentucky Derby Museum.

85 ". . . he'll make a race out of it." Horse Racing, "1979 Kentucky Derby—Spectacular Bid," transcript, YouTube, https://www.youtube.com/watch?v=dc5ROt8HoC4.

85 ". . . others to be considered in there too." Ibid.

86 ". . . make it fast. Hurry up." Inquirer Wire Services, "It's a Different Winner's Circle, and, Maybe, a Different Jockey," *Philadelphia Inquirer,* May 6, 1979.

86 ". . . tell him you love him." Sullivan, "Spectacular Boasts Made Delp's Victory that Much Sweeter."

87 ". . . geared up coming to the paddock." Horse Racing, "1979 Kentucky Derby—Spectacular Bid."

87 ". . . He's ready to run." Billy Reed and Jim Bolus, "Bid and Franklin Simply 'Spectacular' in Run for the Roses," *Louisville Courier-Journal,* May 6, 1979.

87 ". . . Then ride your race." Sullivan, "Spectacular Boasts Made Delp's Victory that Much Sweeter."

87 ". . . Don't misjudge the finish line." Dan Mearns, "The Denouement," *Thoroughbred Record,* May 16, 1979, 1573.

88 ". . . going to draw away like he usually does." Ibid.

88 ". . . mile and a quarter's a pretty long race." Ibid.

88 ". . . "Yeah, I am pretty confident." Meyerhoff Pete interview.

88 ". . . You'll know what to do." Mike Klingarran, "Franklin Recalls Ride of His Life," *Baltimore Sun,* May 15, 2004.

89 . . . as if to ask, "Can this be happening again?" Cindy Morris, "Unflappable Teresa Meyerhoff Hawksworth's Chief Diplomat," *Cincinnati Enquirer,* May 6, 1979.

89 ". . . let him do his own thing early." Mearns, "Denouement."

90 ". . . just made my horse madder." Reed and Bolus, "Bid and Franklin Simply 'Spectacular' in Run for the Roses."

90 ". . . the other horse spit the bit right out." Steve Cady, "Spectacular Bid Takes Kentucky Derby by 2¾ Lengths," *New York Times,* May 6, 1979.

90 ". . . I guess maybe it was Spectacular Bid." Ibid.

90 ". . . he couldn't respond and he was gone." Ibid.

92 ". . . realize he had lapped that horse." Dick Young, "Great Redeemer Sparks Controversy over Maidens in Derby," *Lexington Herald,* May 7, 1979.

92 ". . . Then everything came by like a blur." Associated Press, "Great Redeemer's Great Flop OK with Pretender's Owner," *Newport News (VA) Daily Press,* May 6, 1979.

92 ". . . You is a pro." Ken Denlinger, "Spectacular Bid Surges to Triumph," *Washington Post,* May 6, 1979.

92 . . . Franklin ignored the question. Russ Harris, "Spectacular Bid Roars," *New York Daily News,* May 6, 1979.

92 ". . . glad to come home a winner." United Press International, "Spectacular Bid's Stretch Drive Earns Kentucky Derby Victory," May 6, 1979.

92 ". . . he certainly proved it today." Horse Racing, "1979 Kentucky Derby—Spectacular Bid."

92 ". . . dreamed of coming here with a good horse." Joseph P. Pons Jr., "The Breeders," *Blood-Horse,* May 14, 1979.

92 . . . as the owner of the winning horse. Mark Simon, "The Epilogue," *Thoroughbred Record,* May 16, 1979, 1575.

93 ". . . the longest striding colt in the race." Ibid.

93 ". . . but it won't be Baltimore." Ibid., 1577.

93 ". . . I B.S. a lot. But I never lie." Denlinger, "Spectacular Bid Surges to Triumph."

93 ". . . smartest horse my dad ever had." Associated Press, "Spectacular Bid Settles for Doughnut, *Tallahassee Democrat,* May 6, 1979.

93 ". . . worry about were the ones ahead," he said. United Press International, "Bud Delp No Liar, Talks Triple Crown," *Newport News (VA) Daily Press,* May 6, 1979.

94 ". . . I could run him again Wednesday." Bill Millsaps, "The 'Delpic' Oracle," *Richmond Times-Dispatch,* May 6, 1979.

94 ". . . that should make me sad. It doesn't." Ibid.

94 ". . . Your horse done real good." Will Grimsley, "The Kid Talks, Bid Listens," *Santa Cruz Sentinel,* May 6, 1979.

94 . . . Franklin said, returning the smile. Rick Bailey, "Paster Sent Cruelly Back to West," *Lexington Herald,* May 5, 1979.

94 ". . . *We won the Kentucky Derby.*" Ross Newhan, "Meyerhoffs Love to Horse Around," *Los Angeles Times,* May 27, 1979.

6. Home Again

1. Secretariat's official time in the Preakness was wrong because of a malfunctioning timer. In 2012, after reviewing several other clocked times, Maryland race officials changed his official time from 1:54²/5 to 1:53, which makes Secretariat the record holder for all three Triple Crown races.

Sources by Page Number

96 ". . . the same groom it's all the same." United Press International, "Spectacular Bid Hometown Favorite," *Opelousas (LA) Daily World,* May 17, 1979.

96 ". . . maybe one of the greatest of all time." Andrew Beyer, "Spectacular Bid Surges to Triumph; Spectacular Bid Wins," *Washington Post,* May 6, 1979.

96 ". . . winner of the once-elusive Triple Crown." Russ Harris, "Spectacular Bid Roars," *New York Daily News,* May 6, 1979.

96 ". . . competitive world of Thoroughbred horse racing." Will Grimsley, "Spectacular Bid's Win Was for the Little People," *Kokomo (IN) Tribune,* May 7, 1979.

96 ". . . too much hard early running." Steve Cady, "Spectacular Bid Takes Kentucky Derby by 2¾ Lengths," *New York Times,* May 6, 1979.

96 ". . . Franklin became a pro today." Ken Denlinger, "Spectacular Bid Surges to Triumph," *Washington Post,* May 6, 1979.

97 ". . . 'You can put your head in the air now.'" Will Grimsley, "Bid's Victory Was for 'Little People,'" *Trenton (NJ) Evening Times*, May 7, 1979.

97 ". . . shy awkward boy of his pre-Derby days." Dan Mearns, "Coming Home," *Thoroughbred Record*, May 30, 1979, 1696.

97 ". . . avoiding the chance of disaster." Beyer, "Spectacular Bid Surges to Triumph."

97 ". . . defeated Spectacular Bid on Saturday." Andrew Beyer, "The Bid Belongs in Best; Bid Ranks Right behind Secretariat," *Washington Post*, May 7, 1979.

97 ". . . I'm very disappointed." Rick Bailey, "Paster Sent Cruelly Back to West," *Lexington Herald*, May 5, 1979.

97 . . . taxing Derby and was "sore all over." Dave Koerner, "Owners of Screen King, Flying Paster Expect Better Race in Preakness," *Louisville Courier-Journal*, May 18, 1979.

98 ". . . as he ever came out of a race." Associated Press, "'Bid' Travels to Pimlico," *Louisville Courier-Journal*, May 8, 1979.

98 ". . . He's a dead fit colt." Associated Press, "Churchill Downs Gets OTB Funds," *Louisville Courier-Journal*, May 14, 1979.

98 ". . . does not carry the racetrack with him." Dave Koerner, "Screen King, Paster Owners Are Hopeful," *Louisville Courier-Journal*, May 18, 1979.

99 ". . . when he returned to the barn." Steve Cady, "Preakness Question: Who Will Finish 2nd?" *New York Times*, May 18, 1979.

99 ". . . speed into him now if we need to use it." Ibid.

99 . . . but "put it through the blender." Dave Koerner, "Delp Not Squeezing the Lemon," *Louisville Courier-Journal*, May 19, 1979.

99 ". . . freshest horse that has ever come out of the Derby." Ibid.

100 ". . . seemed like a good thing to do." Billy Reed, "Preakness Win Would Be Music to Opera's Ears . . . Because Bid Paraphernalia Sells for a Song," *Louisville Courier-Journal*, May 18, 1979.

101 ". . . Ronnie Franklin wants outside." Maryjean Wall, "Bid, Flying Paster Are Side by Side in Preakness Field," *Lexington Herald*, May 18, 1979.

101 ". . . expect to see Flying Paster run much better." Paul Nochelski, "Today's Preakness a Race for Second," *Rochester Democrat and Chronicle*, May 19, 1979.

101 ". . . the lesser animals who chase them." Andrew Beyer, "Excuses Will Not Beat Bid," *Washington Post*, May 15, 1979.

102 ". . . in the Preakness field can stop him." Andrew Beyer, "Only a Fast Pace by General Assembly Can Beat 'Bid'; Preakness Should Be a Rerun," *New York Times*, May 17, 1979.

102 ". . . my colt to be on General Assembly's tail." Ibid.

102 ". . . have been here eating crab cakes." Edward L. Bowen, "He'll Take Me to the Wire," *Blood-Horse,* May 28, 1979, 2514.

102 ". . . Damn, you're as crazy as the boss." Steve Haskin, "The Bid: Sustained Greatness," *Blood-Horse,* December 1, 2015, http://cs.bloodhorse.com/blogs/horse-racing-steve-haskin/archive/2015/12/01/the-bid-sustained-greatness.aspx.

102 ". . . 5:40 p.m. winner's circle." Jack Murphy, "Tough Horse, Tough Kid Win Preakness," *San Diego Union,* May 20, 1979.

103 ". . . and get him running." Dave Kindred, "Bid Captures Preakness Spectacularly," *Washington Post,* May 20, 1979.

103 . . . one couple even got married. Tom Yorke, "Bid's Jockey Is Fined for Striking and Kicking Horse," *Washington Star,* May 23, 1979.

103 ". . . seemed to be looking for Franklin." Andrew Beyer, "Bid Captures Preakness Spectacularly; Burst Leaves Leaders up the Track; Franklin Foils Cordero Tactic," *Washington Post,* May 19, 1979.

106 ". . . never saw him explode like that." ABC-TV, "100th Preakness Stakes—Spectacular Bid," transcript, YouTube, https://www.youtube.com/watch?v=Wcs8TPykpFg.

106 . . . Bid "won with resolution." Bob Barnet, "Spectacular Bid?—Heck of a Race Horse!" *Muncie (IN) Star Press,* May 21, 1979.

106 ". . . and I love that horse." Tom Coakley, "Ecstacy [sic] in Dundalk," Meyerhoff Collection, Book 7, Keeneland Library.

106 ". . . clear out to the outside fencing." ABC-TV, "100th Preakness Stakes—Spectacular Bid."

106 ". . . 'Angel, Angel, what happened?'" Joseph Durso, "Cordero Is Accused of Devilish Riding," *New York Times,* May 20, 1979.

106 ". . . down there where he belonged." Steve Cady, "1:54¹/₅ Time Is Near Record before 72,607," *New York Times,* May 20, 1979.

107 ". . . Cordero had to slow down." Kindred, "Bid Captures Preakness Spectacularly."

107 ". . . a race rider just like he is." Billy Reed, "More 'Horseplay' Colors Cordero Preakness Villain," *Louisville Courier-Journal,* May 21, 1979.

107 ". . . America's premier horse races." Kindred, "Bid Captures Preakness Spectacularly."

107 ". . . something else to do, but nothing to prove." Associated Press, "Bid's Win at Pimlico Spectacular," *Lexington Herald,* May 21, 1979.

107 ". . . for Baltimore and Maryland as I am for us." Ibid.

107 ". . . It was spectacular." Ibid.

107 ". . . How great is he, fellows?" Red Smith, "After the Race: Weather Cool, Trainer Mild," *New York Times,* May 21, 1979.

107 ". . . That would be all right with me." Ibid.

107 ". . . I don't talk to dummies." Associated Press, "Meyerhoff's Bid Just Fantastic," *Springfield (MA) Union*, May 20, 1979.

107 ". . . a cinch" for the Triple Crown, he boasted. Kindred, "Bid Captures Preakness Spectacularly."

108 ". . . He is one bad hombre." Mike Klingaman, "A Spectacular Hero," *Baltimore Sun*, May 9, 1999.

108 ". . . guess it was a good thing we won." Andy Belfiore, "A Spectacular Run," *Thoroughbred Daily News*, September 17, 2009, 23.

108 . . . with a few lines of cocaine. Bill Christine, "Still Riding: Jockey Ronnie Franklin Now Races at Pimlico," *Los Angeles Times*, June 4, 1988.

7. One More for the Crown

1. Belmont Park changed the song to "New York, New York" in 1996.

Sources by Page Number

110 ". . . biting, kicking, apparently asking to run." Bob Maisel, "Two in Bid's Supporting Cast Get the Oscars," *Baltimore Sun*, May 27, 1979.

110 ". . . that way with any horse before." "Franklin Beats Horse, Fined," *New York Times*, May 23, 1979.

111 ". . . by kicking him in the belly." Charles Lamb, "Horse Sense a la Delp: 'I Kicked Him in the Belly, Too,'" Meyerhoff Collection, Book 7, Keeneland Library.

111 ". . . to the highest court in the land" if Franklin were suspended. United Press International, "Jockey Franklin in Limbo," *Huntingdon (PA) Daily News*, June 1, 1979.

111 . . . try to keep him off the other horse. "Maryland Stewards Clear Franklin for Belmont," *Louisville Courier-Journal*, June 2, 1979.

111 ". . . isn't one of his characteristics." Bob Barnet, "Ronnie Franklin—Boy Wonder!" *Muncie (IN) Star Press*, June 8, 1979.

111 ". . . speeches can do to a nineteen-year-old kid." Ibid.

112 ". . . control over the horses he rides." Andrew Beyer, "'Blameless' Is Franklin—and Inept; Franklin as Jockey: Few Do It Worse," *New York Times*, June 1, 1979.

112 ". . . beaten because of Franklin's ineptitude." Ibid.

112 ". . . The other ten percent can go pound sand." William Nack, "Some More Yelps from Bud Delp," *Sports Illustrated*, June 11, 1979, 67.

112 ". . . get beat so they can laugh at me." Bill Millsaps, "Derby's Lesson: 'Don't Knock Bid's Jock,'" *Richmond Times Dispatch*, May 7, 1979.

112 ". . . unless he runs into some terribly bad luck." Steve Cady, "Barn 13 Is Home for 'Bid,'" *New York Times,* June 2, 1979.

112 ". . . and that's a lucky number." Ibid.

113 ". . . probably finish second in the race." Steve Cady, "Delp's Only Fear Is the Weather," *New York Times,* June 3, 1979.

113 ". . . but it was a tiring track." "Final Prep for 'Bid,'" *New York Times,* June 5, 1979.

113 ". . . in the country can come close to him." Neil Milbert, "Spectacular Bud Delp Just Along for the Ride," *Chicago Tribune,* June 5, 1979.

113 ". . . seeing that everything is all right with Bid." Ibid.

114 ". . . the day he runs against Affirmed." Neil Milbert, "Delp Going after Bid vs. Affirmed," *Chicago Tribune,* June 7, 1979.

114 ". . . different horse than he has ever met before." Ibid.

114 ". . . talking to animals than sports writers." Jack Murray, "Delp Looks Past Belmont to Meeting with Affirmed," *Cincinnati Enquirer,* May 21, 1979.

114 ". . . we'd probably be pipe-dreaming it." Steve Cady, "Coastal's Belmont Status Is Undecided," *New York Times,* June 6, 1979.

115 ". . . knock him on his ass." Mike Lupica, "Franklin Says: Cordero Threatened to Kill Me," *New York Daily News,* June 8, 1979.

115 ". . . made no effort to take the horse off the boy." Cady, "Coastal's Belmont Status Is Undecided."

115 ". . . important occasion seems questionable." Dale Austin, "N.Y. Stewards Fail to Rise to the Occasion," *Baltimore Sun,* June 10, 1979.

115 ". . . I'm doing mine. We're friends." Steve Cady, "Spectacular Bid Shoots for a Sweep," *New York Times,* June 9, 1979.

116 ". . . we would have scratched." Dan Mearns, "He Could Not Take Manhattan," *Thoroughbred Record,* June 20, 1979, 1928.

116 ". . . Why is he coming in here?" *New York Times* News Service, "Delp Will Remember Bid Fondly," *San Bernardino County Sun,* June 10, 1979.

116 ". . . I wouldn't hesitate a second [to run him]," he said. Andrew Beyer, "Suddenly, Bid Has Belmont Competition," *New York Times,* June 8, 1979.

116 ". . . got that one horse [Coastal] to beat." Ibid.

116 ". . . right on the lead and not fool around." Ibid.

117 ". . . how many lengths he can take this third leg." Buddy Martin, "Triple Crown's Heir Apparent," *New York Daily News,* June 3, 1979.

117 ". . . It should be Bid's easiest race." Jack Patterson, "Surprises in Belmont Challenge," *Akron (OH) Beacon-Journal,* June 8, 1979.

117 ". . . I'll settle for thirty-one and a half." Martin, "Triple Crown's Heir Apparent."

117 ". . . no others in the field that can win." Patterson, "Surprises in Belmont Challenge."

117 ". . .That takes a lot of luck." Jack Kiser, "Bid Goes for Triple," *Philadelphia Daily News,* June 8, 1979.

117 ". . . on the forehead by the Man Upstairs." Ibid.

117 ". . . if I thought anything wasn't just right." Ibid.

118 ". . . Hey boss, this horse is lame." Michael Yockel, "The Great Bid Foiled," *Pressbox,* May 16, 2006, https://www.pressboxonline.com/story/187/the-great-bid-foiled.

118 ". . . It was stuck in there as hard as cement." Bill Christine, "Less than Spectacular Bid," *Los Angeles Times,* June 4, 1999.

118 ". . . you couldn't even see where it came in." Yockel, "Great Bid Foiled."

119 . . . "he would never bother it," Delp said. Ibid.

119 ". . . The ballgame is over." Jack Mann, "Bid and the Pin: The Story Raises a Few Questions," *Washington Star,* June 11, 1979.

119 ". . . a pin prick, and it would probably be fine." Teresa Meyerhoff Pete, interview by the author, January 5, 2017.

120 ". . . We want him to be Buddy Delp." Dick Clemente, "Belmont TV Failed, Too," *Florida Today,* June 10, 1979.

121 ". . . Bid is the only horse shook up." Horse Racing, "1979 Belmont Stakes—Coastal: CBS Broadcast," transcript, YouTube, https://www.youtube.com/watch?v=umZtcw1HeFU.

122 . . . when all four feet are off the ground. Erin Birkenhauer, "Racehorse Lead Changes Explained," West Point Thoroughbreds, January 30, 2015, http://www.westpointtb.com/news-and-blog/blog/2015/01/30/racehorse-lead-changes-explained.

123 . . . when traveling through an airport. Ibid.

123 . . . snapped his fingers and said, "Now." Susan Reimer, "Smiles Turn to Tears and Concern for the Bid," *Baltimore Sun,* June 10, 1979.

124 ". . . We're gonna get beat." "And Here's What They Had to Say," *Louisville Courier-Journal,* June 10, 1979.

124 . . . alluding to the injury. Reimer, "Smiles Turn to Tears and Concern for the Bid."

124 . . . "We are speechless." Ibid.

125 ". . . commit himself a mile away from home." Horse Racing, "1979 Belmont Stakes—Coastal: CBS Broadcast."

125 ". . . to crawl in a hole somewhere." Ron Franklin, interview by Katherine Veitschegger, April 28, 2010.

125 ". . . the best horse won." Billy Reed, "Not the End: In Defeat, Delp Classy," *Louisville Courier-Journal,* June 10, 1979.

126 ". . . He just got outrun, that's all." Ibid.

126 . . . for at least three weeks. Steve Cady, "Trainer Says 'Bid' Ran Hurt," *New York Times,* June 11, 1979.

126 ". . . on the lead with almost a mile to go." Steve Cady, "Coastal Wins Belmont; Spectacular Bid Is Third," *New York Times,* June 10, 1979.

126 ". . . absolutely no sense whatsoever." William Nack, interview by the author, July 9, 2017.

127 ". . . a mile and a half and wind up winning." United Press International, "Some Jockeys Blame Franklin for Spectacular Bid's Loss in Belmont," *Lexington Herald,* June 11, 1979.

127 ". . . outspoken Maryland crew surrounding Bid." Ibid.

127 ". . . shipped around the country for the Triple Crown." Ibid.

127 ". . . I figure I did a good job." Knight Ridder Dispatches, "Franklin Feels Like Crying after Bid for Triple Crown Is Spoiled," *Lexington Herald,* June 10, 1979.

127 ". . . demanding one-and-a-half-mile distance." Andrew Beyer, "Coastal Peaks in Belmont Stretch, Runs Past Bid," *New York Times,* June 9, 1979.

127 ". . . even if he doesn't have a legitimate alibi." Andrew Beyer, "Horses Have No Alibi," *New York Times,* June 12, 1979.

128 ". . . he wouldn't have made no mistakes." Don Pierce, interview by the author, June 3, 2017.

128 ". . . He never choked up before." Ken Denlinger, "Coastal Finishes Bid's Try for Triple," *New York Times,* June 9, 1979.

128 ". . . But I guess it happened." Hal Bodley, "Skittish Hint Begins Less than Spectacular Day," *Sioux Falls (SD) Argus-Leader,* June 10, 1979.

128 ". . . Every turkey has his Thanksgiving." Jim Bolus, "Cordero Gloats over Bid's Loss, Chides Media for Pick," *Louisville Courier-Journal,* June 10, 1979.

129 ". . . was a superhorse. Super shit." Ibid.

129 ". . . I would have if I had been a rider." "And Here's What They Had to Say."

129 ". . . but I'll remember him pretty good." Red Smith, "I'm Always Ready to Lose," *New York Times,* June 10, 1979.

129 ". . . only one who ever had this happen to him." Reed, "Not the End."

129 ". . . then you better take up another profession." Ibid.

129 . . . "There, lady, you got the losers." Smith, "I'm Always Ready to Lose."

8. Growing Pains

1. Technically, this is not a fever, since a horse's temperature can range from 99 to 101 degrees. If Bid's normal temperature ran on the cool side, 101 degrees might be considered a fever.

Sources by Page Number

130 ". . . "They found a needle in a haystack." Mike Klingaman, "A Spectacular Hero," *Baltimore Sun,* May 9, 1999.

130 ". . . would have let the horse run." Steve Cady, "Trainer Says 'Bid' Ran Hurt," *New York Times,* June 11, 1979.

130 ". . . you can count on. He tells the truth." Ibid.

130 ". . . he was a little bit sore on it." Richard Delp, interview by the author, November 6, 2017.

131 ". . . but it's pretty hard to do." "Delp: Bid Was Hurt before the Belmont," *Dallas Morning News,* June 11, 1979.

131 ". . . victory over Golden Act." Jenny Kellner, "Injury Excuse for Bid Not Accepted by All," *Omaha World-Herald,* June 12, 1979.

131 ". . . too bizarre for me to make up." Maryjean Wall, "Delp Should Have Stuck to Original Story without Pinning Blame," *Lexington Herald,* June 14, 1979.

131 ". . . pursuit of an outclassed pacesetter." Joe Piscione, "Spectacular Bid's Jockey Clearly Wasn't," *Trenton (NJ) Evening Times,* June 12, 1979.

131 ". . . not until last Saturday." Russ Harris, "Pin in Bid's Hoof a Real Longshot," *New York Daily News,* June 13, 1979.

132 . . . he might have to be put down. Russ Harris, "Pin Mishap Nearly Fatal to Another Horse," *New York Daily News,* June 29, 1979.

132 ". . . Bid sprint a mile and a half?" Tom Callahan, "From the Start, Arrogance Rode for the Triple Crown," *Washington Star,* June 11, 1979.

132 ". . . And I used him up too early." Ron Franklin, interview by the author, June 3, 2017.

132 ". . . when they put up their hard-earned dough." Will Grimsley, "Delp Duped Bettors by Withholding Safety Pin Incident," *Asbury Park (NJ) Press,* June 12, 1979.

132 ". . . a case of the best horse winning." Tom Yorke, "His Vet Says Bid Could Run," *Washington Star,* June 11, 1979.

133 ". . . may not run fast tomorrow." Skip Bayless, "Only the Horse Knows Why," *Dallas Morning News,* June 13, 1979.

133 ". . . of the rail, but Franklin didn't." Alan Goldstein, "Bid's Bettors Had Right to Know," Meyerhoff Collection, Book 9, Keeneland Library.

133 ". . . we would not do less." Robert L. Ryan, "Sports Editor's Mailbox: Conditions for Belmont Were Fair to All," *New York Times,* July 1, 1979.

133 ". . . It just doesn't seem fair." Jack Mann, "Of Meyerhoffs, the Swans and Bid, and What Still Might Be," Meyerhoff Collection, Book 9, Keeneland Library.

134 "'. . . sons of bitches who called you a liar?'" Michael Yockel, "The Great Bid Foiled," *Pressbox,* May 16, 2006, https://www.pressboxonline.com/story/187/the-great-bid-foiled.

134 ". . . I think he ran with pain," he said. William Nack, "A Simply Spectacular Shoe-in for the Bid," *Sports Illustrated,* September 17, 1979.

134 ". . . he had a very serious injury." Milton C. Toby, "The Travails of a 'Pin Picker,'" *Blood-Horse,* September 15, 1979, 4735.

134 ". . . what we had to do with Spectacular Bid." Ibid.

134 ". . . hung in there and finished." Franklin interview.

135 . . . and exacerbating any minor injury. Robin Richards, interview by the author, May 11, 2016.

135 ". . . after the race he lost thirty pounds." Nack, "Simply Spectacular Shoe-in for the Bid."

135 . . . this was no formal inquiry. "Board to Investigate Bid's Belmont Injury," *Lexington Herald,* June 13, 1979.

135 ". . . can't trust Gilman if he can't trust me." Associated Press, "Bid's Trainer Didn't Trust the Officials," *New Orleans States-Item,* June 14, 1979.

135 ". . . come to the city with a great horse." "Delp: Didn't Tell NYRA Doc 'Cause I Don't Trust Him." Meyerhoff Collection, Book 9, Keeneland Library.

135 ". . . that would affect his racing performance." United Press International, "Board Says Bid Was Fit for Belmont," *Lexington Herald,* June 19, 1979.

135 . . . good horse that had faded in the stretch. Steve Cady, "Spectacular Bid Made No Promises," *Dallas Morning News,* June 20, 1979.

135 ". . . same breath with Secretariat, Seattle Slew, or Affirmed." Ibid.

136 . . . was the father of her five-month-old son. United Press International, "Paternity Suit against Franklin," *St. Louis Post-Dispatch,* June 8, 1979.

136 ". . . wasn't took into court or nothin'." Eric Siegel, "Ronnie Franklin: The Repentant Jockey Rides Again," *Baltimore Sun,* May 11, 1980.

136 . . . a white substance with a razor blade. Associated Press, "Franklin Faces Coke Charge," *St. Louis Post-Dispatch,* June 20, 1979.

136 ". . . anything I can that might pick his head up." "Delp Ponders Punishment for Jockey Franklin," *Louisville Courier-Journal,* June 21, 1979.

136 ". . . didn't say a damn word about being busted." United Press International, "Franklin Suspended by Delp," *Logansport (IN) Pharos-Tribune,* June 21, 1979.

137 ". . . is certainly entitled to a mistake." Associated Press, "Franklin's Suspension Ends after Meeting," *Louisville Courier-Herald,* June 21, 1979.

137 ". . . behind bars for four or five hours." Andrew Beyer, "Franklin Will Ride," *New York Times,* June 22, 1979.

137 ". . . Could have been my fault." Barney Nagler, "Delp Relates Franklin's Side of the Anaheim Arrest," *Daily Racing Form,* June 23, 1979.

137 ". . . he was completely ill-equipped." Andrew Beyer, "Delp Orders Franklin off His Horses," *New York Times,* June 21, 1979.

138 ". . . blame the person who threw him in?" Ibid.

138 ". . . to being a teenage kid." Red Smith, "Delp's Mistake: Having Patience with Franklin," *Palm Beach Post,* June 25, 1979.

138 . . . main reason for replacing him. Tom Meyerhoff, interview by the author, May 30, 2016.

138 ". . . Maybe something else could help." Teresa Meyerhoff Pete, interview by the author, January 5, 2017.

138 ". . . and I'm gonna find it." William Nack, "The Shoe," in *My Turf: Horses, Boxers, Blood Money, and the Sporting Life* (Cambridge, MA: Da Capo Press, 2003), 45.

140 ". . . with silken threads for reins." Ibid., 46.

140 ". . . history's all-time cavalryman." Lou Cannon, "Shoemaker, Bid's New Rider, Forever Young in Saddle," *Washington Post,* August 13, 1979.

140 . . . generally opposed to match races. Associated Press, "Affirmed-Bid Match Race Proposed," *Louisville Courier-Journal,* June 26, 1979.

141 . . . top physical shape before such a race occurred. Associated Press, "Meadowlands Wants Bid-Affirmed Match," *Louisville Courier-Journal,* June 27, 1979.

141 ". . . to make the September races." "Foot Still Tender, 'Bid' Unable to Train Hard," *Daily Racing Form,* July 13, 1979.

141 ". . . bruise is there and he knows it." Associated Press, "Bid to Race Despite Still-Tender Foot," *Dallas Morning News,* July 1, 1979.

142 ". . . horse with two sore feet." Associated Press, "Spectacular Bid's Career in Jeopardy, Tender Feet," *Santa Cruz (CA) Sentinel,* July 25, 1979.

142 ". . . Hell, I don't duck nobody." Ibid.

142 ". . . and run him next year." Ibid.

143 ". . . does his share, but he has to be watched." Jim Naughton, "Ron Franklin: Success, Failure, and Confusion," *New York Times,* July 8, 1979.

143 ". . . I let him get too big too quick." Nellie Blagden, "A Drug Bust, a Paternity Suit—Troubles Come in Battalions for Jockey Ronnie Franklin," *People,* July 9, 1979.

143 ". . . cut a few lines after the races." Richard Kucner, "Ronnie's 'Busted' Life: Can He Put It Together Again?" Meyerhoff Collecction, Book 9, Keeneland Library.

144 ". . . You're in for a ride now." Meyerhoff Pete interview.

144 ". . . he was too far ahead to matter." Associated Press, "Shoemaker, Bid

Smoke Field by 17 in Marlboro Tuneup," *Louisville Courier-Journal,* August 27, 1979.

144 ". . . some of the great ones in the world." Tom Atwell, "Spectacular Bid Breaks Delaware Track Record," *Daily Racing Form,* August 28, 1979.

144 . . . the relationship between weight and distance. Linda Kennedy, *Kelso* (Yardley, PA: Westholme, 2007), 37.

145 . . . the greater the effect. Ibid.

145 . . . the "breaking point" for a horse. Ibid.

145 ". . . swing a bat five pounds heavier?" Nack, "Simply Spectacular Shoe-in for the Bid."

145 ". . . complain about it, but he will." James Tuite, "Affirmed Assigned 133 for Marlboro," *New York Times,* September 4, 1979.

145 ". . . I would not run him." Ibid.

145 . . . deprived of the "race of the century." James Tuite, "Affirmed Is out of Marlboro," *New York Times,* September 5, 1979.

146 ". . . I'm trying to protect their property." Ibid.

146 . . . in the seven-year history of the Marlboro Cup. Russ Harris, "Spectacular Bid Avenges Loss of 'Crown' in Marlboro Romp," *Cincinnati Enquirer,* September 9, 1979.

146 ". . . Bid was not in the same class as Affirmed." Andrew Beyer, "Bid Shoots to Scatter the Critics," *New York Times,* September 7, 1979.

146 . . . called Barrera's actions tasteless and unsportsmanlike. Ibid.

146 ". . . do a little bit of what they did." Nack, "Simply Spectacular Shoe-in for the Bid."

147 . . . alluding to Affirmed's approaching syndication at stud. William H. Rudy, "The Bid Was Affirmative," *Blood-Horse,* September 15, 1979, 4734.

147 ". . . It's still the Race of the Decade." Ibid.

147 ". . . He keeps coming back for more." Ibid.

147 . . . "Got all those pins out?" Dave Koerner, "With New 'Shoe,' Bid 'Rolls' by Five in Marlboro Cup," *Louisville Courier-Journal,* September 9, 1979.

148 . . . boasted, "This race is history." Rudy, "Bid Was Affirmative," 4734.

148 ". . . hadn't asked my horse to run." Russ Harris, "Tribulation, Vindication, Celebration," *Thoroughbred Record,* September 19, 1979, 1176.

148 ". . . was not a true performance by his horse." Andrew Beyer, "Bid Wins Marlboro in a Romp," *New York Times,* September 9, 1979.

148 ". . . Barrera may have decided wisely." Nack, "Simply Spectacular Shoe-in for the Bid."

148 ". . . knocked out for the rest of the year." Harris, "Tribulation, Vindication, Celebration," 1176.

148 ". . . sorry we didn't meet [Affirmed]." Rudy, "Bid Was Affirmative," 4734.

149 ". . . to run back in the Woodward." William Boniface, "Bid to Miss Woodward Stakes," Meyerhoff Collection, Book 10, Keeneland Library.

149 ". . . and some $5,000 claimers, too." Ross Peddicord, "Bid Will Train at Pimlico for the Gold Cup," *Baltimore Sun,* September 18, 1979.

150 ". . . and he knows the surroundings." Associated Press, "Affirmed Is Rated 4–5 Favorite over Bid," *Louisville Courier-Journal,* October 5, 1979.

150 ". . . Rise and shine, you hoss." Tony Kornheiser, "Life in Barn Is a Regular Bowl of Oats," *Washington Post,* October 7, 1979.

150 ". . . save something for this afternoon." Ibid.

150 ". . . He know what comes later." Ibid.

150 ". . . the great ones give off to each other." Ibid.

151 ". . . Anyone got eyes can see that." Ibid.

151 ". . . not going to change his style." William Nack, interview by the author, July 9, 2017.

153 ". . . the outcome might have been different." Dave Koerner, "Affirmed Makes the Best of His Break, Wins Gold Cup," *Louisville Courier-Journal,* October 7, 1979

154 ". . . the pace wouldn't have been that slow." Ibid.

154 . . . he should have gone faster. Timothy T. Capps, *Spectacular Bid: Racing's Horse of Steel* (Lexington, KY: Eclipse Press, 2001), 88.

154 . . . "I only f—— up once [on Spectacular Bid]." Meyerhoff Pete interview.

154 ". . . Shoemaker should have known better." William Boniface, "Shoemaker's Ride Ruined Bid's Chance of Victory," Meyerhoff Collection, Book 10, Keeneland Library.

154 ". . . party's over once he takes control." Steve Cady, "Affirmed Takes Gold Cup," *New York Times,* October 7, 1979.

154 ". . . who could have gotten by him either." Koerner, "Affirmed Makes the Most of His Break."

155 ". . . Arts and Letters succeeded in 1969." Steve Cady, "Affirmed on Mind of Delp," *New York Times,* October 19, 1979.

155 ". . . the continent has to offer." Dan Farley, "The Older, the Better," *Thoroughbred Record,* October 17, 1979, 1533.

155 ". . . can take the pressure a little better." Cady, "Affirmed Takes Gold Cup."

9. The Streak

1. Sham gave Secretariat a run for his money in the Kentucky Derby and Preakness and ran neck and neck with Secretariat for half of his record-breaking Belmont Stakes before Secretariat broke his will. Sham finished last.

2. Round Table was considered the greatest turf horse in American racing. He raced sixty-six times, with forty-three firsts, eight seconds, and five thirds.

3. Damascus was a champion horse that won the 1967 Preakness and Belmont Stakes. He held the track record for one and one-eighth miles.

Sources by Page Number

156 ". . . They could meet next month." Steve Cady, "Affirmed on Mind of Delp," *New York Times,* October 19, 1979.

156 ". . . it might not be necessary." Steve Cady, "Affirmed vs. Spectacular Bid: Racing's Battle of the Bankrolls," *New York Times,* October 20, 1979.

157 ". . . any place, any distance." Ibid.

157 . . . if that would get them together. Ibid.

157 ". . . we'd prefer to have it in California." Ibid.

157 . . . "He does not like the grass." James Tuite, "Affirmed Is Retired as Trainer Decides against Grass Race," *New York Times,* October 23, 1979.

157 ". . . concede Horse of the Year honors to Bid." Ibid.

158 ". . . the same as Affirmed in 1979." William Boniface, "Affirmed's Retirement Bothers Delp," *Baltimore Evening Sun,* October 23, 1979.

158 ". . . he would have whipped Affirmed." Andrew Beyer, "Bid Should Be Horse of the Year," Meyerhoff Collection, Book 11, Keeneland Library.

158 ". . . and heal his feet at the same time." Ross Peddicord, "Bid Will Train at Pimlico for the Gold Cup," *Baltimore Sun,* September 18, 1979.

158 . . . as many as twelve straight stakes. Ross Newhan, "Delp Continues His War with the Establishment," *Los Angeles Times,* December 12, 1979.

158 . . . "Politics were again involved." Ibid.

158 . . . rather than those of the current season. Ibid.

158 ". . . We'll run against anyone anywhere." Ibid.

159 ". . . in Delp's mouth instead of his horse's foot?" John Hall, "Santa Again," *Los Angeles Times,* December 26, 1979.

159 ". . . to restrain him from running quicker." Mike Kiley, "Horse Racing's King Is Treated Like One," *Chicago Tribune,* July 9, 1980.

159 ". . . very slow and never in a hurry." Howard Senzell, "Behind the Bid," Meyerhoff Collection, Book 12, Keeneland Library.

160 . . . "We're gonna win 'em all." Ray Kerrison, "Spectacular Bid's Owners Are as Classy as Their Champion," Meyerhoff Collection, Book 11, Keeneland Library.

160 ". . . I'd like to run him at the Meadowlands again." Associated Press, "Spectacular Bid to Try Same Path as Affirmed," *Louisville Courier-Journal,* December 29, 1979.

160 . . . Delp had said back at the Florida Derby. Eric Siegel, "Ronnie Franklin: The Repentant Jockey Rides Again," *Baltimore Sun,* May 11, 1980.

160 ". . . don't go the way I want them to." Bill Free, "Franklin, Once the Hero, Will Watch Preakness," *Baltimore Sun,* May 12, 1981.

160 ". . . as a hell of a student." Ross Newhan, "The Spectacular Fall of the Spectacular Kid," *Los Angeles Times,* January 29, 1980.

162 ". . . he took off and left the others." Claude Anderson, "Bid Wakes up, Drives to Victory," *San Bernardino County Sun,* January 6, 1980.

162 ". . . like he'd been in his stall all day." Senzell, "Behind the Bid."

162 ". . . the ability and quality of Spectacular Bid." Barry Irwin, "Beginning Another Bid," *Thoroughbred Record,* January 16, 1980, 233.

162 ". . . moving up third on the outside, right to the leaders!" Vintage North American Horse Racing, "Spectacular Bid—1980 Fernando Stakes," You-Tube, https://www.youtube.com/watch?v=Y_-Q_mlMGOM.

163 . . . He paused. "Maybe never." Billy Reed, "Bid's Deceiving if You Listen to Delp," *Louisville Courier-Journal,* January 20, 1980.

163 ". . . with any horse that ever lived." Steven Crist, "$255,692 Haskell to Bid," *New York Times,* August 17, 1980.

163 ". . . is in a class by himself." Barry Irwin, "Trackside," *Thoroughbred Record,* January 30, 1980, 461.

164 . . . excessive weight being assigned to him. Robert Hebert, "Quick Trip for the Quickest Trip," *Blood-Horse,* February 9, 1980.

165 ". . . so I can't say anything new," he told reporters. Associated Press, "Bid Romps in Strub, Shatters U.S. Mark," *Louisville Courier-Journal,* February 4, 1980.

165 ". . . is the only way they'll do it." Hebert, "Quick Trip for the Quickest Trip," 736.

165 ". . . we have no excuses." Ibid., 737.

165 ". . . has been so awe inspiring as Bid." Barry Irwin, "Not since Secretariat," *Thoroughbred Record,* February 13, 1980, 671.

167 ". . . is to tie an anchor on him." Robert Hebert, "Putting the Cap on a Sweep," *Blood-Horse,* March 8, 1980, 1319.

167 ". . . it's up to us if we want to run." Ibid.

168 ". . . that he was coming to Claiborne." Logan Bailey, "Hancock Beat Lot of Competition to Stand 'Bid' at Claiborne Farm," *Daily Racing Form,* March 12, 1980.

168 ". . . All twenty said they wanted in." Billy Reed, "Seth Hancock Is Making It on His Own," *Louisville Courier-Journal,* July 22, 1980.

168 ". . . so we started moving on it yesterday." Associated Press, "Bid Syndicated for $22 Million," *Louisville Courier-Journal,* March 13, 1980.

169 ". . . before he is retired to stud." Howard Senzell, "Syndication of Bid," *Daily Racing Form,* March 12, 1980.

169 ". . . in breeding seasons is a rich man's game." Associated Press, "Meyer-

hoffs Give Delp $1.5 Million Deal," *Louisville Courier-Journal*, April 5, 1980.

169 ". . . we've got an awful lot of horse." Associated Press, "Weber City Miss Takes Susans; Downs Toasts Regret," *Louisville Courier-Journal*, May 17, 1980.

171 . . . a good distance in front of the horse. Mike Kiley, "Horse Racing's King Is Treated Like One," *Chicago Tribune*, July 9, 1980.

172 ". . . it wasn't as serious as the safety pin injury." Howard Senzell, "Delp, 'Bid' Both Survive Big Day Full of Twists," *Daily Racing Form*, June 12, 1980.

172 ". . . who were staying at a hotel in Beverly Hills." Ibid.

172 ". . . shakin' like a leaf." Vinnie Perone, "Spectacular Bid's Trainer Bud Delp Recalls Glory Years of Maryland-Based Superstar," *Baltimore Sun*, October 19, 2000.

173 ". . . wins every time out and a healthy horse." Associated Press, "Bid Passes Affirmed as Top Money-Winner," *Louisville Courier-Journal*, June 9, 1980.

173 ". . . the best horse I've ever ridden." Perrone, "Spectacular Bid's Trainer Bud Delp Recalls Glory Years."

173 ". . . I've got to get him out of here." Ibid.

174 ". . . The rest can eat cake." John Hall, "Bye Bye Bid," *Los Angeles Times*, July 2, 1980.

174 ". . . like he came to me—kicking and playing." Billy Reed, "Delp's Pride and Joy Bids to Be Known as the Greatest Ever," *Louisville Courier-Journal*, July 16, 1980.

174 ". . . kiss your track record goodbye." Neil Milbert, "Spectacular Trainer: Bud Delp," *Illinois Racing News*, August 1990, 25.

175 ". . . and he hadn't raced in several weeks." Associated Press, "Bid Wins Easily, Sets Seventh Track Record," *Louisville Courier-Journal*, July 20, 1980.

175 ". . . by many lengths—we have to offer this season." Dan Farley, "These Are the Good Old Days," *Thoroughbred Record*, July 23, 1980, 394.

175 ". . . to make him carry 137 or 138 [in the Marlboro Cup]." Andrew Beyer, "Monmouth Turns Handicap into Farce," *New York Times*, August 14, 1980.

176 ". . . in the country, if you ask me." Ibid.

177 ". . . carry 140 in the Marlboro if the others tote 137." Ibid.

177 ". . . that trainers and owners rarely appreciate." Andrew Beyer, "Bid Is Challenged," *New York Times*, September 2, 1980.

177 ". . . he will join a very select circle of horses." Ibid.

177 ". . . against 120 for the three-year-olds." Russ Harris, "Why Bid Won't Go in the Marlboro," *New York Daily News*, September 4, 1980.

177 . . . content until they are six years old. "Principles of Bone Development in Horses, Kentucky Equine Research," https://ker.com/equinews/principles -of-bone-development-in-horses1.

178 ". . . know how to handicap a race properly." Andrew Beyer, "Delp Pulls Bid out of Marlboro," *New York Times,* September 5, 1980.

178 ". . . What am I, stupid?" Vinnie Perrone, "Bud Delp—Often 'Indicted'— Now Is Safely Inducted in the Racing Hall of Fame," *Mid-Atlantic Thoroughbred,* October 2002, 55.

178 ". . . to prove it, and he came up short." Ibid.

178 . . . giving Bid 119 or 120 pounds. Russ Harris, "Spectacular Bid Will Miss Saturday's Marlboro Cup," *New York Daily News,* September 5, 1980.

178 ". . . too far from his bush league racing origins." Beyer, "Delp Pulls Bid out of Marlboro."

179 ". . . carrying 136 pounds nine furlongs, bypassing the race." Timothy Capps, *Spectacular Bid: Racing's Horse of Steel* (Lexington, KY: Eclipse Press, 2001), 117.

179 ". . . is truly the greatest horse of modern times." Barry Irwin, "Flying Past Them All," *Thoroughbred Record,* May 28, 1980, 1959.

179 . . . racing's greatest gesture of respect. Brian Landman, "Truly Spectacular," *Tampa Bay Times,* April 28, 1999.

180 ". . . You can go ahead and run him." John Crittenden, "Bid Races Clock and Bankbook," *Miami News,* February 15, 1980.

180 ". . . they were going to do this to us." Tom Meyerhoff, interview by the author, May 30, 2016.

180 ". . . at the Marlboro, where were you?" "Spectacular Bid Learns in Woodward that It's Lonely at the Top," *Louisville Courier-Journal,* September 21, 1980.

182 ". . . We're not looking to set any track records." Associated Press, "Seven Test Spectacular Bid in Gold Cup," *Louisville Courier-Journal,* October 4, 1980.

182 ". . . and had no cause to be concerned." Joe Hirsch, "Didn't Circumvent Racing Rules: Delp," *Daily Racing Form,* October 7, 1980.

182 ". . . when these people have their act together." William Leggett, "The Champ Calls It a Day," *Sports Illustrated,* October 13, 1980, 99.

183 ". . . After that, I don't know what will happen." Ibid.

184 ". . . don't take chances with a $22 million horse." Associated Press, "Delp Calls Report that Spectacular Bid Had Bone Chips in Left Ankle 'a Lie,'" *Louisville Courier-Journal,* October 6, 1980.

184 ". . . It's as simple as that." Leggett, "Champ Calls It a Day."

184 ". . . but there was no point taking a chance." Andrew Beyer, "Injury Ends Spectacular Bid's Career," *New York Times,* October 4, 1980.

184 ". . . probably glad it has come to an end." Dale Austin, "Bid (and the Marylanders) vs. the New Yorkers—It's All Over," *Baltimore Sun,* October 5, 1980.

184 . . . "I'm glad Bid wasn't in there." United Press International, "Spectacular Bid Retired with Ankle Injury," *Muncie (IN) Star Press,* October 5, 1980.

184 . . . the colt was not "one hundred percent fit." Associated Press, "Delp Calls Report . . . a 'Lie.'"

184 ". . . could be said about his owners and trainer." Herb Goldstein, "Bid's People Act in Bad Faith," *Daily Racing Form,* October 7, 1980.

184 . . . Phipps said he did not believe it either. Russ Harris, "Old Ankle Injury Ends Bid's Career; Hill Wins Cup," *New York Daily News,* October 5, 1980.

185 ". . . there was some ill will between them." Tom Meyerhoff interview.

185 ". . . what he never before had done." Dan Farley, "A Day to Praise Caesar, Not Bury Him," *Thoroughbred Record,* October 8, 1980.

Epilogue

1. Genuine Risk was only the second filly to win the Kentucky Derby, the other being Regret back in 1915.

2. "Popping a splint" is an inflammation of the ligament that runs between the horse's splint bone and cannon bone. It can also refer to a fracture in the splint bone.

3. Bid was reshod every three weeks. Early in his career, Delp simply threw the old shoes away, but as the horse became more famous, he donated them to charities to be auctioned off.

Sources by Page Number

187 ". . . we don't have one every year." Ed Golden, "Spectacular Bid Keeps Delp Young," Meyerhoff Collection, Book 14, Keeneland Library.

187 ". . . slighted, snubbed, even maligned." Ross Newhan, "Delp Decides He'll Skip Dinner," *Los Angeles Times,* January 21, 1981.

187 ". . . for the glory of seeing the horse run." Vinnie Perrone, "Bud Delp— Often 'Indicted'—Now Is Safely Inducted in the Racing Hall of Fame," *Mid-Atlantic Thoroughbred,* October 2002, 56.

187 ". . . give something back to the game." Billy Reed, "Claiborne President Seth Hancock Needs a Farm of His Own," *Louisville Courier-Journal,* July 22, 1980.

188 ". . . they have no obligation to it." Herb Goldstein, "Bid's People Act in Bad Faith," *Daily Racing Form,* October 7, 1980.

188 ". . . and thank God for that." Newhan, "Delp Decides He'll Skip Dinner."

188 ". . . probably cost the Meyerhoffs in the voting." Bob Maisel, "Meyerhoffs Merited Eclipse," *Baltimore Sun,* December 18, 1980.

188 ". . . taking all the races and the money." Dale Austin, "Bid (and the Marylanders) vs. the New Yorkers—It's All Over," *Baltimore Sun,* October 5, 1980.

189 . . . "Screw 'em." Russ Harris, "In Trial or Triumph, There's Always Talk," *New York Daily News,* December 26, 1980.

189 ". . . that is now etched in history." Paul Moran, "Bid's Legend Grows in Gulfstream's Garden," *Fort Lauderdale News,* January 9, 1981.

190 ". . . if you sent them out for a gallop." Tom Atwell, "Team Delp," *Daily Racing Form,* May 19, 1994.

191 ". . . who can overcome a weak pedigree." Timothy T. Capps, *Spectacular Bid: Racing's Horse of Steel* (Lexington, KY: Eclipse Press, 2001), 139.

191 ". . . some genes somewhere that just clicked." Associated Press, "Spectacular Bid Destroys the 'Twin Myth' in Racing," *Advocate,* July 16, 1980.

192 . . . "He was a wonderful man." Jim Dunleavy, "Harry C. Meyerhoff, Owner of Spectacular Bid, Dies at 86," http://www.drf.com/news/harry-c-meyerhoff-owner-spectacular-bid-dies-86.

192 ". . . we've had nothing like it ever since." Brain Landman, "Truly Spectacular," *Tampa Bay Times,* April 28, 1999.

192 ". . . because he doesn't want to." "Biographical Sketch Prepared by Jim Bolus for 1989 Breeders' Cup Biography Book," Jim Bolus Collection, Kentucky Derby Museum.

192 . . . "Spectacular Bid never did that to me." Tom Keyser, "Include Removes All Doubt, Edging Albert the Great," *Baltimore Sun,* May 13, 2001.

193 . . . plaque hung in his office for years. "Hall of Fame Trainer Bud Delp Dies," *Blood-Horse,* December 30, 2006, http://www.bloodhorse.com/horse-racing/articles/161967/hall-of-fame-trainer-bud-delp-dies.

193 ". . . reaching the pinnacle of his profession." Perrone, "Bud Delp—Often 'Indicted'—Now Is Safely Inducted in the Racing Hall of Fame."

193 ". . . what a superior horseman he was." Andrew Beyer, interview by the author, July 29, 2016.

193 " . . . I have too much at stake." Ross Newhan, "The Spectacular Fall of the Spectacular Kid," *Los Angeles Times,* January 29, 1980.

194 ". . . his own groceries and cleaning his room." Bill Free, "Franklin, Once the Hero, Will Watch the Preakness," *Baltimore Sun,* May 12, 1981.

194 ". . . should have left him alone, but I didn't." Ibid.

194 ". . . It happens all the time in this business." Ibid.

194 . . . if their package had arrived, attorneys said. Steven Crist, "Fresh Start: Ronnie Franklin Has New Outlook after Time in Jail," *Lexington Herald,* August 10, 1982.

194 ". . . it's up to him." Ibid.

195 ". . . to find happiness in the end." Billy Reed, "The Pressure of Fame Dealt Franklin His Toughest Ride," *Louisville Courier-Journal,* April 15, 1982.

195 ". . . a future [in horse racing] if I work hard enough." "On the Rebound: Jockey Ronnie Franklin Returning to Form at Louisiana Downs," *Longview (TX) News-Journal,* June 26, 1983.

195 ". . . cause for immediate suspension." Kent Baker, "Franklin Gets Md. Jockey License," *Baltimore Sun,* April 1, 1984.

195 ". . . caught on here yet, but he will." Ibid.

196 ". . . couldn't get a license in Hong Kong." Jack Mann, "Franklin Still Has His Dreams, but Riding Days May Be Over," *Baltimore Evening Sun,* September 25, 1986.

196 . . . "I'm all the way back." Clem Florio, "Franklin Gets Exercise License," *Washington Post,* April 2, 1987.

196 . . . "I think I've got it beaten." Dale Austin, "Franklin Can Resume Exercise Riding," *Baltimore Sun,* April 3, 1987.

196 ". . . to do so well in seasons past." Tom Atwell, "Franklin's Road Back Begins to Level," *Daily Racing Form,* October 6, 1987.

196 ". . . serves as a support system." Vinnie Perrone, "Franklin Makes Strides at Laurel; Jockey Overcomes Drug Problems, Regains Form of Early Career," *Washington Post,* March 2, 1988.

196 ". . . or not ride horses anymore." Bill Christine, "Still Riding: Jockey Ronnie Franklin Now Races at Pimlico," *Los Angeles Times,* June 4, 1988.

196 ". . . drugs seem to be a curse." Tom Atwell, "Md. Jockey Ron Franklin Is Suspended Again for Drugs," *Daily Racing Form,* September 21, 1992.

197 "'. . . I should have scratched him.'" *Pressbox,* May 16, 2006, https://www.pressboxonline.com/story/187/the-great-bid-foiled.

197 ". . . Racing is a natural thing for me." C. Ray Hall, "Franklin Puts Troubles behind Him," *Louisville Courier-Journal,* April 27, 2004.

198 ". . . just for jockeys, cocaine would be it." Craig Neff, "Grounded," *Sports Illustrated,* November 6, 1989.

198 ". . . It makes it a lot easier." Hall, "Franklin Puts Troubles behind Him."

198 ". . . I'm not second-guessing nothing." Ron Franklin, interview by the author, March 7, 2016.

199 ". . . and the entire sport will miss him." "Bill Shoemaker 1931–2003," Horse-Races.net, http://www.horse-races.net/library/article-101203.htm.

200 ". . . into a fence and ruined him." Frank Deford, "Riding Horses Is the Pleasure of His Life," *Sports Illustrated,* April 23, 1984.

200 ". . . or because my business wasn't any good." Ibid.

200 ". . . not be as lucky as he was this time." Paul Moran, "Angel Will Be Missed," *Newsday,* May 8, 1992.

201 ". . . wait for you to snap his picture." Associated Press, "A Legend Gone—Spectacular Bid Dies," *Poughkeepsie (NY) Journal,* June 11, 2003.

201 ". . . as any horse in my time." Steve Haskin, "The Bid: Sustained Greatness," *Blood-Horse,* December 1, 2015, http://cs.bloodhorse.com/blogs/horse-racing-steve-haskin/archive/2015/12/01/the-bid-sustained-greatness.aspx.

201 ". . . better than the three years I had him." Bob Mieszerski, "1980 Horse of the Year Spectacular Bid Dies," *Los Angeles Times,* June 11, 2003, http://articles.latimes.com/2003/jun/11/sports/sp-spectacularobit11.

202 ". . . three times in his 1973 season)." Andrew Beyer, interview by the author, July 29, 2016.

203 ". . . the inclusion of Spectacular Bid." Brian Zipse, interview by the author, September 21, 2016.

204 . . . would decline by 27 percent, according to the report. McKinsey & Company, "Driving Sustainable Growth for Thoroughbred Racing and Breeding," August 2011, http://www.jockeyclub.com/pdfs/selected_exhibitss_rt2011.pdf.

205 . . . eight percent from 1990 to 2010. Ibid.

205 . . . horses' legs more fragile. Jeffrey McMurray, "Trainer Backs Jockey; Says He Did No Wrong," *Wisconsin State Journal,* May 6, 2008.

Glossary

Sources by Page Number

214 . . . based on its age, sex, or past performance. "Allowance race," in Industry Glossary, Equibase Company, http://www.equibase.com/newfan/glossary-full.cfm.

Index

Page numbers in italics refer to photos.

Ack Ack, 167
Adams, W. A. "Smiley," 54–55, 58, 70, 73, 93
Admiral Buck, 36
Affirmed, 38, 54, 57, 70, 74–75, 77, 78, 79, 97, 117, 128, *153*, 159, 160, 161, 163, 167, 169, 170, 173, 175, 177, 178, 182; compared to Spectacular Bid, 51, 63, 135, 165, 174, 185, 201; Jockey Club Gold Cup, 149–55, 158; 1979 Woodward Stakes, 148–49; possible match race against Spectacular Bid, 107, 113–14, 135, 140–41, 155, 156, 157, 158; retires, 157; skips 1979 Marlboro Cup, 144–47, 148; syndication of, 168; Triple Crown races with Alydar, 2, 3, 37, 44, 46, 79, 90, 123, 204; wins Horse of the Year, 49, 158
Al (horse), 139
Alameda County Fair, 7
Albert the Great, 192
Alydar, 2, 3, 37, 44, 46, 57, 79, 90, 123, 149, 153, 204
Alysheba, 77, 202
American Derby, 191
American Pharoah, 77, 128, 205
Amy, Jose, 199
Ancient Title, 166
Angelina County (horse), 196
Antley, Chris, 197, 200
Aqueduct Racetrack, 56, 70, 109, 131, 155, 157, 200
Arcaro, Eddie, 87, 105, 117, 139, 140, 145, 166
Archer, Ray, 20
Aristides, 76

Arkansas Derby, 69
Arlington Park, 173
Armada Strike, 143, 144
Arts and Letters, 69, 155
Assault, 77
Associated Press: Horse of the Century poll, 201
Au Point, 199
Austin, Dale, 32, 115, 184, 188

Bailey, Jerry, 67, 197
Baltimore Opera Company, 100
Barbaro, 205
Barnet, Bob, 111
Barrera, Larry, 157
Barrera, Laz, 70, 78, 145–47, 148, 150, 154, 156, 157, 164, 167, 170, 177, 180; criticism of, 146–47; possible match race between Affirmed and Spectacular Bid, 114, 141, 155; wins 1979 Trainer of the Year, 158
Barrera, Luis, 70, 93, 101, 108
Bayless, Skip, 132
Beau's Eagle, 166, 169, 170
Belle's Gold, 70
Belmont, August, 65
Belmont Park, 1, 19, 39, 109, 112, 114, 118, 129, 131, 133, 142, 146, 147, 150, 151, 159, 175, 177, 237n1
Belmont Stakes, 1, 2, 56, 118, 128, 133, 141, 146, 148, 149, 153, 154, 158, 180, 184, 191, 199, 201, 203; Coastal and, 109–10, 116, 122–26, 142; potential Triple Crown winners, 1, 201, 203, 204, 205; Ron Franklin and, 111, 115, 126–28, 137, 138, 162, 197; Secretariat and, 1, 2,

Belmont Stakes (*cont.*)
   245n1; Spectacular Bid and, 63, 99,
      109, 110, 112–13, 116–35, 140, 152,
      157, 172, 201, 206; winners of, 1, 2,
      179, 184, 199, 203, 204, 246n3
Ben Brush (horse), 6
Benser, John M., 27
Bettis, Charlie, 30, 50, 85, 118, 119, 140,
      143, 149, 159, 161, 162, 167, 169,
      171, 183
Beyer, Andrew, 45–46, 54, 66–67, 68,
      73, 76, 79, 84, 96, 99, 101, 103,
      116, 127, 146, 148, 158, 175, 177,
      178, 193, 202, 203; criticism of Ron
      Franklin, 60, 62, 67, 68, 97, 111–12,
      137
Big Brown, 204
Bishop's Choice, 54, 55, 71
Black-Eyed Susan Stakes, 22, 191
Blue Grass Stakes, 48, 70, *71, 72,* 74, 75,
      79, 84, 191
Bold Bidder, 8, *9,* 15, 24, 25, 26, 34,
      164, 165
Bold Forbes, 79
Bold Place, 15, 23, 24
Bold Ruler, 2, 8, 179, 191
Bolger, 173
Bologna, Dominick, 197–98
Boniface, William, 154
Bowl Game (horse), 149, 151
Boyne Valley, 176
Brach's Dancer, 58
Breeders' Cup, 203
Breeders' Cup Classic, 192
Breeders' Cup Juvenile, 190
Breeders' Cup Sprint, 191
Breezing On, 40, 47
Broker's Tip, 6
Buckpasser, 144
Buck Pond Farm, 4–5, 7, 10, 11

Cady, Steve, 96, 99, 113, 126, 155
California Breeders' Championship
      Stakes, 49
California Chrome, 205
Californian Stakes, 160, 171–73
Calipha, 191

Calumet Farm, 1, 4, 37, 54
Campbell, Gordon, 75, 79, 80, 85, 92,
      93, 97, 101, 102, 169, 201
Cannonade, 9, 56, 78
Cañonero II, 1, 14, 105
Cantey, Joe, 184
Caro Bambino, 173
Carry Back, 1
Cassidy, Marshall, 184
Caswell, Ed, 10
Cauthen, Steve, 38, 39, 45, 56, 137
Caveat, 199
Champagne Stakes, 37, 39–41, 46, 47
Charismatic, 204, 205
Chenery, Penny, 85
Chesapeake, 76
Chief's Crown, 190
Churchill brothers, 76
Churchill Downs, 53, 74, 76, 77, 79, 81,
      82, 84, 86, 87, 93, 95, 97, 101, 198
Citation, 1, 63, 77, 100, 103, 117, 145,
      158, 171, 174, 178, 202
Ciulla, Tony, 57, 203
Claiborne Farm, 4, 69; and Spectacular
      Bid, 141, 168, 190, 191, 201
Clark, Meriwether Lewis, Jr., 76, 77
Clever Trick, 41, 44–45
Coaltown (horse), 179
Coastal, 39, 109, 110, 113, 114, 116,
      125, 126, 131, 133, 141, 157, 186,
      197; Belmont Stakes, 122–25; death,
      201; Dwyer Stakes, 142; injures right
      eye, 41; Jockey Club Gold Cup, 149,
      151–53, 155; Marlboro Cup, 144,
      145, 146, 147–48; Peter Pan Stakes,
      110; syndicated, 141; Tyro Stakes,
      36; Woodward Stakes, 149; World's
      Playground, 39
Codex, 199
Colin (horse), 6
Combs, Brownell, 70–71
Combs, Leslie, 189
Considine, Bob, 11
Cool Virginian, The, 176
Cordero, Angel, 86, 95, 114, 116,
      121, 128–29, 132, 137, 156, 180;
      allegations of race fixing, 57, 203;

early life, 56; fines and suspensions, 56, 200; Florida Derby, 57–58; later career, 199–200; Preakness Stakes, 103–7, 112; relationship with Ron Franklin, 60, 94, 106–7, 114–15
Cosell, Howard, 81, 85, 87–88
Count Fleet, 77
Cowdin Stakes, 37, 47
Crest of the Wave, 39, 40
Croatoan, 111
Cullum, Walt, 100
Cuniberti, Betty, 66
Czaravich, 109, 149, 151

Dailey, Jim, 121
Damascus (horse), 79, 87, 144, 168, 174, 175, 246n3
Dancer's Image, 225n1
Davis, Jonathan H. F., 190
Day, Pat, 197
Debary, Pat, 189
Decidedly, 11, 80
Delahoussaye, Eddie, 64
Delaware Park, 20, 21, 37, 193
Delaware Racing Commission, 196
Delp, Brian, 28
Delp, Cleve, 193, 219n3
Delp, Doug, 29, 39, 50
Delp, Gerald, 20, 21, 29, 50, 53, 59, 93, 194
Delp, Grover G. "Bud," 13, 14, *18, 23, 30–31, 32*, 34, 35, 36, 37, 53, 66, 79, 83, 84, 93, 95, 108, 115, 127, 129, 130, 132, 133, 134, 142, 156, 158, 162, 164, 165, 166, 167, 169, 181, 187, 189, 190, 201, 206; Belmont Stakes, 118–26; blames Ron Franklin for Belmont loss, 197; caution in handling Spectacular Bid, 51, 62, 64, 67, 80, 86, 98, 117, 120, 124, 141, 149, 161, 170–72, 173, 174, 182, 183–85; claiming horses, 19, 21–22, 46, 70, 192, 193; confidence, 41, 45, 47, 55, 58, 63, 69, 86, 93–94, 102, 107, 112, 113, 116, 117, 141, 147, 148, 165, 174, 180; criticism, 59–60, 109, 111, 126, 137,

159, 178–79, 184, 188; criticism of Jorge Velasquez, 43; criticism of Ron Franklin, 38, 53, 59, 136, 143; death, 193; early years, 20–21; elected into National Museum of Racing and Hall of Fame, 193; evaluation of Ron Franklin as a jockey, 29, 33, 45, 56, 63, 68, 81, 107, 129, 160, 194; fines and suspensions, 48, 50–51, 136; inducted into National Museum of Racing and Hall of Fame, 193; Keeneland sale, 23–24; Kentucky Derby, 85–94; knowledge of horses, 23, 66, 189, 193; later years, 191–93; looks for another jockey, 38, 39, 43, 61–62, 138; loses horses in fire, 21–22; meets Meyerhoffs, 22; 1979 Jockey Club Gold Cup, 150–54; 1980 Jockey Club Gold Cup, 182; offers Ron Franklin a job, 28; opinion of Coastal, 116; opinion of Flying Paster, 79–80, 163; parts ways with Ron Franklin, 195; personality, 18; Preakness Stakes, 102–7; possible match race with Affirmed, 113, 140–41, 155, 157; rehabilitation of Spectacular Bid, 141, 142, 143; reinstates Ron Franklin as jockey, 43; relationship with horse racing establishment, 18–19, 41–42, 44, 62, 63, 70–71, 75, 112, 135, 142, 158, 178, 184–85, 187–88; relationship with media, 73, 74, 79, 81, 85, 107, 159, 173–74, 178, 184, 188; relationship with other trainers, 44; relationship with race officials, 43–44, 111, 135, 176, 177–78, 179, 180, 183–85; relationship with Ron Franklin, 29, 30, 45, 59, 60, 68, 92, 96, 99, 136–38, 142–43, 193–94; replaces Ron Franklin for first time, 39–40; replaces Ron Franklin permanently, 138; safety pin injures Spectacular Bid, 118–20, 130–33; scratches Bid from 1979 Woodward, 148–49; superstitions, 112, 147; $10,000 horseshoe, 172, 173;

Delp, Grover G. "Bud" (*cont.*)
  temper, 19, 21, 48, 53, 59, 64, 70–71,
  82, 111, 136; training Spectacular
  Bid, 31, 46–47, 51, 52, 62–63, 71,
  73–74, 81, 98–99, 102, 112, 113,
  143, 158, 170, 172, 182; weights on
  Spectacular Bid, 164, 167, 169, 175,
  176, 177, 178; wins 1980 Trainer of
  the Year, 187
Delp, Richard, Jr., 48, 110, 118, 130, 195
Delp, Richard, Sr., 20
Denlinger, Ken, 96
DePass, Richard, 91
Derby Trainers' Dinner, 82
Derby Trial, 83
Desormeaux, Kent, 196, 197
Determine, 11
Discovery, 179
Dispersal, 191–92
Dover Stakes, 37–38, 40
Dr. Patches, 177, 179, 180
Dust Commander, 14
Dutrow, Dick, 21, 195
Dwyer Stakes, 142

Ecole Etage, 15, 23
Eight Belles, 205
El Comandante Race Track, 56
Elliot, Win, 106
Elmendorf Farm, 6, 191
Epsom Derby, 11, 76, 168
Errico, Con, 203
establishment, horse racing, 18–19,
  41–42, 44, 47, 51–52, 62, 63, 65,
  70–71, 75, 82, 86, 112, 130, 158,
  178, 188, 189, 193
Evans, Luther, 54
Evans, William S., 25
Exclusive Dancer, 36
Experimental Handicap, 50
Exterminator, 77, 179, 202

Fair Grounds Race Course, 195
Fantasy 'n Reality, 58–59
Farley, Dan, 155, 175, 185
Feldman, Dave, 49
Ferdinand (horse), 198

Ferrous, 131–32
Firestone, Bertram, 187, 188
Fishman, Bob, 120, 121
Flamingo Ball, 65, 189
Flamingo Stakes, 61, 64, 65, 66–69, 72
Florida Derby, 55–59, 61, 62, 66, 67, 68,
  79, 81, 82, 92, 104, 126, 128, 138,
  160, 189, 202
Flying Paster, 37, 52, 55, 59, 112, 160,
  167; alleged injury, 79, 85, 95, 97;
  comparison with Spectacular Bid,
  69, 72, 73, 77–78, 83–84, 85, 162;
  California Breeders' Championship
  Stakes, 49; Experimental Handicap,
  50; Hollywood Derby, 74; Kentucky
  Derby, 77–78, 79, 82, 83, 85, 88–90,
  92–93, 97; later years and death,
  200–201; Malibu Stakes, 161–62;
  Mervyn Leroy Handicap, 169–
  70; Preakness Stakes, 95, 98, 100,
  101, 102, 103–5, 106; San Felipe
  Handicap, 63–64; San Fernando
  Stakes, 162–63; San Luis Rey Stakes,
  167; Santa Anita Derby, 69, 75;
  Santa Anita Handicap, 166–67; San
  Vicente Stakes, 53; Strub Stakes,
  164–65
Foolish Pleasure, 3, 78, 82, 140
Forego, 82, 144, 145, 146, 147, 177, 179,
  230n2
Fortent, 48
Forward Pass, 116
Fountain of Youth Stakes, 54–55, 58
Franklin, Al, 106
Franklin, Marian, 59, 61, 99, 100
Franklin, Ron, 30, 31, *32*, 41, 44, 50,
  57, *72, 73*, 75, 85, 95, 101, *105*,
  107, 114, 130, 133, 134, 142, 154,
  155, 159, 189, 193; apprentice
  jockey, 32–34, 45, 46, 56; arrested
  for cocaine possession, 136–37;
  arrested for transfer of cocaine,
  194; arrives home for Preakness
  Stakes, 95, 99–100; avoids accident
  during practice, 48; criticism, 60,
  62, 66–67, 68, 80–81, 82, 87–88,
  92, 97, 111–12, 126, 127, 131, 135,

137, 143, 160, 197; death, 198; drug use, 108, 136–37, 142, 194, 195, 196, 197, 198; early life, 26–28; fails drug test, 195, 196, 197; fails to win a race at Santa Anita, 160; fines and suspensions, 68, 110, 115, 136, 196; gets mount on Spectacular Bid, 31–32; inexperience, 37–38, 44, 56, 60, 78, 86, 87–88; keeps mount on Spectacular Bid, 61; loses mount on Spectacular Bid for first time, 39–40; loses mount on Spectacular Bid permanently, 138; marriage and divorce, 195; moves out of Bud Delp's house, 193; paternity suit, 136; personality, 33, 61, 75, 114; regains mount on Spectacular Bid, 43; relationship with Angel Cordero, 60, 94, 106–7, 114–15; relationship with Bud Delp, 29, 30, 45, 59, 60, 68, 92, 96, 99, 136–38, 142–43, 193–94; sentenced to jail, 194; starts working for Bud Delp, 28–29; temper, 110, 111, 160, 194, 195; trains to be jockey, 26, 29; wins Best Apprentice Jockey, 49; wins first two races, 32–33
—RACES ON SPECTACULAR BID: allowance race, 35; Belmont Stakes, 116, 120, 121–28, 129, 132; Blue Grass Stakes, 72–73; Dover Stakes, 37–38; Flamingo Stakes, 66–68; Florida Derby, 58–59; Fountain of Youth Stakes, 55; Hutcheson Stakes, 52–53; Kentucky Derby, 86–92, 96–97; Laurel Futurity, 44–45; maiden win, 34; Preakness Stakes, 103–5, 108; Tyro Stakes, 36; World's Playground Stakes, 37–39
Franklin, Tony, 99, 100
Funny Cide, 201, 204
Futurity Stakes, 47, 190

Gainesway Farm, 9
Gallant Best, 116, 121, 122–24, 127, 132, 149, 151–53, 197
Gallant Fox, 77, 217n1

Gallant Man, 139
Gallant Serenade, 67
Gammon, Clive, 82
Gato del Sol, 203, 217n3
General Assembly, 36–37, 52, 59, 91, 107, 112, 187; Belmont Stakes, 112, 114, 116, 121–24, 129, 132; Champagne Stakes, 39, 40; Cowdin Stakes, 37; Experimental Handicap, 50; Gotham Stakes, 70; Kentucky Derby, 78, 82, 83–84, 85, 88–90; Laurel Futurity, 44, 45; Marlboro Cup, 146, 147–48; Preakness Stakes, 95, 98, 100, 101, 102, 103–5; Travers Stakes, 146; Wood Memorial, 75
Genuine Risk, 187, 199, 250n1
Giacomo, 217n3
Gilman, Manuel, 130–31, 135, 183, 184, 185
Glorious Song, 175, 176, 179
Golden Act, 91, 125, 141, 186; Arkansas Derby, 69–70; Belmont Stakes, 112, 114, 116, 122–24, 131; Kentucky Derby, 78, 82, 83, 85, 88–90; Louisiana Derby, 64; Preakness Stakes, 95, 98, 100, 101, 102, 103–5; San Luis Rey Stakes, 167
Golden Gate Fields, 5–6, 139
Goldstein, Herb, 184, 188
Goodman, Lenny, 38, 39
Go on Green, 6, 7
Gotham Stakes, 47, 70
Go to Goal, 7
Graham, Barbara, 26
gray horses, 11; Kentucky Derby winners, 11, 91, 217n3
Great Redeemer, 83, 89, 91–92, 93
Grimsley, Will, 96, 132
Groton High, 36, 37, 38
Gulfstream Park, 48, 50, 51, 52, 54, 55, 61, 62, 67, 95, 189

Hale, Lenny, 145, 146, 175, 177–79, 180, 185
Hall, Herman "Mo," 20, 33, 53, 58, 59, 73, 85, 86–87, 93, 96, 102, 105, 110, 118–19, 143, 150, 169, 171, 183, 205; asks to be relieved of groom's duties, 140

Hall, John, 159, 173
Halma, 5, 77, 217n1
Hancock, Seth, 69, 141, 168, 190, 191
handicapping, 144–45
Harris, Russ, 41, 96, 131, 146, 177, 184
Harthill, Alex, 74, 95, 133–34, 162, 182, 184, 225n1
Harvey, Randy, 80–81
Haskell Handicap, 175–76, 178
Haskin, Steve, 22, 201
Havre de Grace Racetrack, 179
Hawksworth Farm, 14, 15–16, 17, 30, 34, 37, 66, 101, 110, 133, 169, 222n1
Hawley, Sandy, 61, 88, 90, 127
Hawthorne Gold Cup, 8
Heerman, Victor, 5, 7–8, 10, 14, 24
Heritage Stakes, 46–47
Hernandez, Ruben, 124, 128
Heyman, Nate, 19
Hialeah Park Race Track, 6, 56, 65, 67, 74, 95, 189
High Bid, 8
Highfalutin, 200
Hill, Jim, 14
Hillsdale, 166
Hindoo, 6
Hirsch, Joe, 71, 81
Hold Your Tricks, 174
Hollywood Derby, 74, 78
Hollywood Park, 136, 160, 169, 171, 173, 185
Holy Land, 83
Honest Moment, 38–39
Honest Pleasure, 67, 79, 168
Hopeful Stakes, 37, 47
horse racing attendance, 3, 203, 204
How Rewarding, 161
Humane Society, 205

I Know Why, 31, 222n1
I'll Have Another, 205
Include, 192
Instrument Landing, 42, 75, 78, 181
Irish Derby, 168
Iron Liege, 139
Irwin, Barry, 74–75, 162, 163, 165, 179

Jacobs, Hirsch, 65
Jaklin Klugman (horse), 177
James, Bob, 46, 49
Jason, Madelyn, 5, 6, 7, 9–10, 11, 14, 24, 25, 64, 92, 169
Jatski, 175
Jim Dandy Stakes, 99, 142
Jockey Club, 1, 26, 50, 65, 87, 204, 218n2
jockeys and drug use, 197–98
jockeys, skills of, 29
Jocoy, Jock, 6
John Henry (horse), 167, 181, 184, 198
Johnson, P. G., 178
Johnstown (horse), 6
Jolley, LeRoy, 43–44, 78, 82, 83, 107
Jones, Jimmy, 1, 117
Justify, 77, 128, 205

Kauai King, 1
Keeneland, 13–14, 18, 23, 25, 31, 70, 71, 95, 149, 194, 218n1
Keeneland Association, 71
Kelley, Walter, 6, 191
Kellner, Jenny, 131
Kelso, 21, 144, 145, 146, 177, 179
Kentucky Derby, 1, 2, 22, 30, 34, 35, 37, 46, 47, 48, 50, 51, 52, 53, 61, 63, 70, 79, 96, 109, 117, 181, 191, 197, 225, 245; Flying Paster and, 49, 69, 77, 95, 97, 101; General Assembly and, 75, 98; Golden Act and, 64; history of, 76–77, 80, 81; Ron Franklin and, 96–97; Spectacular Bid and, 54, 60, 71–73, 77–78, 81–94, 98; winners of, 2, 3, 5, 6, 9, 11, 14, 36, 56, 77, 78, 109, 139, 140, 187, 198, 199, 203, 204, 205, 217, 250
Kentucky Jockey Club Stakes, 52
Kessler, Gene, 11
Keystone Racetrack, 46
Kindred, Dave, 107
King Celebrity, 83, 89, 116, 121
Knoop, Grace, 64
Known Presence, 161
Kulina, Bob, 178

Landman, Brian, 179
Lang, Chick, 31, 34, 92, 100, 158
Laurel Futurity, 41, 43, 44–46, 47, 97
Laurel Park, 14, 19, 20, 21, 22, 29, 41,
    43, 44, 48, 181, 192, 196, 197
Laurin, Lucien, 78, 116, 128
Laurin, Roger, 145
Lay Down, 190
leads, 122–23
Leatherbury, King, 19, 21, 222n1
Lenox, Kenny, 176
Lewis, Oliver, 76
Life's Hope, 170
Linfoot, Janet, 7
Linfoot, William, 6, 7
Linkage, 203
Longden, Johnny, 139
Lorine (horse), 114
Lot o' Gold, 52, 54–55, 58, 70, 71–72,
    73; Kentucky Derby, 83, 88–89, 91,
    93
Lotus Pool, 190
Louisiana Derby, 191
Louisiana Downs, 195
Lucky Debonair, 139
Lucky Penny, 35
Luro, Horatio, 51, 68
Lyon, Bill, 19

Mahmoud, 11
Maisel, Bob, 48, 110, 188
Majestic Prince, 1, 36, 69, 75, 109, 126
Make a Mess, 42–43
Malibu Stakes, 159, 160, 161–62, 164,
    182
Mann, Judy, 16, 17
Man o' War, 63, 158, 162, 179, 202,
    219n2
Marengo Road, 192
Mark-Ye-Well, 167
Marlboro Cup, 144–48, 149, 154, 160,
    175, 176, 177–79, 180, 185
Marlboro Nursery Stakes, 41
Marlton Pike, 15
Marshall, Thomas, 4
Martens, George, 127

Martin, Buddy, 117
Martin, Frank "Pancho," 68
Maryland Racing Commission, 195,
    196, 197
McDowell, Thomas Clay, 5
McGee, Marty, 21
McGrath, H. P., 76
McHargue, Darrel, 61, 73, 74, 160
McKinsey & Company, 204–5
McManus, Margaret, 88
Meadowlands, 42, 44, 141, 156, 160,
    178, 185
Meadowlands Cup, 155, 156–57, 181
Mearns, Dan, 21, 97
Medaille d'Or, 52, 58
Mervyn LeRoy Handicap, 169–70, 171
Meyerhoff family, 17, 26, 33, 35, 43,
    46, 53, 55, 66, 67, 70, 73, 84, 95,
    99, 117, 135, 149, 153, 154, 172,
    173, 175, 189, 191; attends 1977
    Keeneland sale, 14, 18, 23–25;
    attends Derby Trainers' Dinner, 82;
    Belmont Stakes, 120, 121, 124, 133;
    changes jockeys, 138; continues to
    race Spectacular Bid, 159, 183, 187;
    criticism, 188; insures Spectacular
    Bid, 42, 54, 64, 100; Kentucky
    Derby, 87–88, 92, 93; looks for
    replacement jockey, 38, 43, 61;
    loses Owners of the Year award,
    187; names Spectacular Bid, 26;
    Preakness Stakes, 103, 106, 108;
    rejects offers to buy Spectacular
    Bid, 46, 49; relationship with
    racing establishment, 52, 65, 71,
    188; retires Spectacular Bid, 183;
    safety pin injures Spectacular Bid,
    120; says Ron Franklin will remain
    Spectacular Bid's rider, 61–62;
    syndication of Spectacular Bid, 168–
    69; Woodward Stakes, 180
Meyerhoff, Harry, 13, 14, 15, 17, 23, 31,
    34, 45, 47, 54, 65–66, 71, 82, 84,
    98, 142, 147, 148, 149, 154, 160,
    169, 189, 190, 192; attends 1977
    Keeneland sale, 23–24;

Meyerhoff, Harry (*cont.*)
  Belmont Stakes, 117, 119, 124, 132,
  133; buys Hawksworth Farm, 15–16;
  death, 192; denies rumors that Bid is
  for sale, 54; divorce, 191; early years,
  14–15; forms Bon Etage Stables,
  15; hires Bud Delp, 22; Kentucky
  Derby, 87, 92, 93, 94; meets Teresa,
  16; personality, 17, 66; possible anti-
  Semitism against, 65; relationship
  with establishment, 65; returns
  to Maryland, 95; syndication of
  Spectacular Bid, 168
Meyerhoff, Jacob, 14
Meyerhoff, Joseph, 14
Meyerhoff, Robert, 14–15, 192
Meyerhoff, Teresa, 14, 17, *23*, 33, 34, 43,
  62, 95; Belmont Stakes, 124, 133;
  changes jockeys, 138; divorce, 191;
  donates sales of Spectacular Bid items
  to Baltimore Opera, 100; early years,
  16; Kentucky Derby, 84, 87, 88, 89,
  92, 94; meets Harry, 16; personality,
  16, 66; Preakness Stakes, 103, 104,
  107; relationship with establishment,
  65; safety pin injures Spectacular
  Bid, 119
Meyerhoff, Tom, 14, 15, *23*, 26, 34,
  49, 53, 64, 84, 172, 190, 191, 192;
  attends 1977 Keeneland sale, 23–24;
  Belmont Stakes, 117, 120, 123, 124;
  changes jockeys, 138; early years,
  17; Kentucky Derby, 87; Preakness
  Stakes, 101, 107, 108; proposes
  match race with Affirmed, 157;
  relationship with establishment, 180,
  184; sells Spectacular Bid items for
  Baltimore Opera, 100
Middleburg Training Center, 26, 29, 30,
  31, 34, 100, 123, 134
Milfer Farm, 190, 201
Miller, Mack, 179
Mohamed, James Allison 83
Monarchos, 217n3
Monmouth Handicap, 8
Monmouth Park, 20, 35, 37, 175, 176, 178

Moran, Paul, 189
Morris, Tony, 202
Morvich, 78
Murray, Jack, 114
Murray, Jim, 140
Musical Phantasy, 58
My Fair Lady Stakes, 7
Mystic Era, 116, 122

Nack, William, 40, 126, 140, 148, 151,
  152
Nashua, 37, 69
National Museum of Racing and Hall of
  Fame, 8, 65, 167, 185, 193, 194, 200
National Turf Writers Association, 188
Native Dancer, 37
Need More Time, 67
New York Racing Association (NYRA),
  115, 133, 135, 175, 177, 179, 180,
  183, 184–85, 188
New York State Racing and Wagering
  Board, 57, 135, 198
Niatross, 185
Nijinsky II, 168
Noor, 165
Northern Dancer, 51, 77, 144
Northern Prospect, 52–53
Not So Proud, 144

Omaha, 77, 217n1
Onion, 176
Our Rocky, 21

Paint King, 173
Passmore, Bill, 196
Peregrinator, 169–70
Perry, William Haggin, 114, 116
Petrucione, Joe, 51
Phelps, Frank, 19
phenylbutazone (Butazolidin), 97, 133,
  182, 225n1
Phillips, William, 34
Phipps, Dinny, 115
Phipps, Ogden Mills, 184
Pianist, 71, 72, 83
Picturesque, 116, 121

Pierce, Don, 37, 64, 69, 74, 78, 79, 87, 90, 94, 104, 106, 127, 163, 165, 167, 170, 198
Pimlico Race Course, 14, 19, 22, 28, 31, 33, 34, 35, 92, 95, 96, 97, 99, 100, 101, 106, 110, 111–12, 133, 135, 136, 143, 150, 155, 158, 193, 199
Pimlico Special, 22, 192
Pincay, Laffit, 102, 152, 154
Pioneer Patty, 32–33
Piscione, Joe, 131
Pity the Sea, 144
Pleasant Colony, 203
Pole Position, 63
Poona's Day, 140
Port Ebony, 42
Preakness Stakes, 1, 2, 15, 63, 70, 93, 95–108, 110, 112, 117, 130, 148, 151, 203, 245; Secretariat and, 8, 234n1; winners of, 8, 199, 203, 204, 246
Prix du Palais Royal, 190
Prix Maurice de Gheest, 190
Promised Land, 7, 34
Proskauer, George and Susan, 5, 10
Protagonist, 47, 54
Proud Clarion, 79

Quack, 165
Quiet Crossing, 116, 121
Quigley, Bob, 141

Randall, John, 202
Rasmussen, Leon, 69
Real Quiet, 204
Reed, Billy, 19, 60, 62, 81, 187, 195
Relaunch, 162–63, 164–65
Renick, Sam, 130
Replant, 170, 173
Reynolds, Jack, 141, 166, 172
Richards, Robin, 134
Ridder, B. J., 37, 69, 79, 92, 167, 170
Rivalero, 54–55
Riva Ridge, 78
Roman Coffee, 83
Rosie's Seville, 161
Round Table, 144, 166, 167, 168, 189, 246n2

Rubigo, 200
Ruffian, 3, 140, 147

San Antonio Stakes, 180
San Felipe Handicap, 63–64
San Fernando Stakes, 159, 160, 162–63, 164, 176, 182
Sangster, Robert, 54, 169
San Luis Rey Stakes, 167
San Pasqual Handicap, 164
Santa Anita Derby, 69, 75
Santa Anita Handicap, 159, 164, 166–67
Santa Anita Park, 8, 49, 52, 139, 140, 159, 160, 162, 174, 180, 182, 193
San Vicente Stakes, 52, 53
Sapling Stakes, 37
Saratoga, 13, 19, 99, 142, 194, 200
Saratoga Special Stakes, 37
Schaap, Dick, 115
Schapiro, John, 22
Schultz, Randy, 66
Screen King, 70, 75, 78, 114; Belmont Stakes, 112, 116, 121; Kentucky Derby, 82, 83, 84, 85, 89, 93; Preakness Stakes, 96, 97, 98, 100, 101, 103–7, 108
Seabiscuit, 167, 201
Seattle Slew, 2, 14, 40, 46, 51, 54, 63, 77, 78, 128, 135, 145, 157, 177
Secretariat, 36, 46, 52, 77, 78, 79, 82, 85, 97, 117, 124, 128, 132, *139*, 148, 173, 176, 177, 178, 189, 219; and General Assembly, 15; and Preakness Stakes, 8, 234n1; and Sham, 68, 245n1; compared to Spectacular Bid, 54, 63, 68–69, 91, 113, 116, 129, 135, 165, 185, 202; syndication of, 69, 168; Triple Crown winner, 1, 2, 54
Seethreepeo, 31, 86, 222n1
Shafter V, 139
Shake Shake Shake, 57
Sham, 68, 74, 162, 245n1
Shamgo, 83, 89, 156
Shoemaker, Bill, 43, 61, 127–28, *139*, 156, 178, *181*, 189, 191;

Shoemaker, Bill (*cont.*)
   calls Spectacular Bid best horse he's
   ever ridden, 173; career, 138–40;
   early life, 138; later years and death,
   198–99; replaces Ron Franklin as
   Spectacular Bid's jockey, 138
—RACES ON SPECTACULAR BID:
   allowance race, 143–44; Californian
   Stakes, 173; Haskell Handicap, 176;
   Jockey Club Gold Cup, 151–54;
   Malibu Stakes, 161–62; Marlboro
   Cup, 147–48; Meadowlands Cup,
   156–57; Mervyn LeRoy Handicap,
   169–70; San Fernando Stakes, 162–
   63; Santa Anita Handicap, 166;
   Strub Stakes, 164–65; Washington
   Park Stakes, 174–75; Woodward
   Stakes, 180
Silent Cal, 149, 151
Silent King, 191
Silent Native, 35
Silver Charm, 204, 217n3
Sir Barton, 77
Sir Ivor Again, 58, 83, 89
Ski Pants, 114
Slew o' Gold, 199
Smarten, 70, 157
Smarty Jones, 204
Smith, Mike, 48
Smith, Robert, 49, 64, 110, 150, 159,
   169, 171
Smith, Tim, 199
Snider, Steve, 1
Snowden, Harold, 189
Snow Goose Handicap, 196
Spectacular, 5, 7–10, 11, 14, 26, 34, 201
Spectacular Bid, *72, 73,* 74, *105,* 110,
   125, 147, *153,* 171–72, *181,* 185,
   189, *202;* attempts to buy, 46, 49;
   becomes richest Thoroughbred in
   history, 173; birth, 5, 10; compared
   to Affirmed, 51, 63, 74–75, 135, 165,
   174, 201; death, 201; doughnuts,
   35, 85, 93, 98, 100, 133, 161; early
   days, 10–12; "higher gear," 31,
   40–41, 45, 55, 59, 67, 163, 166, 176;
   high weights, 166, 171, 174, 175,

176–77; injury to ankle, 182–85;
   insurance for, 42, 54, 64, 100, 187;
   leads Experimental Handicap, 50;
   legacy, 185–86, 201–3, 205–6;
   misses Sapling Stakes, 37; moves
   to Claiborne Farm, 188–89; moves
   to Milfer Farm, 190; named, 26;
   offspring, 190; personality, 159;
   physical makeup, 31; potential,
   30, 35, 46, 47; racing style, 31, 70;
   rehabilitation, 141–43; safety pin
   injury, 118–20, 133–35; scratched
   from 1979 Woodward, 148–49;
   scratched from 1980 Jockey Club
   Gold Cup, 181–85; scratched
   from 1980 Marlboro Cup, 177–
   79; sold, 14, 23–25; syndicated,
   168–69; training, 51, 71, 73–74,
   81, 98, 99, 112, 113, 116; training
   at Middleburg Training Center, 26;
   versus Flying Paster, 69, 77–78, 85,
   90, 161, 162–63, 165, 166–67; wins
   1978 Champion Two-Year-Old Male
   Horse, 49; wins 1979 Champion
   Three-Year-Old Male Horse, 158;
   wins 1980 Horse of the Year, 191
—RACES OF: allowance race (1978),
   35; allowance race (1979), 143–
   44; Belmont Stakes, 112, 116,
   117, 118–29; Blue Grass Stakes,
   71–72; Californian Stakes, 171–73;
   Champagne Stakes, 44–45; Dover
   Stakes, 37–38; Flamingo Stakes,
   67–68; Florida Derby, 57–59;
   Fountain of Youth Stakes, 55;
   Haskell Handicap, 175–76; Heritage
   Stakes, 46–47; Hutcheson Stakes,
   52–53; Jockey Club Gold Cup,
   151–53; Kentucky Derby, 60, 71, 73,
   77, 81–94; Laurel Futurity, 43–46;
   maiden win, 31, 33–35; Malibu
   Stakes, 161–62; Marlboro Cup
   (1979), 144–48; Meadowlands Cup,
   156–57; Mervyn LeRoy Handicap,
   169–70; Preakness Stakes, 102–6;
   San Fernando Stakes, 162–63; Santa
   Anita Handicap, 166–67; Strub

Stakes, 164–65; Tyro Stakes, 35–36; walkover in Woodward Stakes, 179–81; Washington Park Stakes, 173–75; World's Playground Stakes, 38–39
Spectacular Joke, 190
Spectacular Love, 190
Spendthrift Farm, 70, 157
Spring Switches, 48
Stage Door Johnny, 116
Star de Naskra, 146, 147
Steelwood, 176
Stephens, Woody, 23, 78, 116, 199
Stop on Red, 6–7, 191
Strike the Main, 66
Strike Your Colors, 34, 38, 42, 50
Strub Series, 164, 166
Strub Stakes, 8, 159, 164–66, 167, 174
Suburban Handicap, 177
Sunday Silence, 77, 191, 202, 204
Sun Watcher, 47
Swaps, 69, 77, 139, 144, 176, 202
Swaps Stakes, 156
Switch Partners, 64, 74

Tammaro, John, 21
Tanforan Racetrack, 6
Tannenbaum, Joe, 54
Tanthem, 178
Tanton, Bill, 17
Taylor, Mickey, 14
Taylor Manor Hospital, 195
Temperence Hill, 179, 180, 181, 184
Terrific Son, 47
Tesher, Howie, 131
Tetrarch, The, 11
Text, 147, 156–57
Thoroughbred Racing Association, 6, 188, 199, 205
Thumbs Up, 167
Timbo, 162
Tim Tam, 1
Tim the Tiger, 37, 39, 40, 44, 45, 50, 82
Tomy Lee, 139
Top Knight, 47, 54
Touch Gold, 204
Travers Stakes, 57, 142, 143, 146, 179
Triple Crown, 1, 2, 30, 38, 46, 47, 49,

54, 107, 116, 117, 126, 132, 204, 205, 234n1; Spectacular Bid and, 30, 41, 46, 47, 49, 54, 63, 69, 96, 100, 107, 110, 112, 113, 116, 117, 119–20, 127, 129
Trombetta, Michael, 192
Troy (horse), 168
Tunerup, 176
Turf Classic, 155, 157
Turner, Billy, 78
Twice a Prince, 1
Tyro Stakes, 35–36, 37, 39, 41, 42, 52, 53, 84, 98, 109, 176

Unconscious Lad, 83

Valdez (horse), 156–57, 164–65, 180
Valenzuela, Pat, 197
Vallance, D. Robert, 132, 133
Vandernat, Reinier, 15
Vasquez, Jacinto, 61, 199, 203
Veitch, John, 37, 43, 44
Veitch, Sylvester, 44
Velasquez, Jorge, 39, 40, 41, 42–43, 56, 57, 58, 60, 62, 66
Victory Gallop, 204

Wadler, Gary, 200
Wall, Maryjean, 192
War Admiral, 77, 201
War Emblem, 204
Washington, DC International Stakes, 181
Washington Park Handicap, 8, 173
Washington Park Stakes, 173–75
Western Playboy, 191
Whirlaway, 77
Whisk Broom II, 179
White, Charlie, 22
Whiteley, David, 109–10, 114, 116, 124, 126, 142, 146, 147
Whitney Handicap, 176
Williamson, Ansel, 76
Wimbledon Farm, 10–11
Winn, Matt, 77
Winning Colors, 217n3
Winter's Tale, 177, 179

Wolfson, Louis and Patrice, 140, 145, 146
Woodbine Farm, 196
Woodhouse, Bob, 56
Wood Memorial, 75, 78, 79
Woodward Stakes, 146, 148–49, 154, 160, 177, 178–81, 186

World's Playground Stakes, 38–39, 41, 45, 109
Worswick, Doug, 178

Young America Stakes, 42–43, 75

Zipse, Brian, 39, 202

Horses in History

Series Editor: James C. Nicholson

For thousands of years, humans have utilized horses for transportation, recreation, war, agriculture, and sport. Arguably, no animal has had a greater influence on human history. Horses in History explores this special human-equine relationship, encompassing a broad range of topics, from ancient Chinese polo to modern Thoroughbred racing. From biographies of influential equestrians to studies of horses in literature, television, and film, this series profiles racehorses, warhorses, sport horses, and plow horses in novel and compelling ways.